Philip Tocque

Kaleidoscope Echoes

Being Historical, Philosophical, Scientific and Theological Sketches from the Miscellaneous Writings

Philip Tocque

Kaleidoscope Echoes
Being Historical, Philosophical, Scientific and Theological Sketches from the Miscellaneous Writings

ISBN/EAN: 9783337097134

Printed in Europe, USA, Canada, Australia, Japan

Cover: Foto ©ninafisch / pixelio.de

More available books at **www.hansebooks.com**

KALEIDOSCOPE ECHOES

BEING

HISTORICAL, PHILOSOPHICAL, SCIENTIFIC, AND
THEOLOGICAL SKETCHES, FROM THE
MISCELLANEOUS WRITINGS

OF THE

REV. PHILIP TOCQUE, A.M.

EDITED BY HIS DAUGHTER
ANNIE S. W. TOCQUE.

"Gather up the crumbs that nothing may be lost."

It is said of the Venerable Bede that besides his regular exercises of devotion he made it his pleasure every day "either to learn or to teach or to write something."

TORONTO:
THE HUNTER, ROSE COMPANY, LTD.,
PRINTERS AND BINDERS.
1895.

These Sketches were written at different intervals, and make no pretentions to originality. Part of the materials have been drawn from authors of the most unquestionable authority, whilst the rest came under the writer's own observation and enquiry. It is thought the subjects would be interesting and convey information to the general reader.

ANNIE S. W. TOCQUE.

TORONTO, Dec. 1st., 1895.

CONTENTS.

	PAGE
Groaning and Grumbling	9
Pastoral Visiting	12
Sermons to the Children	14
"Nothing Succeeds Like Success"	15
Church Schools	18
"Life on the Ocean Wave"	22
Family Worship	32
He Is Nobody	35
Slavery of Debt	38
Woman's Rights	42
Fashionable Amusements	47
The Celebrated Pusey Family	53
Toronto in 1894	56
Concomitant Evils of Modern Civilization	61
Yellow-Covered Literature	67
Labor Day, 1895	68
Physical Necessity of Labor	71
Old Men Not Wanted in the Pulpit	78
International Conference at Ottawa, 1894	83
The Pan-American Congress	88
The Secular and Religious Press	91
Incineration	94
"Tradition"	100
Popularity	104
Newfoundland as a Health Resort	108
Reminiscences	125
Temperance	131
Expedients for Raising Money	147
First General Synod of the Church of England in the Dominion of Canada, 1893	152

	PAGE
Extempore Preaching	157
Plagiarism in the Pulpit	160
"Music as Religion and Religion Music"	163
Personal Recollections of Kossuth	166
Incidents of a Visit to New York	168
Education for the Church	176
A Summer Holiday on the Mediterranean of the Province of Quebec	182
The Phocas of Terra Neuve	192
Extempore Listening	201
Our Mother's Chair	204
Preachers and Preaching	205
The Fur Seal	210
Church Union	214
Evangelists	224
Permutation of the Clergy	228
Hades, or the Intermediate State	231
"The Uncrowned King"	236
Degrees and Titles	239
The Bocothics or Red Indians of Newfoundland	242
The Cod Fisheries of Newfoundland	253
Fires of St. John's, Newfoundland	261
Mineral Resources of Newfoundland	272
Agricultural Developments of Newfoundland	283
Aggressive Work of the Church	298

ILLUSTRATIONS.

	PAGE
Sealing Steamer in the Ice taking on board Seals	211
Mary Marsh, Red Indian or Bocothick of Newfoundland	243
Conception Bay, showing the Stages and Fish Houses of the Fishermen	255
Church of England Cathedral, as it appeared before the fire of July, 1892, St. John's, Newfoundland	263

KALEIDOSCOPE ECHOES.

Groaning and Grumbling.

THERE is a class of persons who are constantly grumbling about every occurrence in life, instead of trying to make the best of everything. No matter which way the wind blows or the state of the weather, they are sure to find some fault with it, no matter how excellent any thing is in itself, if it has any deficiency they are sure to spy it out, and comment thereon in no measured terms. They are like the poor woman that we once read of, who thought that a little money would make her completely happy, and having been asked by a benevolent and eccentric gentleman, how much would answer for this purpose, answered, one hundred pounds, which sum being at once handed to her; scarcely was the worthy donor out of hearing when she remarked, I wish I had said two hundred. It is just so with grumblers, nothing will satisfy them, and when their ideal mark is reached, they querulously object to allowing its excellence. This sort of people not only make themselves miserable, but become a nuisance to their neighbors and the society which tolerates them. Besides the habit is a useless and unphilosophical one. When things go wrong, it is certainly much better by patience and persevering exertions to try and set them right, than to grumble. There are those who can never speak of the Church they belong to without "groaning" spiritually, financially, numerically, they find occasion for groans, everything cheerful and hopeful is hidden from sight. What a number of persons and things makes them groan. They begin with the clergyman. Their first charge is that he does not visit, and then his calls are not spiritually profitable, then these calls are partial—some are overlooked and others are regarded too much. Some, notorious for passion, evil speaking, lying and kindred vices, "groan" because the minister is not pious enough for them. They are afraid he will get too proud. They are greatly exercised for his humility. It is necessary to that end to keep him poor. But they do not so reason as to themselves, for they may be adding house to house and field to field yearly without interfering with their own humility. Then the sermons are too long and prosy. If there was more scripture and less poetry, or if they were more deeply experimental, how much better it would be. The groaners, who are followers of "Lo, here, and Lo, there," grieve because some specific topic is not brought into the sermon, they want an artificial excitement on the topics of the day. It may be intemperence or secret societies, Sunday profanation, dancing, gambling, theatres, or other worldly conformity. They groan when a discourse closes without these things being unsparingly denounced. They grumble about variegated altar cloths, stained glass windows, flowers, cushioned pews, crosses, banners, surpliced choirs, bowings, genuflections and ritualism. They see a worldly mindedness and temporizing spirit in the minister which compels them to groan. In the summer the minister's absence for vacation is a staple cause of "groaning." If he loved souls as he ought, would he be willing to be absent from his flock, and spending his days in idleness and perhaps croquet. The services should be more attractive. One groaner suggests striking and amusing sermons, full of anecdotes; another bright music. Another thinks the clergyman altogether too doctrinal, another gives it as his opinion that the man is stiff and awkward in the pulpit, and do not like his voice—that he was never cut out for a clergyman, and has mistook his calling. Another thinks he ought to gesticulate more. Some grumble because he flings his arms about and nods his head so much. If he is a single man a host of young ladies in his congregation are his warmest friends. They embroider for him slippers and manufacture his dressing gowns, until, to their surprise, he comes home one day bringing with him a young wife from a distant city. Then attention is diverted from the "parson" and fixed upon his help-meet. One of the groaners complains that she is too gay and frivolous, not suited for a minister's wife. Another that she is too extravagant, too expensive things all over the house; she is too dressy, she ought to dress more plainly and set a good example; some of the congregation think there is too much company at the parsonage; others, not enough. All claim a good share of visits from both inmates of the parsonage. How would these groaners and grumblers like being picked to pieces the way they dissect the minister and his family with their tongues. How easy it is to criticize the parsonage while the grumblers live as they please in their own homes without being found fault with. Then these people groan over the members of the Church. They remember faults committed years ago. No single tergiversation from right do they forget. Some people can hardly enter the sanctuary but their presence elicits a groan. The whole estate of the Church, its lack of spirituality, its formalism and ceremonies are causes of perpetual groaning. To remedy this complaining, these groaners and grumblers must have the "wit of geese," which pick up the kernels and leaves the chaff.

Pastoral Visiting.

Next to the preaching of the Gospel is pastoral work, which in many respects bears the same relation to the public preaching that the preparation of the ground and the cultivation of the crop does to the planting of the grain. The parable of the sower illustrates this truth. The prepared ground alone yielded fruit. Every minister should visit his people, either at their homes or places of business, or both, as occasion requires. Establishing an influence in one's field of labor is an important factor in the preparation of the soil for the reception of spiritual seed. But the great question is, how is this work to be performed? It is impossible to lay down rules that will apply to every case. There are two extremes to be avoided: one consists in engaging in pastoral work to such an extent as to interfere with pulpit preparation, and the other is a total neglect of it—supposing that pulpit ministrations are sufficient. I have met with families who had not been visited for years by the clergyman of the church where they attended. Pastoral work ought not to be habitually neglected. Just as a sportsman looks to see the effect of his shot, or a physician observes the effect of his medicines, so should every minister observe the effect of his sermons on the congregation. Whatever effect may be produced by sermons should be promptly followed up by pastoral work, until the people at least realize that their pastor is in earnest about their salvation. The visits should be so conducted as to be sources of real pleasure to the families. The visits should never be inopportune, not too protracted.

Pastoral visiting may afford an opportunity of meeting and speaking with those who never or seldom attend church, and thus may lead to their reformation. If the people will not come to church, the church should be taken to the people. The pastor should not only look after the resident citizens who fail to attend public worship but also to visit strangers who move within the parish to invite them to the house of God. An efficient prosecution of this work will do much to fill the sanctuary and to build up the church. Strong congregations become careless concerning attention to strangers, to the young, the poor, and others whom they can help. There is not too much said in these days about "hand shaking Christianity." The minister should fire pocket pistols as he passes about on week days, as well as big guns on Sundays. Poor preaching has driven many of the poor from preaching. Vapid discoursing lies at the bottom of the indifference of the working classes to the house of God. If they had been interested they would have continued to attend, but much of the preaching they have never been able to understand. There is a great deal of "toplofty transcendentalism" that passes for preaching that is utterly incomprehensible to common people. Some men will absurdly persist in putting their fodder so high that only a giraffe can reach it. Such guardians do not carefully " watch " the "flock," nor trouble the "lost sheep" with a vigorous pursuit. There is a great deal of pointless preaching. The hearer is often led to inquire: What is all this for? What is the preacher's object? What end has he in view? So aimless and pointless is the discourse. No preacher, however, was ever so attractive that he could, in and of himself, draw a single sinner to Christ.

It is, no doubt, the experience of a large number of ministers that strangers fail in their duty to the church. Numbers hold themselves aloof from the church services. They should make themselves known, and hold themselves ready to receive attention. They should let their voice be heard in the service of song and prayer. They should let the influence of their dollars and cents be felt in the revenue of the parish and in the benevolent offerings.

Sermons to the Children.

There is a widespread complaint over the absence of the children from the preaching service, and there are some who are ready to pronounce against the Sunday-school itself as being somehow responsible for this deplorable alienation. The Sunday-school is a human institution but the preaching of the Gospel is a divine command. Some ministers seek to remedy the difficulty by preaching a five minutes' prefatory sermon to the children, and directing the remainder of the service to the older people Others still, have adopted the plan of an occasional sermon to the children, expressed in words so high that the little people, for whose special benefit the sermon was prepared, cannot reach it, and delivered in such a dry, formal manner as not to interest them. Men and women are but children of a larger growth. The children of the Sunday-school should attend the public preaching in the church with the children of a larger growth. The children are the future hope of the Church. The most effectual method of successful ministerial work is by reaching and entertaining the children. If a pastor can gain the confidence and love of the little ones, his success is guaranteed. Children naturally fear a minister of the Gospel. In many cases the reserve of the minister increases this. If we would occasionally make ourselves as children we might hope to win them to Christ. Some parents discard all obligation to teach their children what they profess to regard the truth in respect to the distinguishing doctrines, the worship and government of the Church of England, and large numbers are entirely indifferent on the subject. This is all due to the defective training in the parents themselves. They were never taught, or at least they never learned the teaching of the Church. Generally, those who have wandered from the Church have never really been taught the right way.

The education of the young in the principles of religion, and the knowledge of God's word, is the best antidote for every crime. The religious training of the young is in a great measure left to the Sunday-school. The family altar and home training may suffice for those who are fortunate enough to have such, but what of the thousands who have no such advantages. The impressions of early life next vanish, and the streets and lanes of our cities are poor schools for morality. We have an instrumentality of great power in the Sunday-school, but it should never be made to take the place of preaching the Gospel.

"Nothing Succeeds Like Success."

THAT nothing succeeds like success is a false maxim. It is only partially true. Failure is very often the direct path to success in the very object we are seeking. The fact is, nothing has ever succeeded in the world like failure. Men fail in one business to find another for which they are better suited. Men are fitted by failure in their affairs to accomplish personal success. Here are a few instances of failure being a success: An intimate companion of my youth entered into mercantile business, but he had no liking for that pursuit and abandoned it. He next went into Canada, bought a farm, and commenced farming in the village of Compton, in the eastern township of Lower Canada, where he continued two years, but had to give up farming as a failure. He next spent a year as tutor to a gentleman in the State of Alabama. His next move was to the West Indies, where he spent two years studying the birds of Jamaica; after which he returned to England and became a writer of books for the Society for the Promotion of Christian Knowledge. I believe he has written some thirty or forty volumes, with about a dozen titles of honor to his name. Well versed in literature and art, skilled in drawing, painting and etching, a good singer. He made all the drawings and paintings for his books, most of them from nature. He has a son equally clever as himself. A niece of mine paid a most delightful visit to him at his English home last summer. The person of whom I speak is Philip Henry Gosse, the great English naturalist, whose writings are well-known among English speaking people throughout the world. I knew a young man, a poor fisherman, he had received a good education ; I urged him repeatedly to give up fishing and do something else. He began writing editorials for a newspaper, went into politics, became a Member of Parliament, had Hon. attached to his name, retired from politics, and took a Government appointment with a salary of $6,000 a year. I knew a commercial clerk, quite a philosopher, but a clerkship was not to his taste. He became a successful journalist in Boston, U. S. I know another clerk who gave up clerking—wrote a poem and obtained the prize which was offered for it. He studied theology and became a prominent minister of the Church of England in a city where he still resides. I knew another clerk who resigned his position, migrated, and became a Bishop of the Church of England. I knew a young man who commenced business as a merchant, but he had no love for buying and selling and getting gain, and, therefore, gave it up. He had a very defective education, having only received the mere rudiments of learning—such as reading, writing, and arithmetic. He was from a boy a great reader. After his failure as a merchant, he began to officiate as lay reader and preacher. He began to read upon theology, and notwithstanding that he did not know English grammar and could not conjugate a verb, and unacquainted with the classical literature of Greece and Rome, yet he was well versed in the English classics, and passed a most credible examination in theology by the learned Professors of a College, was ordained a minister of the Episcopal Church, and became an assistant to a Bishop. Elihu Burritt learned the trade of blacksmith, but failed in that business. He then turned his attention to journalism. I was personally and intimately acquainted with him, having assisted several months on a paper which he started called the *Christian Citizen*, and taken part with him at great public meetings. After some years he gave up the paper and became American Consul in one of the cities in England. He wrote several books, was a great lecturer, and was a member of nearly all the learned societies. Mr. Burritt informed me that he understood twenty languages, and could speak eight or ten of them. I was personally acquainted with John Tilley, a poor fisherman, who taught himself to read and write at twenty-six years of age. The first time I entered Mr. Tilley's house I observed a piece of mechanism —he said it was something on which he was experimenting, on hydrostatic principles. He made himself familiar with Homer's Iliad, in the Greek. He found pleasure and profit too, in scientific and learned pursuits. He gave up fishing. He was the first man to commence brickmaking, and preserving salmon in tins in Newfoundland. This "horny handed son of toil" rose from obscurity to eminence, as a man of science and learning. Three years ago I met his daughter, Mrs. Bremner, at London, Ont., where I spent a pleasant evening with her at her son's residence. Her three sons are assistant editors on the London *Free Press*, and the *Daily Advertiser*. I knew another fisherman, John Soaper, who fished until he was over forty years of age. He then studied medicine, taught himself surgery, performed some difficult operations by cutting off legs, cancers, etc., and became a most successful medical practitioner; was a great book-worm, I have heard him quote nearly the whole of Milton's "Paradise Lost" from memory. I knew a carpenter who became a most eloquent Methodist minister and filled some of the most important stations in the gift of the Conference to bestow. He afterwards entered the Church of England, and is now the rector of an important parish. Take our own ex-Premier, Mr. McKenzie, who left the business of a stone-mason to find another for which he was better fitted; and in which he could do nobler work. Men are wrought by failure as by a sculptor's chisel, out of hard blocks into personal success—like Hugh Miller. I could give many more cases which came under my own personal observation, where failure has resulted in personal success.

Church Schools.

THE celebrated Robert Hall says: "This is not the season for half measures; danger is to be repelled by intrepid resistance, by stern defiance, not by compliance and concession; it is to be opposed, if opposed successfully, by a return to the wholesome dialect of purer times."

If party spirit, or a love of popularity, or a foolish desire of being thought liberal, or a mean subserviency to the political views of others, if these or any one of these motives possess the heart, and incline it to prevaricate in so sacred a cause, then it is a wilful sacrifice of divine truth to worldly feelings and worldly interests. It is by religious instruction that the moral regeneration of the rising race is to be accomplished. The religious educator is endeavoring to create mind. But the vaunted education which the schoolmasters are to give, is one which leaves out the Master science of the world, which concerns the soul of man and his interests through all eternity. I would just appeal to all history in proof of the position that education without a knowledge of the true God is vain. There was a great march of science in Greece and Rome, but what was their polity, what were all their improvements? Where are Greece and Rome now? Learning is not religion. Look at France and Germany, nearly all their men of learning are rationalists and sceptics. If you give knowledge without religion, you give the power of the steam engine without the fly to regulate and direct its action. To lead children through the knowledge of time to that which is connected with the world to come, you purify the mass out of which future generations are to be formed, and prepare elements for a better state of society.

Intellectual training has usurped the place of moral discipline, because we, as a people, are setting a higher value upon money and those things which money will procure, than upon virtue and religion. It is because we are not so devout and religious as we should be, that our schools are given up to just those studies which have reference to trade and the business of the world. There has been a compromise in education, by which definite religious education has been almost wholly excluded from our common schools, a compromise in which many good sort of people glory, as if it were not fatal to the wellbeing of society.

The Common School system of Canada is not directly injurious to morals, but it is true that our Common Schools have become almost wholly secular, they are divorced from religion, which is the only basis of morals, and many of the most earnest advocates of popular instruction regard this feature with especial favor.

Those incessant witnesses—the prison returns of the Dominion for the past year, have again borne fearful testimony to the extent of moral darkness which still broods over large portions of our population.

It may be that the evils must grow much greater before people will perceive that it is not fine schoolhouses, and improved methods of teaching geography and grammar, that are going to arrest the progress of vice.

Clifford, late Governor of Massachusetts, says: " I have a general impression, derived from a long familiarity with the prosecution of crime, both as District Attorney and Attorney-General, that the merely intellectual education of our schools in the absence of that moral culture and discipline, which, in my judgment, ought to be an essential part of every system of school education, furnishes but a feeble barrier to the assaults of temptation and the prevalence of crime. Indeed, without this sanctifying element, I am by no means certain that the mere cultivation of intellect does not increase the exposure to crime by enlarging the sphere of man's capability to minister, through its agency, to his sensual and corrupt desires." So, also, Mr. Pierce, one of the School Inspectors for Massachusetts, has called attention to the absence of the moral element in the Public Schools. In former times, the Assembly's Catechism was taught every week in nearly all the schools of the New England States, and what few Episcopalians attended the schools were examined in the Church Catechism separately. But all this has passed away. But the difficulty is, that the Catechism has been gradually worked out, and nothing has come in to take its place.

The Rev. Dr. Townley says: " One of the most popular objections against denominational schools is that they will increase the bitterness of religious party strife. It appears to me that the objection is so groundless, that it must be made either in culpable thoughtlessness, or hypocritically, especially as the parties making it are often those who most vehemently urge the influence of Sunday Schools as a substitute for week-day religious instruction. But clearly, if denominational schools, on a week-day, will increase religious strife, they must do the same on a Sunday. I repeat then, the objection is little better than clear hypocrisy. But what is the design of religious instruction? Why, however seriously the different denominations may differ as to the means of accomplishing it, their aim is one ; namely, to implant in the human bosom love to God and man. Where sin yet lurks, earnestness on any subject, will sometimes produce bitterness towards those who oppose it; but in order to remedy this evil, shall we train our children in utter indifference not only to all distinctive truth, but to whatever else can excite any interest in either head or heart? and yet, this indifference is the only method by which those who advocate secular as opposed to religious training, can hope to lessen party strife. Verily the cure is worse than the disease."

In 1835, the Government of Newfoundland passed an Act for the encouragement of education, but, owing to the objection of the Roman Catholics to the reading of the Scriptures the schools failed. In 1844, a new Education Act was passed by the Legislature, giving each denomination its proportion of the education grant according to the number belonging to each, which gave great satisfaction. For a period of forty years, education in Newfoundland has been wholly denominational, and works well. For many years, in the United States, where they possibly can, they establish Church Schools. There is nothing to hinder Church Schools from being established in the diocese of Toronto. Nearly every church in the city has a fine parochial schoolhouse, which could be utilized for a week-day school; and lots of young men in every congregation well qualified to teach a Church School. All that is required in the Common Schools is the three R's—reading, writing, and arithmetic, with geography and grammar. Any man thus qualified, is competent to do any kind of business in the Dominion or in the World. A great deal of time and labor are lost in the Common Schools by the pupils studying unnecessary things, by having too long vacations, too many holidays, too much drilling—marching, counter-marching. I have known boys going to school until they were twelve and fourteen years old, and afterwards had to attend nightschool, to get a knowledge of the three R's. Mr Blake says there should be four R's, the fourth being Religion.

"Life on the Ocean Wave."

It has been calculated that the sea occupies nearly three-fourths of the surface of the globe. Or suppose the surface of the earth to be divided into 1,000 parts; there are then 266 of land and 734 of water. "The sea comprises five oceans: the Atlantic, so named from the Atlas mountains; the Pacific, from *pacificus, peaceful;* the Portuguese gave it this name because of its tranquility when they entered it. Balboa, in 1513, discovered it from the summit of the mountains which traverse the Isthmus of Darien. Magellan sailed across it from east to west in 1521. The Indian, so called from its proximity to India; the Arctic, from the Greek word *arktos, the bear,* or *the north;* and the Antarctic, from the Greek word *anti, opposite to,* and *arktos.* The Pacific Ocean is the largest and the Arctic the smallest. The Pacific occupies more than half the surface of the globe." As these form only one body of salt water, there are no precise limits at which it can be said that one ocean terminates and another begins. The ocean is a world within itself containing thousands of hidden objects that the curiosity of the human mind has never reached. The sea holds a prominent place among the sublimest objects of nature. It astonishes every beholder who surveys the vast expanse of its mighty waters, glittering and dancing in the summer sun, then lifting its foaming waves and roaring in the winter storm; the flux and reflux of its tides; and the consideration that on its ample bosom the stately ship bears the fortunes of thousands, displays the wonderful adaptation of nature to the wants of man.

The tides are supposed to be produced by the revolution of the earth on its axis, the action of the winds, changes of temperature, inequality of evaporation, and the attraction of the sun and moon. It has been observed that the current has a tendency towards the east. It is found that the waters of the ocean are higher upon the eastern than upon the western coasts. It is said that the waters of the Red Sea maintain a constant elevation of four or five fathoms above the neighboring waters of the Mediterranean, at all times of the tide; and that in the Gulf of Mexico and the Caribbean Sea the surface is higher than the surface of the Pacific Ocean on the western coast of America.

The ordinary velocity of the tide is calculated to be about one mile and a half per hour, though in some countries near the shore it runs at the rate of a hundred miles per hour. The tide appears to extend to no great depth below the surface, and its great force is only felt near a coast. It is not unusual to see currents running close by each other in different directions. The highest tides in the world are said to be in the Bristol Channel, in England, and in Basin of Mines, Bay of Fundy, on the coast of Nova Scotia. At the former place it rises and falls forty-two feet, and at the latter place sixty feet. The greatest tide on the Newfoundland coast is near St. Shotts, about twenty miles west of Cape Race, which has been the scene of a number of shipwrecks. Several of H. M. Ships having been lost here, as well as steamers and sailing vessels. A strong current sets in there from the eastward at the rate of four miles an hour, and it is always greatest at the full of the moon. Vessels bound from Canada, New Brunswick and Nova Scotia are frequently wrecked upon that coast, in consequence of their not making proper allowance for the force of the current. No inconvenience is experienced in Newfoundland from the rushing of the tides. The waters generally do not rise or fall more than six or eight feet.

Kurisewo, or great Japan current, of the Pacific Ocean, which is estimated to be a mile deep and five hundred miles wide off the coast of California, and which regulates and equalizes the climate along the shore line. This great body of water never varies more than three degrees from a temperature of fifty-eight degrees.

H. M. S. *Challenger*, on an exploring expedition in 1875, traversed the Atlantic twice:—round the Cape of Good Hope—the Antarctic Regions—Australia—Torris Straits—China—and round Cape Horn, the whole distance being about 70,000 miles; and taking sounding at 300 different places.

Prof. Sir Wyville Thompson, one of the exploring party says:—

"Everywhere we went we took soundings, and the greatest depth which we got was something about five miles. At a depth of about four miles we were always able to dredge and trawl with very considerable certainty. In fact, under favorable circumstances, we could use one of the large trawls, such as are commonly used to catch flat fish on the south coast of England and in the Firth of Forth, without difficulty or risk, and almost with the certainty that the trawl would come up with its freight quite right from that depth. It seemed almost wild to make such an attempt at first; but we found the little iron dredge we were using so unsatisfactory, on account of the small quantity of material it brought up, that I think it was Captain Nares who suggested that we might try the trawl. We did so, not expecting ever to see it come up again; but it did come up, and brought with it a lot of fish of all kinds, none of which we had had ever seen before. The trawl after that almost entirely replaced the dredge. Instead of using a small Ball's dredge about eighteen inches long, a trawl with a beam of twenty feet across was dragged across the bottom of the Atlantic and Pacific Oceans; and in that way we covered a considerable amount of ground, and obtained a far better idea of the larger organisms of these regions. No doubt we missed a great many of the smaller things. Little hard and heavy bodies fell through the net; but we got, nevertheless, a very good idea of the *fauna* of the bottom of the sea. A number of the forms from these extreme depths were comparatively large and spiny, and these stuck in the large dredge net. The depth of the Atlantic apparently averaged something about two thousand fathoms, and that of the Pacific about twenty-five hundred fathoms. There did not seem to be any great difference between the Atlantic and Pacific Oceans—a general characteristic being that the bottom of each was a tolerably level expanse with slight undulations. In the temperature of these great depths we took a great interest, for we expected that by determining the temperature at the bottom we would be able to trace the direction in which the water was moving in any particular way, because water is an extremely bad conductor, and it maintains for a great length of time, unless there is some special reason for its mixing with other water, the temparature of its source. We usually, at most of the stations, determined correctly the bottom temperature, and then that of the various strata from the bottom up to the surface; and without going over these observations, I may say that we were inclined to come to the conclusion that the great mass of the water we found in the troughs of the Atlantic and Pacific is derived from the southern sea. At various localities in the Pacific and Atlantic the temperature of the water precisely, or very nearly so, agreed with water at the same depth in the southern sea, and the temperature of the bottom water in the Atlantic or Pacific at any one locality depended apparently upon the height of the barrier which separated that particular portion of the ocean from the southern sea from which it is derived. Thus in this way all over the Atlantic and Pacific Oceans we could almost tell by the temperature of the water the height of the ridges which separated it from its source."

In the Gulf Stream, that great Sargasso Sea, that strange ocean meadow with the many forms of life, that like the weed itself are to be found nowhere else in the world. It was this vast meadow of tangled seaweed that so disturbed the minds of Columbus' sailors that they were ready to mutiny, fearing hidden shoals.

Humboldt is of opinion that this weed is produced in large beds, at the bottom of the ocean, and that from these beds it is detached in a ripened state, and collects in large masses on that part of the Atlantic called the Sargasso or Weedy Sea. Other writers are of opinion that it grows along the sea-coast, and is carried to sea by means of winds and currents.

The New York *Sun* says:—

"Vessels very rarely visit the great sea in the middle of the ocean, but occasionally they are driven there by storms or adverse winds. Strange sights meet the gaze of the sailors at such times. Wonderful stories—partly true and partly false—have been told by sailors returning from a forced trip to the vast Sargasso Sea. The surface of the sea is covered with floating wrecks, spars, seaweed, boxes, fruits, and a thousand other innumerable articles. It is the great repository or storehouse of the ocean, and all things which do not sink to the bottom or are not washed upon the shores are carried to the centre of the sea. When one considers the vast number of wrecks on the ocean, and the quantity of floating material that is thrown overboard, a faint idea of the wreckage in the Sargasso Sea may be conceived. Derelicts or abandoned vessels frequently disappear in mysterious ways, and no accounts are given of them for years by passing vessels. Then, suddenly, years later, they appear again in some well-travelled route to the astonishment of all. The wrecks are covered with mould and green slime, showing the long, lonesome voyage which they have passed through. It is generally supposed that such derelicts have been swept into the centre of the pool and remained in the Sargasso Sea, until finally cast out by some unusually violent storm. The life in this sea is interesting. Solitary and alone the acres of waters, covered with the debris, stretch out as the vast graveyard of the ocean, seldom being visited by vessels or human beings. From all trading routes of vessels, the sight of a sail or steam vessel is something unusual. The fishes of the sea form the chief life of these watery solitudes. Attracted by the vast quantities of wreckage floating in the sea, and also by the gulfweed on which many of them live, they swarm around in great numbers. The smaller fishes live in the intricate avenues formed by the seaweed, and the more ferocious denizens of the deep come hither to feed upon the quantities of small fish. In this way the submarine life of the Sargasso Sea is made interesting and lively. The only life overhead is that made by a few sea birds, which occasionally reach the solitude of this mid-ocean cemetery. A few of the long flyers of the air penetrate to the very middle of the ocean, but it is very rarely that this occurs. Some have been known to follow vessels across the ocean, keeping at a respectful distance from the stern. Other birds have been swept out to sea by storms, and have finally sought refuge in the Sargasso Sea. Still others, taking refuge on some derelict, have been gradually carried to the same mid-ocean scene. There is sufficient food floating on the surface, or to be obtained from the fishes which live among the forests of seaweed, to support a large colony of birds. It is surmised that many of those found in the sea have inhabited those regions for years, partly from choice and partly from necessity. Birds swept out there by storms would not care to venture the long return trip to land, and finding an abundance of food and wrecks on which to rest and rear their young, they might easily become contented with their strange lot. Just how far the strong-winged sea-birds can fly without resting is all conjectural; but it is doubtful if many of them undertake such a long journey seaward with no better prospects ahead than dreary wastes of water."

The wide expanse of ocean teems with life; a population made up of beings of various habits and of various forms range its gloomy deeps. Here we behold the whale, the monarch of the deep, plowing the waves, and lashing the ocean into storm. A shoal of porpoises racing on the crested wave. The seal, the sword-fish and the dolphin gamboling. Here, too, the shark revels in his ocean home.

"In the war of 1812, numerous British cruisers were on the look-out for American vessels all over the world. One day an English corvette sailed into Port Royal harbor, Jamaica, with a prize she had taken on suspicion of being a Yankee; but as there were no papers on board, and no flag but the English, she could not be convicted. She was therefore left in the harbor with a prize crew on board, and the cruiser sailed out. Two days after leaving Jamaica, she fell in with another British cruiser on the same station, and came near enough for the captain of the corvette to board the other. He was met on the quarter-deck by the other captain, and they compared notes. The captain of the corvette said he had taken a prize, but was afraid he could not convict her, as there were no papers on board. 'What is her name?' asked the other. 'The Nancy.' 'Oh, I know her, The Nancy, Captain Brush; supercargo, John Williams.' 'Why, where did you see her?—that is the captain's name, and also the supercargo's.' 'Well, walk aft; I will show you a shark we caught this morning, and we are drying a part of the contents of his stomach on the poop.' They walked aft, and the captain handed his visitor the ship's papers, which Captain Brush had thrown overboard on being chased, and the shark had picked them up for his breakfast. The two cruisers, on making this discovery, made sail for Port Royal together, where they arrived. The Nancy was convicted by the papers found in the fish, and the two British cruisers shared equally in the prize."

Every ebb of the sea exhibits to our view the sea-urchin, the crab, the mussel, the lobster, the clam, the razor-fish, and hundreds of other animals. Few persons ever cross the mighty deep without beholding fleets of creatures sporting and frisking on the ocean wave.

Of what incalculable benefit is the sea to man! Without it trade and commerce could not be carried on. It has been an agent in the civilization of the world. It has led to the building of ships, by means of which the distant nations of the world are brought near each other. Could we take a view of all the ships which pass and repass the ocean, with their cargoes of corn, wine and oil, what a panorama of life on the ocean would pass before us. The Atlantic is now crowded with "floating palaces," filled with goods and multitudes of passengers, who are careening joyously over the ocean which is crossed in a few days. The great world of waters was almost unknown until the invention of the mariner's compass, in the beginning of the twelfth century. It was then found that a piece of iron rubbed against a loadstone, pointed due north and south. This was shortly after applied to navigation. Two ends of an iron needle being rubbed against a loadstone, and balanced on a pivot, so as to turn round freely, acquired the singular property of always pointing to the north. This needle being fixed in a round box, with a card marked with thirty-two points, forms the sea-compass. The loadstone is sometimes called magnetic iron-stone.

It is somewhat harder and more heavy than iron ore, and it is found in most iron mines. As yet, philosophers have not been able to explain the cause of the extraordinary powers of attraction possessed by this stone. Previous to the invention of the compass, the ancients steered their ships at night by the moon and stars. Pope beautifully describes it in his translation of Homer:

> " Placed at the helm he sat, and marked the skies,
> Nor closed in sleep his ever watchful eyes.
> There viewed the Pleiades, and the northern team,
> And great Orion's more refulgent beam,
> To which around the axle of the sky,
> The Bear revolving, points his golden eye,
> Who shines exalted on th' ethereal plain,
> Nor bathes his blazing forehead in the main.'

The first advantage resulting from the invention of the compass was the discovery of a passage round the south of Africa, by the Portuguese. The next and most important was the discovery of the Bahamas, called then St. Salvador, in the West Indies, and the continent of South America, by Columbus, in 1492; five years after which, Newfoundland and the continent of North America were discovered by John Cabot, a Venetian, who sailed from Bristol under a commission from Henry VII. of England. The following interesting account of why the compass points north, is taken from *Golden Hours*.:—

"The needle of the compass points north because practically the earth is a magnet, not differing essentially in its magnetic properties from a bar of magnetized steel, says *American Notes and Queries.*

"It has two poles of greatest intensity, and, like most large steel magnets, there are several supplementary poles of lesser intensity. Just as the poles of one bar magnet attracts the end of another, so the magnet poles of the earth behave toward poles of the compass-needle, unlike poles attracting and like poles repelling each other.

"But it is not correct to say that the needle always points north; as a matter of fact, there are but few localities on the earth where it does so, and even those are constantly changing.

"An irregular line drawn from the mouth of the Orinoco river through the east coast of Hayti, Charleston, S. C., and Detroit, Mich., represents very nearly the line in which there is no variation at the present time.

"In all places east of this line the north end of the neddle swings slightly to the westward; in all places west of it to the eastward. At the mouth of the Columbia river the variation of the compass is about 22° east; in Alaska it is from 40 to 60° east; midway between New York and Liverpool it is about 35° west.

"Of course there is reason for this variation, and the explanation is that the needle does not point to the North

Pole, as many people suppose, but to the *magnetic pole*, which is something entirely different.

"The magnetic north pole is at present on or near the north-western shore of Boothia peninsula, in the northern part of North America. Its position is constantly changing, and in the last six hundred years it has moved about half the distance round the geographical pole.

"During a period of three hundred years, in which observations have been carefully made at the Magnetic Observatory in Paris, the variations have changed from 11° 20' east of north to 22° 10' west.

"In the United States the rate of the change invariation differs much in different parts of the country. In Washington State it changes at the rate of about 7' a year; in Arizona and New Mexico it is stationery; in the New England States it is from 1' to 3' per year."

If some of the undiscovered rocks and shoals could become decimated and vocal, they would sing in mournful strains—

> "Of the ship that sunk in the reefy surge
> And left her fate to the sea-bird's dirge—
> Of the lover that sailed to meet his bride,
> And his story left to the secret tide—
> Of the father that went on the trustless main,
> And never was met by his child again—
> And the hidden things which the waves conceal,
> And the sea-bird's song alone can reveal."

Poetry has decked the grave of the sailor-boy with pearls, and shaded it with coral branches, whilst spirit forms have been created to hover around it with soft airs, and to sing, and sail, and sleep on the "breast of the billow." But there is something more than poetry in dying at sea, to be washed overboard in the darkness of the night, to grapple with death on the foaming billow, to listen to the ocean's roar and tempest moan, singing our funeral dirge.

Who hath not paused with deep emotion to gaze on the

vast expanse of the mighty deep, whether it is spread out calm and mirror-like or lifted into liquid mountains by the fierce breath of the storm ? Who has not thought of the

"Mariner who compasses the globe,
With but one plank between him and the grave."

What anguish must the shipwrecked sailor feel, as he clings to portions of the wreck on the dark-blue waters, when thoughts of home and loved ones gather around his heart—when he thinks of his aged mother, his loved sister, and his expectant wife, as he sinks into the ocean depths, and sends his wild cry of anguish along the troubled world of waters !

"Then think on the mariner toss'd on the billow,
Away from the scenes of his childhood and youth—
No mother to watch o'er his sleep-broken pillow ;
No father to counsel, no sister to soothe."

Family Worship.

FAMILY worship has been on the decline in the cities as well as in the country. In only a few houses is family worship observed daily, in others it is observed only on Sundays. But in the great majority of houses no worship is kept. The Bible is hardly ever read. No blessing is asked upon meals, no thanks expressed. The heathen blindly bowed to wood and stone, but in this land of gospel light many parents do not so much as observe the very form of bowing before the Lord. In some homes the difficulty is to get the members together at a suitable hour. In the morning all is hurry and confusion, and in the evening the engagements are so many and the hours of retiring so different, that no convenient time can be found for the service. So on one plea or another the parent excuses himself from the duty, and the family goes without the morning and evening blessing. All Christian people are agreed that it is of the utmost importance that family worship should be conducted regularly in the home. It was the practice of General Gordon during his first sojourn in the Soudan to lay a pocket handkerchief at his tent door half an hour each day. This was respected by all as the signal that he was at his devotions. The best time for evening worship, where there are children, is immediately after tea. There ought if possible to be praise as well as reading and prayer, and the children should be encouraged to take part in the reading, as it gives them a greater interest; and if they begin to take an interest in the worship in the home, they would also take an interest in it in the Church. Need we be surprised if our children drift away from the services of the Church, when family devotion is neglected in the home. There will be more life in the heart, in the Church, in the home, in all Christian effort, when there is more prayer in the home. It is a matter deeply to be deplored that in many families there is no such thing as family worship. There may be religious members in the family, but that in itself will not constitute family religion, and indeed it is difficult to see how there can be family religion where there is no family worship. No teaching is so powerful as example. It was when the disciples heard Jesus pray that they said, "Lord teach us to pray." When children hear their parents pray, they are beginning to bear upon them the most powerful influence to lead them to pray. The Rev. John Ryland, the predecessor of the celebrated Robert Hall, at Cambridge, being on a journey was overtaken by a violent storm, and compelled to take shelter in the first inn he came to. When the hour of rest approached, his host informed him that his chamber was prepared whenever he chose to retire. "But," said he, "you have not had your family together." "I don't know what you mean," said the landlord. "To read and pray with them," replied the guest. The landlord confessed that he never thought of doing such a thing, "Then, sir," said Mr. Ryland, "I must beg you to order my horse immediately, I had rather brave the storm than venture to sleep in a house where there is no prayer; who can tell what may befall us before morning." The landlord called the family together, when Mr. Ryland conducted family worship, which resulted in much good to the family and neighborhood. Rowland Hill when travelling, was once placed in precisely similar circumstances. It is said that "a family without prayer is like a home without a roof, exposed to all the injury of weather and to every storm that blows." In Greenland, when a stranger knocks at the door, he asks, "Is God in this house?" and if they answer "Yes," he enters. The direct influence of family prayer is to bring down the benediction of God upon the children of the house. We live in the days of multiplicity of engagements, and many parents are excusing themselves on the plea that they have not time for family prayer. The father has to rush off to business; he has time, it is true, to read his morning paper, but no time to gather his family around him, and by the hand of faith put them under the sheltering wing of God. In the evening he is tired and wearied, and thus family worship is neglected. He suffers his business to consume his time, so as to deprive him of opportunities for prayer, reading the Bible, and real communion with God, his services of mammon eat up his service of God. A Frenchman, it is said, visited his chapel in Paris to say his family devotions, but he found no priest in attendance, and the building undergoing repairs. He walked up to the altar, laid his card on it with a low bow and withdrew, well satisfied with the homage he had paid to the Lord. It is to be feared that too many of the morning prayers of the family are little more than laying a card upon the altar, a complimentary presentation of respects.

But nothing less than such a communion with God as touches the heart and draws forth earnest desires can be any safeguard to us in the busy scenes of the day. In some families the father is nominally a Churchman, the mother may be Presbyterian, Methodist or Baptist, but the children are Godless, know no religion. With how many the consideration of supposed want of time has been allowed so to weigh that in their homes there has come to be no family altar. No one who believes that God answers prayer will think of omitting either secret or family devotion for want of time, even when business is unusually urgent. The plea of want of time none should urge it, but those who regard prayer as an empty mockery. There must be real communion with God and not a mere formal prayer.

He Is Nobody.

How often do we hear it said of one of no position, wealth or influence, he is nobody! As we grow older we see things in a different light. The nobodies, as they are contemptuously called, are an overwhelming majority of the human race. Of the fourteen hundred millions of people on the globe to-day, how many have ever been heard of beyond the narrow circle of their neighborhood? Certainly not one in a million. A few friends know them, and recognize them when they meet, but a few miles from home they are as unknown as if they lived in the remotest part of the world. Of the millions of millions who have lived and died since Adam, how few have left any memorial. Of how few do we know the names even. What they did and what they were we know not. They are as indistinguishable as the grains of sand on the ocean floor. If, then, nobodyism is the common lot, why should not we be willing to be nobodies? The men and women who have been discontented with the common lot, who have scorned the idea of being nobodies, have too often mistaken notoriety for fame. The world cares more for what is startling and sensational than what is useful. It prefers to be astonished or even shocked to being instructed. Some people have pushed themselves into notoriety by eccentricities, some embezzlement, some great fraud, or some startling crime. The honest, plodding man is not spoken of. The best people, as a rule, are the least known, and the best part of human life does not get into history. History, for the most part, is a record of wars, catastrophes, of vices and crimes, rather than of the real progress of the race. However successful any man may have been in the world, he will confess that life has been full of disappointments. This, indeed, is the verdict which we must all pass upon it. When we begin life we are full of hope and spirit; the world is all before us, and we dream of great enjoyment. The future is all bright, our pathway looks as if it stretched away through a land of milk and honey. We do not think of any desert land, nor of any enemies. But we have found that the objects on which we set our heart have not yielded us, when we obtained them, the enjoyment we expected.

We have found that honor, wealth, pleasure and fame are broken cisterns that hold no water. Let the nobodies of the world be consoled, assured that the labor-loving, frugal and industrious and virtuous among them possess joy and happiness which the rich know not and cannot appreciate. It was the remark of a celebrated London physician, who enjoyed the most lucrative practice, that he had witnessed such harrowing scenes at the death-beds of the aristocracy, that he shrank with instinctive dread when called upon to visit persons of this class in their sickness. The nobodies have no cause to envy the men of fame, honor or riches. Gibbon, in his history of the rise and fall of the Roman Empire, gives an account of one of the Caliphs of Bagdad, one of the wealthiest sovereigns that ever lived, who luxuriated in magnificence and pleasure, who reigned fifty years, but during a life-time only enjoyed fourteen days of happiness. Look at the vanity and emptiness of mere worldly fame in the closing scenes of the lives of Cardinal Wolsey, Bonaparte, Mary Queen of Scots, Tallyrand, Sir Walter Scott, Lord Byron, Burns, Jane Shore, Lady Hamilton, Lady Hester Stanhope, and a host of others, showing the vanity and illusory nature of all human ambition and greatness. If everybody was eminent in literature and science, nobody would be eminent. If everybody was famous, fame would be like the billows of the ocean, none of which is distinguishable from the rest.

Where are those who began the journey of life with us, or joined us at any point on the march? Few can look back on happy hours without thinking of those with whom they spent them; and then comes the sad question, Where are they now? If we were to have a roll-call of all our earthly friends, and of all who were associated with us in any way, or known to us in youth, how many would respond to the call? Comparatively few indeed. Who could then have forecast how it would be with us when fifty years had come and gone. Where, then, are those with whom in life we started? Alas, all along the road they dropped out of the ranks and turned aside to die. And with this constant diminution of friends there comes a sense of loneliness, which no bustle of life and no accession of new friends can altogether remove. As we grow older this sense of loneliness deepens.

One of the greatest curses of the ancient Romans was "May you outlive your friends." The world is a world of changes; there are changes in the natural world, changes in the political world, the commercial world, changes in our homes. We fail to see the children of yesterday in the busy men and women of to-day. The times have changed, and we have changed with them. Is there anything unchanging? We cannot find it in ourselves, we cannot find it in our surroundings. If we wish for something on which we can rest with unshaken confidence through the vicissitudes of life, we must find it in God. Then, of how little consequence will it be, that we have been placed among the nobodies!

Slavery of Debt.

"WHAT we wish you particularly to tell us is, how a man stands in the future world dying in debt," etc. It used to be the saying of an old planter in Newfoundland, "My grandfather lived and died in debt, my father lived all his life in debt and died in debt, and I myself am deeply in debt which I hope to get rid of; but all these generations of indebtedness have arisen mainly from high prices of goods and bad fisheries." We know nothing of man's status in the future world, except what the Bible tells us. Who among us has not asked, in the deep necessities of his immortal spirit, what shall become of me when I die? Where shall I go when I leave this world? You have taken me outside the gates of this world to mentally explore what John Wesley calls "A land of deepest shade, unpierced by human thought." James Montgomery says:—"Ye dead, where can your dwelling be? The place for all the living come and see." And Blair, in his beautiful poem, says:—" O, that some courtly ghost would blab it out: What 'tis you are and we must shortly be." The present is an age of profound religious enquiry. What a mine of speculation this subject opens up to query! How vain are most of the descriptions and speculations concerning the future world! There is a veil that separates us from the invisible world, which the hand of the philosopher cannot lift to show us what is doing on the other side. The scripture only can tell us of our destiny. God will forgive our being in debt, like all our other short-comings, because "His blood cleanseth from all sin." To the vilest sinners repentance and remission of sins are commanded to be offered. The first offers of grace were made to the people who, of all others, hated and despised Him—the Jews. They persecuted His prophets and apostles and crucified Himself. Christ chooses the greatest offenders against His laws to make them the greatest example of His mercy, unlike our human laws which visit the greatest punishment on the greatest criminal. Do you say that your sins are scarlet? God says, "They shall be as white as snow." Do you say that they are red like crimson? God says, "They shall be as wool." Do you say that you are five hundred pence debtors? God says he will "Frankly forgive you all." "He pardoneth and absolveth all them that truly repent and unfeignedly believe His holy Gospel."

You cannot go into a city, town or village where you will not find some persons in debt. In Newfoundland it used to be the practice with the merchants to give their dealers the same amount of credit, whether they were in debt or out of debt. I recollect, when I was a youth, I was put to draw off accounts in my father's office. Some of those accounts were very long. I used to feel annoyed that, after all my trouble and labor making out accounts fifteen or twenty pages, most of the planters refused to take them, because, as they said, "What is the good of an account to us? We don't want them." They got all they wanted and they were so deeply in debt that they gave up all hope of ever paying it. A long time ago, it was the custom in Turkey that when a person died in debt, the body lay above ground until his friends came forward and paid his debts. I have heard of an old clergyman who never preached without ending his sermon with this good advice: "Be careful, friends, not to run into debt." Debt is one of the discomforts to individuals and to families, and one of the worst evils that can afflict society. Debt leads to a thoughtless, inconsiderate and wasteful course of living, and blinds the eyes to the common rights that men owe to their fellow men. Persons who form the habit of living in debt seem to be insensible of the fact that they are living on what is not their own, which when strictly and rigidly viewed, is not honest. Debt makes a man a slave, and is a galling burden on life, mentally and morally. He who makes purchases without money, for the necessaries and the unnecessaries of life, lives on the chance or chequer game of the future, with all its uncertainties of health or sickness, of business, of changing circumstances, and of misfortune in its various forms. He has no certainty of future ability to pay those liabilities, especially if they are large in proportion to his means, and hence, how often have creditors to suffer losses, and virtually pay for the unwisdom, and for the frequent luxuries of those who go into debt. We preach to the people the exercise of self-denial. We ought to practice it in respect of our means of income and outgo. What a blessing it would be to the church and the world were the apostles advice adopted by families generally: "Owe no man anything." And if this principle had a practical embodiment in the doings of Christian men and women, the example and influence thereof would doubtless tell against the over-spending tendencies of our times, and also there would be the possession of greater means to be devoted to Christian liberality.

"There was a good prayer I knew a man to offer once —a very good prayer. A brother was praying with much noise for faith—soul-saving faith, sin-killing faith, devil-driving faith. There was a quiet friend next to him, to whom the noisy brother owed a long bill. 'Amen,' said the quiet friend; 'Amen, and give us debt-paying faith, too.'" There are congregations who run in debt to their minister. The obligation of a congregation to pay the minister's stipend as soon as it is due, is as much a matter of business as their obligation to pay the merchant, or the doctor, or the lawyer. A minister stated to his congregation that they were behind in their payment five hundred dollars, and that it was making him dishonest, as he could not pay his own liabilities, as he promised; but if they would pay him two hundred dollars, he would forgive the balance. Another congregation voted a hundred dollars more to the minister's salary, but he positively refused it, for said he, "I have to go round and beg, and plead, and importune for the three hundred salary you voted (all of which I have not received), and to go round and have to beg for another hundred would kill me." Nations cannot repudiate their debts without losing their character; but some congregations think nothing of it. To cast off the incubus of debt, brings the comforting and pleasing thought that the clothes I am wearing, and the clothes my sons are wearing, and the dresses in which my daughters go to school and church, and the meals on our table from day to day are really my own, because they are all paid for. Money is a mere instrument—a means to an end. What men want for personal use is not money, but the things which money will purchase. We cannot eat money, nor wear it as clothing. The man who has money to offer, can go to the shop and get what he wants in exchange for it; but he who makes purchases without money, has no certainty of paying for them. Let us endeavor to follow the command of the Apostle: "Owe no man anything."

Woman's Rights.

CARDINAL GIBBON says, in his book entitled "Our Christian Heritage," published in 1889:—"The Catholic Church, following the maxims of the Gospel and of St. Paul, proclaims woman the peer of man in origin and destiny, in redemption by the blood of Christ, and in the participation of His spiritual gifts. ' Ye are all,' says the apostle, ' the children of God by faith, which is in Christ Jesus. There is neither Jew nor Greek; there is neither servant nor freeman; there is *neither male nor female.*' The meaning is that in the distribution of his gifts God makes no distinction of person or sex. He bestows them equally on bond and free, on male and female. And as woman's origin and destiny are the same as man's, so is her dignity equal to his. As both were redeemed by the same Lord, and as both aspire to the same heavenly inheritance, so should they be regarded as equal in rank on earth; as they are partakers of the same spiritual gifts, so should they share alike the blessings and prerogatives of domestic life. In the mind of the Church, however, equal rights do not imply that both sexes should engage promiscuously in the same pursuits, but rather that each sex should discharge those duties which are adapted to its physical constitution and sanctioned by the canons of society. To some among the gentler sex the words *equal rights* have been, it is feared, synonymous with *similar rights.* It is fearful to contemplate what would have become of our Christian civilization without the aid of the female sex. Not to speak of the grand array of consecrated virgins who are fanning the flame of faith and charity throughout the world. Women, it is true, are debarred from the exercise of the public ministry and the celebration of the Sacred Mysteries, for they are commanded by the Apostle to "keep silence in the churches." But if they are not apostles by preaching, they are apostles by prayer, by charity and good example. If they cannot offer up the sacrifice of the mass, they are priests in the broader sense of the term; for they offer up in the sanctuary of their own homes and on the altar of their hearts the acceptable sacrifice of supplication, praise and thanksgiving to God. Viewing, then, woman's dignity and her work in the cause of Christ, well may we apply to her these words of the Prince of the Apostles: 'You are a chosen generation, a royal priesthood, a holy nation, a purchased people.' The noblest work given to woman is to take care of her children. The most important part of her apostleship should consist in instructing them in the ways of God." In 1850, forty-five years ago, I attended with Mrs. Tocque "A Woman's Rights Convention," held in the City Hall, in the City of Worcester, in the heart of the State of Massachusetts. It was the first Woman's Rights Convention ever held in America. Mrs. Earle, an intimate friend of ours, a Quakeress, a lady of the highest intellectual endowments, and moving in the upper strata of society, presided at the meeting. Her husband, a Quaker, was editor and proprietor of the *Worcester Spy*, the oldest newspaper published in the State of Massachusetts. The ladies who spoke at the meeting were not only eloquent, but displayed gems of thought flashing with the light of intellect and reflecting all the hues of Christian graces.

That woman has rights no one will deny. That she has in time past been neglected, oppressed and degraded is true. She has not even now risen to her true sphere in every respect. She constitutes the better part of creation. She occupies a position that man never could occupy, discharges duties that he never could discharge, and possesses those qualities of mind and character which, if rightly cultivated, fit her to adorn society and bless the world. She is peculiarly adapted to have the care of the sick. There is a large class of female physicians in England, France, Germany, Italy, the United States and Canada.

They have taken prizes at the Universities. They are students of law and theology. They have soared high in astronomy, dug deep in geology, and ascended the highest pinnacles of Panassus. They have far exceeded the achievements of men in astronomy, poetry, literature and religion. Women were now found occupying the mission field in every part of the world, not only among Roman Catholics, but also among all the Protestant denominations. Female exertion in the cause of Christianity is one of the most prominent and characteristic distinctions of the present age. Of woman it might be said :

> "Not she with treacherous lips the Saviour sung
> Not she denied Him with unholy tongue,
> She when apostles fled could dangers brave,
> Last at His cross and earliest at His grave."

Everywhere she has performed deeds of heroism. She has filled positions in the Government offices, post offices, telegraph offices, and other positions in Europe and America. She votes in municipal elections, school boards, and in Toronto for members of Parliament. On the temperance question she wields a power and influence that men cannot reach. In the family and school her influence is greater than man's can be. There are no positions occupied by men in banks, government, or anything else that women cannot fill. They should therefore have equal advantages with men in all departments of life. In physical endurance and rough labor, women far outstrip men. In most of the farm houses I have stayed at, the women had to get up cold winter mornings, light the fires, and draw the water, while the men have been lying in bed. They often cut and saw wood, and in addition to which, do all the cooking, washing, mending, spinning, knitting and baking, while the men were sitting round the stove smoking their pipes. The women had to work the garden, raise the beans, tomatoes, cucumbers and other garden vegetables, because the work was *too hard for the men.*

The men must have a plough and a pair of horses to break up the ground for them, but the woman must take her spade and break up the ground with her own hands. The man sits on the reaper and drives the horses to cut the grain, but the woman has the hard work. It is she who gathers the grain into sheafs, binds them, pitches them in and out of the waggon, drives the horses to the barn and stows them away for threshing. She makes the hay, milks the cows, churns the butter and prepares it for market. Women do most of the marketing. I have seen them riding along Queen Street, Toronto, sometimes in the coldest, stormiest weather. Sometimes they come alone to market. I often pity the poor woman, sitting in the open, unsheltered waggon, cold winter mornings, around the Toronto Markets doing the selling, while the men are walking about quite comfortable after taking their whiskey punch. In lots of cases, in every kind of business in Toronto, if women did not manage the business instead of the men, their families would be ruined. Many women have been, and are, tailors, shoemakers, barbers, printers, editors, painters and artizans of every description. Some years ago I stopped with the Misses Wiswell, at Wilmot, N.S., aunts of the present Dean of Halifax, Dr. Gilpin; their father was a clergyman of the Church of England in America, but left soon after the revolution and settled in a parish in Nova Scotia. The Misses Wiswell, after the death of their parents, set to work themselves, gathered brick clay, burnt brick for a large house, carried the brick and mortar to the bricklayers, and otherwise toiled attending on them. I have spent days at their large and elegantly-furnished house. They worked the farm with their brother; they were the managers; they used to work on the farm some nights until 12 o'clock; they kept no servants. Some time after they started a boarding school for young ladies. One of the sisters married Mr. Smith, one of the wealthiest bankers in St. John, New Brunswick. Mr. Smith one time at

Boston went to the Revere House, at that time the principal hotel of the city, and asked at the bar if he could get a room. As he was not dressed in the highest style of fashion, the clerk hesitated some time, and said he did not know. Mr. Smith asked for a cigar; on receiving it he took a piece of paper out of his pocket to light it; but, before doing so, he showed it to the clerk of the bar. It was a thousand dollar bill. A room was found for him immediately, and every attention paid to him. After the above little digression, I have to say Mary Longhurst, with her little daughter, residing in the county of Simcoe, Ontario, with whom I was personally acquainted, took a free grant farm at Muskoka, chopped the trees, burnt and logged them, built a shanty, sowed the grain, planted the potatoes, gathered in the crops, &c., and did such hard work as most men would shrink from. She is now in comfortable circumstances. Hannah Lauder, in the Province of Quebec, at whose house I often spent a week, used to plough the farm, put up the fences, sow and reap, shear the sheep, knit the wool, milk the cows, churn the butter, salt the pork, look after the cattle, horses and poultry, cut and draw firewood. In the evenings she would dress in style, play the organ and sing. She has often brought me a delicious fish caught by herself. She was a good fisher. Last summer I spent a little time with her in her splendid new house. In Newfoundland at Hermitage Bay and other parts of the coast, women used to fish; they cure the codfish. In St. John's they used to work in loading and unloading vessels, and throughout the country women work the gardens, and do all sorts of drudgery work. I do not remember seeing a single man working in a garden when I was on a visit to Newfoundland two years ago. Some of the girls are quite literary, and contribute articles in prose and poetry to the press. We have heard of women being in the army; and who has not read of the heroic Amazons, an army all composed of women, and the Maid of

Orleans, who led the French army on to victory. Among the ancient Greeks and Romans women took the field, and in some heathen countries at the present day the women fight like the men. At the time of the Buccaneers women commanded some of the ships. Some have been sailors. See how Grace Darling could handle her boat in the stormiest weather, and rescue men from death. We find women stewardesses on the ocean and lake steamers, and also on some sailing vessels. A woman is now filling the highest position on earth, swaying the sceptre of the greatest nation in the world, as Queen of Great Britain and Ireland and Empress of India. Wherever the waters roll, the name of Queen Victoria is known.

Fashionable Amusements.

CERTAIN things there are, which are institutions, having long been used to lead people astray, such as theatre, opera, card-table, dance and horse-race. Some go to the opera because they "love music." Others say a game of cards is no harm, and yet the defiling touch of gamblers has for centuries made the game leprous. Not a few say there is nothing wrong in the dance, that it is simply the "poetry of motion;" these institutions for thousands of years have been the gilded gateway to ruin. I never learned how to dance or to play cards. Bishop Coxe, who is the Protestant Bishop of Western New York, one of the ablest men of the United States, says:—"You are welcome to quote me anywhere and everywhere as regarding the modern dance, waltz, German, or whatever else they call it, as immoral. My standpoint in the Scriptures, as understood in the Primitive Christian age, when 'renouncing the world' meant anything but conformity to licentious and heathenish indecorums of that 'excess of riot' which disgraces the Laodicean religion of these times. These shameless dances, with play-going and social parties, are all denounced by the spirit of the New Testament, discouraged by the example of saints and martyrs, and everywhere discountenanced by moralists. Not to the Puritans belongs the exclusive honor of setting their faces against such things. Nowhere has play-going been so written down as by the pen of Jeremy Collier, the stout old High Churchman. I have strong convictions on the subject." It is said most of the fallen women in the cities first commenced their downward course at the waltz. Some of the Roman Catholic clergy of New York City have denounced this style of dancing in the strongest terms. Where I usually stop at, on St. Denis Street, which is one of the principle streets of the City of Montreal, has one of the aristocratic French families residing the next door, and almost every Sunday evening they have a social dance. They do not think it any harm to have a little recreation and amusement after attending mass. The head of the Roman Catholic Church in the United States, His Eminence the Cardinal Archbishop Gibbon, of Baltimore, says :—" There is little doubt that the revulsion in public sentiment from a rigorous to a loose observance of the Lord's Day can be ascribed to the sincere but misguided zeal of the Puritans, who confounded the Christian Sunday with the Jewish Sabbath, and imposed restraints on the people which were repulsive to Christian freedom, and which were not warranted by the Gospel dispensation. The Lord's day to the Catholic heart is always a day of joy. The Church desires us on that day to be cheerful without dissipation, grave and religious without sadness and melancholy. She forbids, indeed, all unnecessary servile work on that day; but, as 'the Sabbath was made for man, not man for the Sabbath,' she allows such work whenever charity or necessity may demand it. And, as it is a day consecrated not only to religion, but also to relaxation of mind and body, she permits us to spend a portion of it in innocent recreation. In a word, the true conception of the Lord's Day is expressed in the words of the Psalmist : 'This is the day which the Lord hath made, let us rejoice and be glad therein.'" At the meeting of the Shaker Quakers, part of their worship consists of a religious dance. The men dance on one side and the women on the other side of the building. "A dancing Christian felt it his duty to try and win one of his associates to Christ. 'Oh,' says he, 'I long to see you a Christian.' 'For what?' 'Why, for salvation; don't you want to be saved?' 'Yes, I do.' 'Do you pray?' 'No, do you?' 'Yes,' said the 'Name To Live,' 'I pray for you.' 'For me! When, I'd like to know? Monday night you were at the dance; Tuesday night I met you at the ball; Wednesday night I saw you at the sociable, and like the rest of us you carried on like sixty; Thursday night I don't know where you were, but if cards could testify they would tell what you and I were up to until two o'clock Friday night; and now it is Saturday, and for the life of me I can't tell what time you've had for prayer this week or when you could have felt like it. As far as I can see, you seek your happiness just where I do—in the world and the things of the world soon becomes a passion.'"

Playing cards for pastime is regarded as an innocent amusement, but soon becomes a passion, and leads one to forego home, family, business and pleasure for the exciting scenes of the card-table. The presence of culture and intellect may embellish, but can never dignify it. It cannot recommend itself to the favor of Christian people. Dr. Holland, the accomplished American writer, says:—"I have at this moment ringing in my ears the dying injunction of my father's early friend, 'Keep your son from cards. Over them I have murdered time and lost Heaven.' Fathers and mothers, keep your sons from cards in the 'home circle.'" What a great amount of money is spent by people who have " renounced the world," attending theatres, circuses and public balls. Not long ago, at a ring performance in a tent in Virginia, the circus clown thus addressed the audience:—" We have taken in $600 here to-day—more than most ministers of the Gospel receive for a whole year's service. A large portion of this audience is made up of members of the church, and yet when your preacher asks you to aid him in supporting the Gospel, you are too poor to give anything. But you come here and pay dollars to hear me talk nonsense. I am a fool because I am paid for it. You profess to be wise, and yet you support me in my folly. Now, isn't this a pretty place for Christians to be in? Don't you feel ashamed of yourselves? You ought to." Baldwin, Bishop of Huron, in his address to the delegates of the Prison Congress, says:—" What were the results of the 'Life of Jack Sheppard' upon the community? Was it not to encourage the crime of robbery? and what can these scenes of blood and violence do but encourage murder. Who put temptation in the way that made the criminal? Amid the swell of voluptuous music, amid the glitter of the theatre, amid the deadly scenes of the circus that heart was led on, it knew not how, until the hand had the glittering dagger within it, and the foul crime was perpetrated that ended in the scene of the gallows." Sir Walter Scott says:—" Christianity, from its first origin, was inimical to the institution of the theatre." When speaking of the immoral influence of genteel comedy in particular, he says:—" It is not so probable that the 'Beggar's Opera' has sent one from the two-shilling gallery to the highway, as that a youth entering upon the world, and hesitating between good and evil, may, for instance, be determined to the worst course, by the gay and seductive example of Lovemore or Sir Charles Easy." It is said that several actors, while representing the Christian religion, and throwing it into ridicule before the Roman Emperor, were led to embrace Christianity, and some of them suffered martyrdom. Four of them were canonized by the Roman Catholic Church. Dr. Young, author of the "Night Thoughts," wrote a tragedy called "The Brothers," which was performed at Drury Lane Theatre in 1726; but when he went into orders the play was withdrawn. About thirty years after the Doctor consented to have his tragedy acted again at the same theatre. In mitigation of this circumstance, it is stated in Davies' Life of Garrick, that the Doctor formed a design of giving a thousand pounds to the Society for the propagation of the Gospel. It is said the profits of the play were insufficient to make good the sum, but that the Doctor made up the deficiency. Addison lamented the immoral tendency of the stage. He wrote a dramatic piece entitled "Cato," which, for sublimity of expression and depth of reason is considered some of the finest poetry in the English language, but it was never popular on the stage, on account of some of its moral sentiments. The moral beauties of Shakespeare bear but a small proportion to the mass of his writings. He had to pander to the vitiated taste of the age in which he lived. "He wrote," says Dr. Johnson, "without any moral purpose." In the reigns of Elizabeth, James, the Charles' and Georges', the stage was considered the fourth estate of the realm, and was regulated by acts of Parliament. Thousands obtained their knowledge of history and poetry by attending the theatre. Numerous proofs might be given to show that, in the reigns of George the third and fourth, the theatre was the nursery of immorality and vice. I never attended a theatre but three times during my life. The first at a small theatre at St. John's, Newfoundland, nearly sixty years ago, where I saw Miss Davenport, then a little girl, take part in Richard III. with her father. She afterwards became a celebrated actress in Europe and America. On that occasion the theatre was lit with tallow candles. It was in the hottest weather of the summer, the house was packed, which made the heat intense; by and by the candles began to melt; I was in the gallery, but I could not help laughing at seeing the melted tallow running down on the heads, faces and clothes of those who were in the pit. The place was so densely crowded that those in the pit could not get out of the way of the running tallow. Every candle in the theatre melted, and we were left in total darkness until more candles were procured to light up the building to finish the performance. The next theatrical performance I saw was at Boston Museum. After seeing the museum a play was acted. Mrs. Vincet, who was an actress there, was a regular attendant at the daily service and a communicant in the Church of the Advent, where I officiated. The greater portion of her income was given to the poor and other benevolent objects. The third theatre, and last I ever was at, was at the Howard Theatre, forty-five years ago, where a lady from England performed an opera. Horseracing is a scene of the most extensive gambling. It is the place where fortunes are made and lost. The necessities of our being demand recreation and amusement of some description. There are some kinds of recreation which, though they have no inherent sinfulness, still possess such a fascination as to make them dangerous. No limit can be prescribed for all persons beyond which indulgence in amusement is sinful. Each one must determine for himself.

The Celebrated Pusey Family.

THE Puseyites, so-called, are only of a higher type of the old-fashioned High Churchman. Intellectually and theologically, Dr. Pusey was one of the greatest men in the English Church. Miss Sarah B. Pusey, who has been a correspondent of mine for many years, with her sister, has been making a tour of the United States. She writes me some charming descriptive letters of places visited. In her last, she says: "We had quite a pleasant visit to West Grove, Chester County, Penn. The weather was charming. My father's sister's home is the old homestead of the Pusey family, dating back 150 years ago. We paid a visit to the large rose-growing establishment of Dingee & Co." It may interest you to hear something of the family history of so distinguished a man as the late celebrated Rev. Dr. Edward B. Pusey, who had so long been a central figure in the Church of England. Miss Pusey, some time ago, wrote me the following interesting account of her ancestors: "Caleb Pusey, the first of the name who immigrated to America was born in Berkshire, England, in 1651, and went to America in 1682. Caleb Pusey had no male issue, but left two daughters. He was followed to America by his two nephews in 1700. One of these, William Pusey, married Elizabeth Bowater, and settled in London Grove, Chester County, Pa., the other, Caleb Pusey jr., settled in Marlborough in the same county. Both left numerous descendants, and, as far as is known, all persons of American birth, bearing the Pusey name, may trace their origin to one or other of these two brothers, or to their uncle, Caleb Pusey, through his married daughters. The manor and village of Pusey, situated in the hundred of Ganfield, Berkshire, lie south of London Road, twelve miles from Oxford, and about five miles east of Farringdon. Here the family have resided from the time of the

Danish King Canute, fifty years before the Norman conquest. The tradition is that about the year 1016, during the bloody contest for the English Crown, between the Danes under Canute and the Saxons led by Edmund Ironsides, the hostile forces, having manœuvred for position, lay encamped a few miles apart, the Saxons on White Horse Hill, and the Danes at Chesbury Castle, a hamlet of Charney, when William Pusey, an officer under Canute, entered the Saxon camp in disguise and discovered a plot there formed for a midnight surprise and massacre of the Danes. As a reward for this perilous service, which saved the Danish army from destruction, King Canute presented the daring officer with the manor lying contiguous to the camping ground, giving him as evidence of the transfer the horn of an ox bearing the inscription; 'kyng knowde gene Wyllyam Puvte thys home to holde by thy lond." The horn was presented by Canute to the original William Pusey, with much ceremony on the beach of Southampton, and a plastic representation of the scene hangs in the hall of the present Pusey mansion. The old horn, by the delivery of which the estate was granted and is still held, remains in possession of the family. It is believed to have been the drinking horn of King Canute. It is a dark brown or tortoise shell color, two feet in length, one foot in circumference at the large end, and two and a quarter inches at the small end.

To continue the description of the horn presented to William Pusey by King Canute: Rings of silver gilt encircle it at either end, and a broader ring or band surrounds it near the middle. To this band are affixed two legs with feet resembling those of a hound, by which the horn is supported upon a stand. It could also be used as a hunting-horn. Cornage was a species of tenure in old England, by which the grantee not only received, but bound himself to blow a horn to alarm the country on the approach of an enemy, and tradition asserts that the delivery of this old horn imposed upon its receiver a special obligation to keep a vigilant watch and blow a warning alarm against all the King's enemies. The inscription on the middle band of the horn is believed to belong to a much later age than that of Canute.

The estate thus granted by the old Danish King to William Pusey has remained in possession of the family and their descendants down to the present day. In the year 1155, the manor was held by Henry de Persye; 1307, by Richard de Pose; that Henry de Pusey was lord of the manor in 1316; Henry de Pusey 1343; William de Pusey, 1377; John de Pusey in 1468; Thomas a Pyssey de Pyssey in 1597; by Philip, Wm., and Richard de Pyssey, in 1542, 1580, and 1655, and by Charles Pusey in 1710. At the death of Charles Pusey in 1710, the estate passed to his nephew, John Allen, who took the name of Pusey. Both John Allen and the sisters of Charles Pusey having died without issue, the estate passed to Hon. Philip Bouverie, nephew of Allen Pusey's wife, who was daughter of Sir William Bouverie, Bart. Philip Bouverie in succeeding to the estate in 1789, assumed the name of Pusey, and married Lucy, widow of Sir Thomas Cave, and daughter of the 4th Earl of Harborough. He died in 1828; his son Philip succeeded him, who became a member of Parliament for Berkshire. His brother next in age was Dr. Edward B. Pusey, Canon of Christ Church, and Regius Professor of Hebrew in the University of Oxford, widely known as leader of the so-called 'Puseyite' or Anglo-Catholic movement in the Church of England. Hon. Philip Pusey married Lady Emily Herbert, daughter of the second Earl of Canarvon; he died in 1855, and was succeeded by his son Sydney Edward Bouverie Pusey, the present possessor, who married a daughter of Lord William Harvey in 1871. The Bouveries who thus succeeded to the Pusey manor are descended from Lawrence des Bouvies, of the Low Countries, driven to England by religious persecution in the time of Queen Elizabeth.

Miss Sarah Pusey's parents and all the family were born in Pennsylvania, U. S. She has no brothers, but three sisters, who, with herself, were educated at Paris and England. Two of her sisters, within the last five years, got married, one of them to a nephew of Sir Wm. Howland, ex-Governor of Ontario, the other to an extensive hardware merchant. Sarah is the youngest, all of them very talented. Mr. Pusey is largely engaged in mining and manufactures. They are not like their ancestor, Anglo-Catholic or High Church, but all of them *Low Church*.

Toronto in 1894.

TORONTO is not only called the "Queen City," but also "Toronto the Beautiful," and certainly a more beautiful city cannot be found on the continent. I propose in this brief article to give the natives who have not been out of Newfoundland, some idea of what sort of a city Toronto is. It will be remembered that at the beginning of the nineteenth century this place was only a swamp. It was the camping ground of the Indians. It was a French stockade and trading post. Toronto, the name given it by the Mohawk Indians, signifies "a place of meeting,"— called later on "Muddy Little York,"— from which has emerged, magnificent Toronto. Less than a hundred years ago, Indians roamed through the site of Toronto, hunting deer, bears, wolves and other wild animals, and fever and ague were rampant where now exist over 315 miles of beautiful streets, 210 miles of sewerage, and 70 miles of street railway. In 1871 the employed of the city numbered 9,000 which now number 26,300. In the same year the products aggregated $13,690, which are to-day over $45,000,-000. In 1872 Toronto could have been bought for

$5,000,000, to-day her assessed value is over $150,000,000. When Henry John Boulton left Toronto to assume the Chief Justiceship of Newfoundland, the population of Toronto was 4,000, the population of St. John's was over 26,000. Now Toronto has a population of over 200,000, and St. John's 25,000. The census of Toronto has been taken by the assessors and also by the police, but the "City Directory" just published gives the ponulution 219,000. A few decades more will probably see Toronto a city of 500,000. It now takes rank with the cities of the second class as to population throughout the British Empire. There are only forty-seven larger cities in the British Dominions, and England has only eighteen which have a greater population. Toronto is larger than Aderdeen, Cork, Waterford, Plymouth and Preston. There are only seven larger cities in Germany; nineteen in the United States; seven in France and seven in Russia. The professions are well represented in Toronto, there are 368 physicians, 310 barristers, 73 dentists. There are 136 newspapers and periodicals published in Toronto, and 100 printing offices, and 90 stationers. Toronto can retain its name as the City of Churches. There are 179 places of worship. Montreal has not half that number. The Church of England is the strongest Protestant body in Toronto, numbering 46,084. The Methodist number 32,309. The Presbyterians number 27,445, are third in rank, while the Roman Catholics take fourth place, numbering 21,830. Of Baptists there are 6,909, and of Congregationalists, 3,102. There are 1,425 Jews, with some hundreds belonging to various minor sects. The number of shipping arriving at Toronto for 1893 was 2,918. Steamers loaded 1,289; light 2. Propellers loaded 121; light 94. Schooners loaded 1,347; light 65. The amount of coal received by vessels was 161,559 tons. The amount received by rail: anthracite 171,997 tons; bituminous 195,988. There is no soft coal brought by vessels to this port now. The cattle trade seems to be increasing. According to returns from the Toronto cattle market in 1892, the number of cattle received was 102,571; sheep, 49,382; hogs, 74,116. There are now 75 new yards in the cattle market annex, drained and supplied with water. Toronto's Industrial Exhibition is now one of the attractive institutions of the city, with numerous buildings. The grand stand is 675 feet long and capable of seating 12,000, with a half-mile track, is and considered one of the finest grand stands on this continent. The ground floor and walks round the building are paved with granolithic pavement. Every building on the grounds in September last was occupied to its fullest extent with the finest productions of the factory, farm, garden and studio ever gathered together in the Dominion. The marvellous progress that has been made from year to year in this exhibition, in the number of entries, the quality of exhibits and the thousands of visitors who come from all parts of the Dominion and the United States each year, all testify to the wonderful results that have been attained. The Toronto is the premier exhibition of the Dominion and one of the largest on the American continent. The grounds are beautifully laid out with lawns, shade trees, and flowers. A number of the most distinguished persons from all parts of the world, who were at the World's Fair at Chicago, came to visit the Toronto Exhibition and pronounced it finer than the Chicago Fair, only not so large. While Montreal, London, Detroit, Buffalo and other places did not pay the expenses of their exhibitions, Toronto made a profit of thousands. The steamboat and railway facilities of Toronto are not surpassed by any city in America. You can take the cars in Toronto and check your luggage through to Yokahama, Japan, or Hong Kong in China. Toronto is fast becoming the wholesale centre of the Dominion. Steadily, year after year, Montreal houses have been opening branches, or removing their entire business interests to Toronto. The "Queen City" seems to be marching ahead of the commercial and manufacturing procession of the entire Dominion.

On every hand are to be seen evidences of material wealth and prosperity, of comfort and luxury, of taste, culture and refinement. The principal thoroughfares are lined with mammoth and magnificent mercantile establishments, banks and halls. The streets are broad, well-paved, and kept in good order. In the architecture of her halls, colleges, and churches, Toronto is in advance of any city of equal size in the Western Hemisphere. In every department of industry, commerce and trade, Toronto is progressing. It is true that just now, like as in every part of the world, there is a depression of trade, but it is only temporary. Toronto is a city of homes numbering among its citizens more actual householders than any community of the same area and population in the Dominion. Several Newfoundlanders own lots and built houses for themselves in the outskirts of the city. Working people, as a rule, own their houses. This beautiful and flourishing city, with its vast and ever-increasing industrial, commercial and financial interests, is growing in favor and patronage of seekers of health and recreation from all parts of the Dominion of Canada and the United States. Toronto is as good a summer resort as can be found; cool nights and refreshing breezes in the day from the lake. The city is intersected by a cordon of splendid parks, the most attractive the island, which is opposite the city, two miles distant; it is a beautiful place, with its lagoons, drives and amusements; hundreds of the citizens of Toronto have their summer residences there. In the centre of the island is a beautiful park to which thousands resort from the city. Apart from the island ferry boats and excursion steamers, there are also regular lines of steamships running to all points, and numerous yachts and sailing craft make Toronto their port of entry and exit. There is a line of wharves and warehouses extending a mile along the water front. Toronto is a dead flat extending for miles on Lake Ontario. About three miles north of the city a ridge gently rises studded with beautiful villas and palatial residences rivalling those of New York. The lake is 85 fathoms deep and looks like the ocean. During a gale the white caps and combing waves are seen. The lake supplies Toronto with water to drink and for cleansing purposes. The lake abounds with fish in great variety. There are numerous places of resort in the environs of Toronto. Boating of every description is resorted to, from the single canoe to the steam yacht. Toronto covers more ground in proportion to population than most other cities. Perhaps Toronto is the healthiest city on the continent. It has a mild and salubrious climate. The thermometer is rarely down to zero. The public buildings of Toronto excel many of the public buildings in the United States. Several American gentlemen said, the colleges—such as the Toronto University; Victoria College, Methodist; McMaster College, Baptist; Knox College, Presbyterian; Trinity University and Wycliffe College, Church of England; St. Michael's College, Roman Catholic; Parliament Buildings, and some of the Banks surpassed in beautiful architecture most of their buildings. There are public and private schools of every grade, and four medical colleges. I have thus, in as brief a manner as possible, grouped together a few things about Toronto.

Concomitant Evils of Modern Civilization.

Mrs. Chauncey says: "We have been having very fine missionary meetings all over the city, in which the people have been very much interested and quite delighted with the stirring and eloquent speeches delivered," etc. Have you ever thought of the sins which follow the introduction of civilization into heathen lands. It is humiliating that many great evils accompany the introduction of civilization into heathen lands, which are a great hindrance to the progress of Christianity, and which can be only successfully counteracted and removed by the gospel of Christ. Though somewhat paradoxical, this concomitance is true. The Rev. William Mellan, of the American Board of Missions, says:—"With the introduction of our civilization, rum and immorality, and sins such as natives never knew, will come in, as well as missionaries and bibles. There are some things we can learn from the heathen. 'Dr. Livingstone was kindly treated by tribes which had never before seen the face of a white man. His waggon, left exposed in Central Africa, was found safe by him nearly seven years after he left it. The boxes, with their contents, with which the waggon was loaded, had been untouched by the natives through all those years. They did not steal; there were no jails or penitentiaries among the natives; but if a person should steal and be convicted, they would send him where he would certainly not steal again. There they kill the guilty and save the innocent; here they pardon thieves and assassins, and their victims are the ones who suffer and perish. In America, missionaries even must lock the doors and fasten the windows. There are no harlots; they would not be tolerated. They would be either banished or killed. An illegitimate child would be a curiosity there. But we must not think they are pure. They are more immoral in thought, word and deed than I dare express. They are not so bad as the most immoral in your midst, but on the other hand we have none of the good you have here. We had no drunkenness there until the white man brought it. In the interior they had pow-palm wine which would intoxicate. I have not heard so much profanity in twenty-five years there as I have heard in a half a day here. They must learn English in order to know how to swear.'" In his remarkable speech before the Church Congress, the Rev. Canon Isaac Taylor says:—" Islam is the most powerful total abstinence association in the world, whereas the extension of European trade means the extension of drunkenness and vice, and the degradation of the people. The Moslem brotherhood is a reality. We have over-much 'dearly beloved brother' in the reading desk, but over-little in daily life. The strictly regulated polygamy of Moslem lands is infinitely less degrading to women and less injurious to men than the promiscuous polyandry which is the curse of Christian cities, and which is absolutely unknown in Islam. Let us remember that in some respects, Moslem morality is better than our own. In resignation to God's will, in temperance, charity, veracity, and in the brotherhood of believers, they set us a pattern we would do well to follow. Islam has abolished drunkenness, gambling and prostitution, the three curses of Christian lands!" Bishop Southgate, who resided several years at Constantinople, informed me that he saw many things among the Moslems which Christians ought to follow. There was no dishonesty, wine-drinking, or drunkenness among them. A person could enter a bazzar—weigh or measure any article he wanted (the price being marked) lay down his money and depart without seeing anybody. A merchant in Christian Toronto could not trust his goods exposed in such a manner, left to the honesty of every passer to pay for them. Captain Moresby, in his surveys of New Guinea and the Islands in Torres Straits, found some of the native races intelligent and advanced in civilization. Many gross instances of kidnapping came under his notice. Once where a Christianized island had been nearly depopulated, the able-bodied men had been enticed on board a schooner by invitation *to receive the sacrament.* When the men had been made prisoners, the women and children were beguiled in the same way. After a trip in a boat along the north coast of New Guinea, Captain Moresby thus describes his impression of the coast : " A shore more beautiful and luxuriant than words can describe. At times I found myself drawing a contrast between the squalid poverty so often seen in humble life in England, and the plenty and cleanliness that met us here at every step where the small cane houses that lay in villages rich as the Garden of Eden, and no man had to go more than a stone's throw from his own door to find all the necessities of his simple life. They possess cocoanuts, the bread-fruit, citron, oranges, and sago by the bounty of nature, and they cultivate yams, taro, bananas, and various other roots. They are great fishers and traders, passing from island to island in large canoes, forty and fifty feet long.

What have these people to gain from civilization ? Pondering on the fate of other aboriginal races when brought into contact with the white, I was ready to wish that their happy homes had never been seen by us. We were not responsible for the issues, and Providence may surely be trusted to work out its ends." In the leaflet of the " Society of the Treasury of God," we read :—" Of all the contrasts in the world, there is perhaps none greater than that between heathen-giving and Christian-giving. The hope of gain, physical, pecuniary, or social, or the fear of the devil they worship seems to exercise a power over the former, and to offer greater inducements to part with their money for religious purposes, than all the love of the Heavenly Father, all the self-immolation of his Son, who died on the cross for the redemption of man, exercise over the hearts of the latter. If the religious state of the world in future depends upon money, it would seem as if, humanely speaking, there was danger of its becoming heathen and not Christian." The Rev. Dr. Beerends says :—" Civilization taxes men more than savagery, and makes toil more unremittent, severe and universal." The English *Catholic Magazine* for May says :—" The people, though now in danger of being carried away with the impulse of the new Japanese civilization, are surprisingly quiet and peaceable, and being acquainted with rum, guns, and other implements of civilization, have some chance of continuing to live up to their own designation of themselves, ' as the nation that observes propriety.' " Dr. George McDonald speaking of the sunken masses in London, says :—" It would have been a sad thing for the world if the Lord of it had not sought first the lost sheep of the house of Israel. One awful consequence of our making haste to pull the mote out of the heathen brother's eye while yet the beam is in our own, is, that, wherever our missionaries go, they are followed by a foul wave of our vices." The evils here referred to are great and deplorable. All missionaries unite in complaining of them, and that the wicked practices of professed Christians are of the greatest hindrances to the success of their work. The gospel is the true foundation of the highest and most enduring form of civilization that has blessed the earth. How strange, how paradoxical, that there rests upon us an obligation to send missionaries to counteract the effect of the evils concomitant with the introduction of our Christian civilization into heathen lands. It is estimated that about 400,000,000 nominal Christians are scattered over the world, divided as follows :—Greeks and Eastern Communions, 85,000,000 ; Roman Catholics, 195,000,000 ; Anglicans and all Protestant Communions, 135,000,000. On the other hand we find Mohommedans, 173,000,000 ; Hindoos, 200,000,000 ; Buddhists and their allies, 400,000,- 000 ; outlying, barbaric heathens, 200,000,000; total yet without the Gospel of Christ, 973,000,000. Besides these there are about 7,000,000 Jews. In the early age of the Christian Church, the seven Churches of Asia, because of their unfaithfulness, their candlesticks were removed, and they died out. The whole of North Africa, from the Red Sea on the East, to the Pillars of Hercules on the West, were, in the early ages of Christianity, mainly Christian. Here lived those who are called the Fathers, such as Clemens and Tertullion, Origen, Cyprian and Augustin. Here were flourishing Churches. Now, north of Africa is Mohommedan. The crescent is now in the place of the Cross.

How is the vast mass of heathenism to be reached? The last command of our Lord will never be fulfilled by leaving the proclamation of the Gospel to a class of men specially set apart. Many old prejudices against evangelistic work by laymen, are fast falling away, and to-day there is a large number of laymen doing all kinds of work in the Church of England, with the bare exception of the administration of the sacraments. Even in the time of Wesley, the Roman Catholic Church sent out laymen on a mission, and which it still continues to do. The history of the early ages of the Catholic Church, shew that large bodies of devoted religious men and women seem to have been specially raised up for the conversion of Europe. The history of *preaching friars*, who were laymen, gives abundant proof that in the ages which were most exclusive, it was allowed that it was open to any devout layman to give himself up for life, and without ceasing to be a layman, to the work of preaching the Gospel to his fellowmen. The Rev. Dr. Pierson, of Philadelphia, one of the greatest Presbyterian ministers in the United States, says:—" Let us suppose there were on earth to-day but *one true disciple*, and that, during this year, he leads to the cross *one more*, and then these *two* go forth a second year, each winning one new soul, and these four, during a third year, thus double their number; how long on this principle of geometrical progression would it take to gather a multitude of converts equal to the present population of our globe? Only *thirty years*. At the end of ten years, 1,024; of fifteen, 32,568; of twenty, 1,042,176; of thirty, 1,323,441,224. Now mark, here is an aggregate within thirty years, of more than 1,300,000,000 converts in less than the average lifetime of *one generation*, and yet one the simple practical basis that each converted soul shall disciple *one other soul every year*! Now face this fact, that nearly nineteen centuries have gone by since the first disciple bowed before the cross, and yet but about one-tenth of the population of the earth is even *nominally* Christian, and what overwhelming proof is there that the bulk of professing Christians *practically do no work whatever in discipling others*. They seem to think that all they are to do is to secure their own salvation. The whole question of service in saving others is forgotten." In all the English and Canadian Dioceses there are now *Associations of Lay Helpers* to assist in the spiritual work of the Church. Among them are found persons in all ranks of society, from the nobility down to the humblest tradesmen and workingmen. The Church of England, in common with the Catholic Church believes in the Communion of Saints, which means the mutual society, help and comfort which Christian people should be one to another in spiritual matters, in this world. The communion of saints with many of us, is very much of a dead letter. How immense would be the change in the effective force of the church for self-propagation, if the devout laity, who go up to her altars, and there "offer and present themselves, their souls and bodies to be a reasonable, holy, and living sacrifice" to their Lord, could be brought to engage in the spiritual work of the church.

Yellow-Covered Literature.

THERE can be no doubt that the reading of dime novels and sensational detective stories have a damaging and pernicious influence over the mind. Two-thirds of the books taken out of the public library here are novels, and that is the case in all the cities of Europe and America. All classes of society, religious and irreligious, indulge in novel reading. Only a generation ago it was considered improper for anybody professing to be a Christian to read novels. And there are those who even yet look upon all novel readers as persons given over to dissipation. Who among the great men of the world have not read the Arabian Night's Entertainment, Scott, Dickens, Disraeli, Thackeray, Hawthorne, and other celebrated novelists? The studies of some clergymen have not all been in the line of homiletics or theology. "We must agree that a novel is good for us now and then," said a clergyman at a Methodist meeting. "He read them to secure entertainment, to relieve the mind after difficult study, and to assist the imagination, both in its expansion and chastening. In these respects the novel has a real usefulness, and some most devoted ministers and profound theologians employ it as a recreation and pleasure. I think John Wesley abridged some novel for his people to read. I cannot now recollect the name of the novel without referring to Wesley's writings. Forty years ago I was preaching on Sunday in the city of Boston; referring to the immorality of the soul, I gave a passage from one of Bulwer's novels. The next day the bishop said to me: "Some ladies told me that part of your sermon was from one of Bulwer's novels; was it so?" I said "yes." I did not mention the name of Bulwer, but the ladies, it appears, were quite conversant with Bulwer's novels. I brought the MS. sermon to the bishop and read the passage from Bulwer to him. He said it was very beautiful and very appropriate, and here it is:—" It cannot be that earth is man's abiding place. It cannot be that our life is cast up by the ocean of eternity, to float a moment upon its waves and sink into nothingness. Else why is it that the high and glorious aspirations which leap like angels from the temple of our heart are forever wandering about unsatisfied? Why is it that the rainbow and the cloud come over us with a beauty that is not of earth, and then pass off and leave us to muse upon our faded loveliness? Why is it that the stars, which hold their festival around the midnight throne, are set above the grasp of our limited faculties, for ever mocking us with their unapproachable glory? And finally, why is it that bright forms of human beauty are presented to our view and then taken from us, leaving the thousand streams of our affections to flow back in Alpine torrents upon our hearts? We are born for a higher destiny than that of earth, there is a realm where the rainbow never fades, where the stars will be spread out before us, like islands that slumber on the ocean, and where the beautiful beings which here pass before us like shadows, will stay in our presence for ever."

Labor Day, 1895.

THE annual procession of organized labor took place at Toronto on the 2nd September, 1895. It was a great demonstration, the parade was the largest in the history of the labor organizations of Toronto—over four thousand representatives of the great industrial army that are endeavouring to secure to the workingman a fair share of the fruits of his labor. The procession paraded the principal streets of the city. It is estimated that 50,000 persons lined the thoroughfares through which the procession passed, showing their appreciation by continued applause and cheers. Floats, representing all branches of the world of labor, were distributed throughout the parade. There were bakers, bookbinders—the bakers wore white caps and costumes—the bookbinders were headed by a great leather-bound ledger. The cigar float, with cigar makers at work, were headed by a gaily-decorated billy goat. The bricklayers' float contained a brick tower. The iron moulders and metal platers had two floats. The Machinists' Union were headed by a male bicyclist in female garb. Journeymen Tailors' Union, carpenters and joiners and slaters had two floats. The stonecutters had a float drawn by horses. The varnishers, painters and decorators had floats. Typographical Union, stereotypers and electrotypers made the biggest show in the procession. Picture-frame makers and delivery rigs of all kinds. All the trades were at work on the different waggons, showing the *modus operandi* in the manufacture of the different wares. The finest portions of the procession were the light and firemen, with their red tunics and glistening helmets, they made a magnificent appearance on the march, and evoked cheers all along the line. The different organizations had their bands. Centre Island park was the objective point of a large proportion of the workingmen and friends. Early in the afternoon thousands began to move towards the docks, and the ferry steamers carried over immense loads to Centre Island Park. The programme there consisted of games, a band concert, and addresses on questions of interest to labor. Mr. Edward Hylton, the chairman, introduced the speakers, and among those on the platform were: His Honor Lieut.-Governor Kirkpatrick, Alderman Shaw, acting mayor; Rev. Father Ryan, Rev. C. O. Johnston and others. The chairman Hylton spoke a few words in favor of unionism and of making a united effort to secure proper representation in Parliament. He urged that they should sink politics and religious differences in their union for a common cause. Squabbling over religious questions was worse than useless. What mattered it about the route to the better world, so long as all got there. The Rev. C. O. Johnston, Methodist, was the first speaker. He upheld labor, and claimed to belong himself to the army of industry. Canada, he said, was a strong young land, great now and growing greater in spite of the party politicians. They made a great many blunders and a great many offices. A statesman, he said, was a man who wanted to do something for his country. A politician was a man who wanted his country to do something for him. Labor must send to Parliament men who would die rather than become recreant. He was frequently cheered, and made a vigorous speech. He closed by an expression of pleasure that on this labor platform they had the Lieut.-Governor and men of various religious denominations. His Honor Lieut.-Governor Kirkpatrick said, he came not as a politician, but as a representative of the constitutional government of the country. He expressed his sympathy with honest labor, and congratulated the unions. Labor day was a recognition of the dignity of labor. It was the greatest achievement of the century. Several serious questions are knocking at the door. Better houses for the poor, with proper sanitary conditions; protection for the aged and infirm; annihilation of that hydra-headed monster, intemperance; and the crushing out of the sweating-system; devising a scheme for the co-operation of capital and labor, so that the worker should have more interest in the returns of his labor than merely his wages. He particularly warned against foreign agitators, and the red flag of anarchy. No good can come from riot and revolution. Acting-Mayor Shaw expressed his gratification, and said the Church should unite with the State to elevate labor. The cause of the many was the cause of the Church. Great men had bestowed much thought on the labor problem, but as yet no satisfactory, comprehensive scheme of alleviation had been evolved.

The Rev. Father Ryan (a native of Newfoundland) delivered a stirring address. He called the labor-men his fellow-workers and friends. He had seen the parade, and it was a credit to any land. He was delighted to be present, and with his Methodist brother who preceded him, speak to them of a subject so important to them all. Labor was not a thing, but an individual. His church had expressed itself on that subject, through Pope Leo XIII., Cardinal Manning and Cardinal Gibbons. The laborer was worthy of his hire. The whole question was one of ethics, as well as economics. "Thanks be to God," he said, "bigotry has disappeared from the labor platform, and is going from the pulpit, too." He closed with an appeal to them to cast off the saloon, a sentiment that was heartily cheered.

Physical Necessity of Labor.

I KNOW of nothing which can solve the social problem but real *practical Christianity*. I often look at a man poorly clad, poorly fed, and living in a poor habitation, with this thought growing in my mind: that individual has a soul as immortal and as precious in the sight of God as the greatest personage on earth. There is no difference between the value of the soul of a king and a beggar.

"He was my equal at his birth,
 A naked, helpless, weeping child,
And such are born to thrones on earth,
 On such hath every mother smiled.
My equal he will be again,
 Down in that cold, oblivious gloom,
Where all the prostrate sons of men
 Crowd without fellowship the tomb.'

Physical necessity to labor is one of the greatest blessings conferred upon the race. That sterility of the ground which obliges man, in the sweat of his face, to eat bread, wards off innumerable diseases, increases mental vigor, and is a powerful help to the formation of moral and religious habits. Some have rendered the passage, "Cursed is the ground for thy work (Gen. iii. ch., 17 v.); I have cursed the ground for thy labor; or idleness and viciousness would destroy thee." In climates which most abound with temporal delights, the period of life is shortest. In the temperate zones where men have to labor, they are happier, because less indolent and degenerate, than in the torrid zone where the earth yields her increase almost spontaneously. The physical necessity to labor is a great blessing to the human race. But the mass of mankind still look upon it in the light of a curse, and it is difficult to convince men that it is not really so, for the idea is associated with our earliest religious impressions, and various causes have tended to strengthen these impressions. It is the light in which we look at the labor we have to do, which settles the question where we count it mere drudgery or a desirable service. The details of every-day business in a counting-house are one thing to a clerk who has no thought beyond earning his wages, and quite another thing to a partner in the house who expects to make a fortune through attention to those details. And when a clerk is fired with ambition to prove himself so useful there, that he also shall become a partner, the more he has to do the better. What is treadmill stepping to his companions is ladder-climbing to him. Toiling up a mountain-side is wearisome work to one who thinks only of the rugged path and cheerless surroundings, but it is one inspiriting effort to the enthusiastic lovers of nature. It might, perhaps, promote a better feeling in case of labor troubles that occur so often, if all could remember that it is for the interests of capitalists that the laborer should be well off, for he will be also a consumer and furnish a good home market, while as it is, he suffers for want of the products of industry, while industry languishes for want of consumers of products. It is hard to find any good reason why other than that many of our habits, customs, and modes of thought are traditional, but we are certain that there does exist in every community a disposition to exalt what are called the learned professions to an undue position in the scale of society, and to pay that deference to mere book learning and the use of it, which is seldom or ever paid to the highest manifestations of talents in other departments of mental or corporeal activity. We ought to ask ourselves what there is or can be in the occupation of an individual, that makes one man a clown and another a gentleman, which prompts society to greet the man of starch and broad-cloth with a fraternal embrace, and hustles the skilful artizan out of the parlor. There is no exaggeration in saying what every one knows to be true, when we say that there is not a village or town in the country where the lines are not as distinctly drawn between what are called the professional and working classes, in regard to the intimacies of social life, as if there was something in the title of a profession or the nature of an occupation which ought to give a preponderance of influence and a ready acquiescence from the many, no matter how much the few may be lacking in sterling principle and intellectual ability. We are tempted to smile sometimes at the ludicrous figure which some of this class make when they undertake to set themselves off to the best advantage, by exalting themselves in railing at their equals. What dignity of manner persons of this school assume when expressing an opinion upon any of the social, moral, or political questions that now excite the attention of the community and the world. In their sweeping denunciations of all that is "vulgar," they seem to forget that they oftentimes inflict a blow upon their own parents, who may have been shoemakers, carpenters or cart-men, and run such rigs upon the "lower classes," as they call them, as though themselves only were part of the primary formation of the human society strata, and always intended to be at the foundation of things. The workingman belongs to the universe, and the universal world has a claim upon him. We are all members of one great family. The world is a joint-stock company in which we are all shareholders. All mankind are our brothers and sisters, and we all have a direct personal interest in the management of all affairs connected in any degree with the welfare of humanity; a wrong done to a single human being, whether in Boston or in London, in India or in Mexico, in Halifax or Toronto, is a wrong done to any one of us. A bad principle laid down, an unjust precedent established, an oppressive law enacted or enforced, though so far removed from us that we do not directly feel its exactions, nevertheless imposes upon us responsibilities and duties that we cannot escape, and not to attempt to evade by the subterfuge of our unfavorable position.

It is not enough that we think right; we must, whatever the sacrifice, do right. The world has had enough of theory to have reformed a hundred worlds; what it most needs is practice. Plenty of breath has been expended, and not a little ink, to make men better, and wiser, and happier; but deeds, always more effective than words, have been wanting. Twenty-six years ago I met the Rev. Dr. Newman Hall, of London, Eng., in Toronto, when I told him that, many years ago, when delivering a lecture in Nova Scotia, I quoted largely from his eloquent lecture "On the Dignity of Labor," etc. Immediately after, Mr. Hall gave that same lecture in New York city. I now quote a little bit from it here:—"The dignity of labor—consider its achievements! Labor fells the forest and drains the morass, and makes the wilderness rejoice and blossom as the rose. Labor drives the plough and scatters the seed, and reaps the harvest and grinds the corn, and converts it into bread—the staff of life. Labor, tending the pastures and sweeping the waters, as well as cultivating the soil, provides with daily sustenance the fourteen hundred millions of the family of man, and distributes that sustenance throughout their habitations."

Carlyle says: "All true work is sacred; in all true work, were it but true hand labor, something of divineness. Labor, wide as the earth, has its summit in Heaven. Sweat of the brow; and up from that to sweat of the brain; sweat of the heart; which includes all Kepler calculations, Newton meditations, all sciences, all spoken epics, all acted heroisms, martyrdoms, up to that agony of 'bloody sweat,' which all men have called divine. Two men I honor and no third. First, the toilworn craftsman that, with earth-made implements, laboriously conquers the earth, and makes her man's. Venerable to me is the hard hand, crooked, coarse; venerable, too, is the rugged face, all weather-tanned, besoiled, with rude intelligence, for it is the face of a man living manlike. Toil on, thou art in thy duty, be out of it who may, thou toilest for the altogether indispensable, for daily bread. A second man I honor, and still more highly. Him who is seen toiling for the spiritually indispensable; not daily bread, but the Bread of Life. Is not he, too, in his duty?" Dr. Arnold wrote an essay on "The Social Condition of the Operative Classes." He maintained that society "should put the poor man, being a free man, into a situation where he may live as a freeman ought to live." The late Bishop Fraser of Manchester was sometimes called the "Bishop of the Laity," so ready was he to co-operate with all Christian workers. The Labor Question, and the subordinate matters of Trade's Unions, and co-operation exercised his mind during all his episcopate. One of the most interesting developments of Christian Socialism in England is the Oxford University movement in the city of London. A few years ago, Arnold Toynbee, tutor and treasurer of Baliol College, Oxford, and a company of his friends, graduates of that Institution, took hold of the almost hopeless task of reforming East London. Toynbee set himself resolutely against some of the extreme socialistic views of men who had been excited by agitators, and misled by theorists. He was the true friend of the working man. After his death, his friends took up his social mission and established a colony of Oxford graduates in East London, the working men's quarter's. Money was raised and Toynbee Hall was erected. There these students lived and worked. Between twenty and thirty University men were engaged last year working for humanity in business of every day life. East London people are proud of having University men living among them, and would perhaps send them all to Parliament, to represent the labor party, if that were possible by a *plebiscite*. The church is neither the peculiar heritage of the capitalist or laborer. Within her sacred precincts alone all men are equal before God. It is on the line of her mission to be the friend of the poor and oppressed. The rich we do not always have in the church, but we do have the poor; one is a shifting factor, the other is constantly with us. The poor are the rich in prospect. By the revolving wheel of time, men on the highest spokes of their classes are brought down, and those on the lowest spokes are brought up. Why do we see so much want and misery in the world, but because men of power and of business, whose love should be universal, narrow down their senses and their sympathies to the love of gold, of power and of self.

They regard their neighbors, not as men and women to be served, but to be used. Their solicitude is not how much happiness they can confer, but how much they can extract; not how much good they can do to others, but how much they can compel others to do for them. The workingmen have resolved that the right shall be done—not clinging to the past, which means caring for the few rather than the many—shall prevail. It is the

Christian spirit that is showing itself in the demand for fairness, for entire equality of rights. The church must adopt what socialism is aiming at, the triumph of sympathy, practical, lovely Christian brotherhood. Christian socialism, which means organized and personal efforts to regenerate the lowest state of society, is fast spreading over England, springing from the love of God.

Nothing but Christianity can solve the social problem. Not mere "hand-shaking Christianity," but practical Christian love springing from the love of God. Love is the *materia medica* for the social wrongs, the therapeutics for healing the social element. Let us not lose sight of the command, "Honor all men, love thy neighbor as thyself." We are to love God and love our neighbor. The one cannot be separated from the other. The sentiment, "Am I my brother's keeper?" is the exponent of the feelings of the natural man. It expresses the principles which governs his actions. It may be reduced in one word—selfishness: every man caring only for his wants, and unconcerned for the wants of his brother. To carry out this principle would lay in ruins every hospital, asylum and prison, for what are these institutions but the efforts of society to protect and support the weak and helpless. The same principle, if carried out, would destroy every charitable and missionary and reform institution in the world. It would undermine and overthrow the family, the Church and the State; for these are but the machinery God has set up through which we are to extend a helping hand to others. Christianity regards the race as one brotherhood, and seeks to infuse into this one body a keener sensibility in regard to each other's interests. It makes us feel that we are made of one blood, that we are members one of another. The theory of the Gospel binds rich and poor together in mutual offices of charity and good will, but the modern practice of the Church realises little or nothing of this Divine ideal— that fellowship of love which the Redeemer ordained as a characteristic of His Church. I have long observed even among those who kneel together around one altar, and receive a common spiritual food, there is too little personal knowledge of one another's welfare, or one another's woe. The spirit of Christian love is the reverse of selfish; it is expansive, it is diffusive, it embraces the whole world, and especially the universal household of faith. "Whatsoever ye would that men should do unto you, even so do unto them; for this is the Law and the Prophets."

The social problem is the focus in which many of the burning questions of the day are concentrated. What is capital, and who are capitalists. Capital is not the outcome or product of selfishness and tyranny, or the work of a silent enemy of man. It is labor; money is coined labor. Mechanical skill and force are capital. A good character is capital; it is a product. If people would cease to rate a man's consequence by his money, there would be an end of the discontent that comes from comparing ourselves with others, both among the rich and among the poor.

Old Men Not Wanted in the Pulpit.

THAT there is a "dead line" in the ministerial career we have no doubt, but that it can be determined by years is not true. Some men are dead while yet in the theological college, and show no progress except to become "deader." Their education, perhaps, has contributed to this. To some students, poetry and light reading would be better than constant study of mathematics and root-digging in the languages. When a minister ceases to do genuine pastoral work he has passed the "dead line," no matter if he preaches like Apollo. He will get old, and will either preach doctrines in doctrinal formulas or platitudes, or it will be imaginary characters rather than real. The minister also who never introduces anything new in his sermons from the Word of God, or from an experience which shows growth in grace, is dead at any age. If he always shapes his sermons in the same mould, the interest in them will wane. A man who has plenty of old things on hand, will always find plenty of new to say about them. And let it not be forgotten that whenever a man has to give a re-hash of his old sermons, he has crossed the dead line. As a general thing, when a man changes parishes because he wants to use his old material, he is lingering on the brink of the line. There are but few, even in dire distress, who will wear old clothes until they are made over. The minister who keeps on the sunny side of age will not be carried away by the crazes of the day. Temperance is a subject that lies close to the heart of the gospel; but some clergymen have given themselves to this subject until they have become prematurely dead, while others have gone to seed on the subject of hermeneutics, or become experts in social questions, until they have been branded as bores in the pulpit when they have reached their fortieth year. A young lady said: "I like to have a young clergyman or curate to play tennis with; or a game of whist or checkers, or take a private part in private theatricals, or concerts, or picnics, but then there is nothing religious in such things. But when I get into the blues about my spiritual condition, and I cannot satisfy my conscience about some things, I really could not have much confidence in my young friend as my spiritual adviser, although he had the Rev. before his name. We must, of course, have young clergymen before we can have old or elderly ones, and new wine before we have the old, which is better. But we prefer the old wine to be that of the last vintage." Why is it that old men are not sought after for the pulpit? In other professions to be young, or even to look young, is rather a drawback. Who chooses a physician because he is young and has had no experience worth mentioning? No client ever thinks of turning aside from a lawyer because he is old, to hunt up a young lawyer for advice on grave and weighty questions. Who, when far-reaching plans have to be made and acted upon, involving peace or war, life or death, votes for a statesman to have charge of those plans because he is young? And is it not the case in the clerical profession, too, that greater skill and experience demand greater age? In other professions age and experience count for something and give men standing. But in the ministry age is rather against a man. Why is this? Our young men begin to think of laying their seniors on the shelf when they have reached sixty years of age, although they are then in the height of their intellectual vigor. How different the present estimate put upon the experience of age, from that which characterized a certain period of the Grecian Republic, when a man was not allowed to open his mouth in cases of political meetings who was under forty years of age. Dryden, in his sixty-eighth year, commenced the translation of the Iliad, and his best productions were written in his old age. We could give many examples of some of the most learned men commencing studies in their old age.

Is it necessary that a man should offer a defence because he is growing old? That grand elixir of life, so earnestly sought after by the old alchemists, with its wonderful transmuting power, has not yet been discovered; we therefore have to submit to the inevitable. We were all young once, and if it please God to permit, we shall grow old. The aged man, by diligence and experience of many years, is fitted for positions of responsibility and usefulness which the young is not prepared to occupy. Shall we conclude when a man has attained a certain age, irrespective of any other consideration, that it is his duty to cease labor, stand aside, and allow the young to take possession of the field? The memorials of human life will bear me out in the statement, that if a man has dealt fairly with mind and body, when he has reached, say, his three-score, he is better prepared than ever before to do the most important and valuable work in life. He will do more actual work, either of body or mind, or combining both, and with less complaining than many a fledgling whose pinions have scarcely been tried, but who is ready to say to the sexagenarian, "stand aside, and see how I can soar." I refer to that class of aged ministers who have kept "abreast of the times:" preachers who are not satisfied to preach the same sermons, word for word, preached a quarter of a century ago. The Word of God is an inexhaustible mine of gold, but whoever would load himself with its treasures must dig for them in person. There is no doing this work by proxy. Try to borrow or steal from others enough for the supply of your own wants, and see if you are not speedily reduced to poverty. No doubt one may often preach over his old sermons with manifest advantage. We shall need but little research throughout the pages of history to find many brilliant examples of very great labor combined with very great old age. Look at the great statesmen of England and other countries. Think of Chatham, Eldon, Palmerston, Derby, Russell, Brougham, O'Connell, Beaconsfield, Shaftesbury, Bismarck, Thiers, and a host of others, most of whom for half a century have occupied more space in the mind of the world than any other men, and some of whom are performing more efficient labor than many who are forty years their juniors. Think of Salisbury, and the "Grand Old Man," W. E. Gladstone, although 84 years of age, is now a grander man than when he was only 30 or 40 years of age, and better furnished and fitted for his difficult duties. So there are clergymen who are 60, 70 and 80 years old who are far better fitted, mentally, spiritually and bodily for their duties than most young men. Old ministers, like old wine, are the best. Their freedom from earthly ambition, their deep experience of men and things, their simplicity and evident nearness to heaven, all unite to invest their preaching with an interest such as seldom attaches to that of young divines. Think of the aged and hardworking bishops of the Church of England and clergymen of other denominations of the present day. Of John Wesley and his ceaseless travels, writings, preachings, up to beyond the eighties. Of George Whitefield, his physicians perpetually prescribing—the patient declaring a better remedy to be " perpetual preaching "—better for him than a seaside vacation. But every one familiar with the biography of distinguished men will recollect individual cases such as Cato, Plutarch, Sir Henry Spelman, Colbert, Franklin, Cardinals Manning and Newman and hundreds of others who commenced hard study in their old age. The aged man will be a safer guide, a wiser counseller, a more tender sympathizer than he was forty years ago. Nobody who has been active and useful likes the feeling of being laid on the shelf. I am afraid that younger ministers, unwittingly probably, do much harm by pandering to the false sentiment which obtains so extensively about ministers advanced in life. They, at least, wink at it and tacitly encourage it, instead of opposing it and frowning it down. They seem not to reflect that they are whetting a knife which, in fifteen or twenty years, will be used to cut their own throats. Deal gently with those who are on the downhill of life. Your own time is coming to be where they now are. There is probably no class of men who are less imbued with the feeling of *esprit de corps*, and who, alas, are readier to play each other slippery tricks and supplant and undermine each other than some ministers. Hundreds of clergymen, thoughtlessly perhaps, are guilty of the unspeakable meanness of slandering some brother for the purpose of stealing a march upon him in the gaining of some coveted position. The pastoral relationship is looked upon as a mere business arrangement, to be dissolved on the slightest pretext, and for the flimsiest of reasons.

International Conference at Ottawa, 1894.

THE recent meeting of the Colonial Delegates at Ottawa was one of the most important meetings ever held in this " the greatest colony of the greatest Empire the world has ever seen." The accredited delegates and the *personel* of them, in brief, are as follows :—Great Britain, the Earl of Jersey, late Governor of New South Wales ; and Mr. W. Mercer of the Colonial Office. New South Wales, Hon. F. B. Suttor, M.L.A., Minister of Education, Vice-President of the Executive Council, a native. For fifty years Mr. Suttor has sat continually in the legislature. Cape of Good Hope—Hon. Sir Henry de Villiers, K.C.M.G., descended from admixture of French and Dutch ; Hon. Sir Charles Mills, Welsh descent, Agent General ; and the Hon. Jan. H. Hofmeyer, M.L.C., a native of Cape Town, Dutch descent, belongs to Dutch Reformed Church, formerly a journalist, and one of the leading politicians of Cape Colony. South Australia—Hon. Thos. Playford, born in London in 1837, a veteran politician, had a long and varied experience in Australasia. New Zealand—Hon. Alfred Lee Smith, a Yorkshireman by birth, but has lived in the Antipodes since 1869. Victoria —Sir Henry Wrixon, K.C.M.G., Q.C., Ex-Attorney General, an Irishman, but a long time in the colony ; Hon. Nicholas Fitzgerald, M.L.C., Irish by birth, 30 years in Council, graduate of Trinity College, Dublin, and of some other Irish college ; he is an eloquent speaker. He is regarded as the mouthpiece of the Roman Catholic party in the Upper House. He also represented Tasmania, formerly Van Dieman's Land, Botany Bay ; Hon. Simon Fraser, M.L.C., been in Australia 40 years, a native of Pictou, Nova Scotia, of Scotch descent, belongs to the Presbyterian Church, and Grand Master of the Orange Order of Victoria. Queensland—Hon. A. J. Thynne, M.L.C., a minister, born in Ireland, belongs to the Roman

Catholic Church, studied law in Ireland. Hon. William Forrest, M.L.C.; Honolulu Chamber of Commerce—Mr. Theodore H. Davies. The Canadian delegates were the Hon. Mackenzie Bowell, Sir Adolphe Caron, Hon. George E. Foster and Mr. Sanford Fleming. Newfoundland and the West Indies were the only self-governing portions of the empire not represented at the conference.

Sir William Harcourt made the statement in the House of Commons, "That it had never been conceded in connection with the ' most favored nation ' treatment in commercial treaties ; that the colonies were included in the words ' other nation or other country.' " If true, this is most important in view of the Ottawa conference, as showing the power of all parts of the empire to make what internal commercial plans they choose without reference to foreign nations.

The first meeting of the Conference was opened at Ottawa on the 29th June. The Hon. Mackenzie Bowell, Minister of Trade and Commerce, was unanimously chosen President, and Sir A. P. Caron was elected Vice-President. The chief subjects for discussion were, first, closer trade relations between Canada and the Australian and African colonies; and, second, the laying of the Pacific cable of an exclusively British character. The Earl of Aberdeen, the Governor-General, addressed the meeting, after which he called on the Earl of Jersey, and the delegates from the various colonies, who addressed the meeting. Also, Sir John Thompson, the Premier of Canada, and others. The Conference if looked upon as a prelude to others, leading to imperial federation, when there will be a great federated parliament of the empire meeting in London. The first practical result of the Conference. After discussing the Pacific cable project for three days, the delegates passed a resolution of the Hon. F. B. Suttor, expressing the opinion that immediate steps should be taken to provide telegraphic communication free from foreign control between the Dominion of Canada and

Australia. A resolution was unanimously adopted, asking the Imperial Government to undertake a survey of the ocean bed of the proposed routes, the expense to be borne in equal proportions by Great Britain, Canada and the Australian Colonies. Cable to be extended to the African Colonies. A resolution was also adopted :—

"That this Conference is of opinion that any provisions in existing treaties, between Great Britain and any foreign power, which prevent the self-governing dependencies of the Empire from entering into agreement of commercial reciprocity with each other, or with Great Britain shall be removed."

The following resolution was adopted by the Conference :—

"*Whereas* the stability and progress of the British Empire can be best assured by drawing continually closer the bonds that unite the Colonies with the Mother Country, and by the continuous growth of a practical sympathy and co-operation in all that pertains to the common welfare ;

"*And whereas*, this co-operation and unity can in no way be more effectually promoted than by the cultivation and extension of the mutual interchange of their products ;

"*Therefore resolved*, that this Conference records its belief in the advisability of a customs arrangement between Great Britain and her colonies, by which trade within the Empire may be placed on a more favorable footing than that which is carried on with foreign countries ;

"*Further resolved* that until the Mother Country can see her way to enter into customs arrangement with her colonies, it is desirable that, when empowered to do so, the colonies of Great Britain, or such of them as may be disposed to accede to this view, take steps to place each other's products, in whole or in part, on a more favored customs basis than is acceded to the like products of foreign countries ;

"*Furthermore resolved*, that for the purposes of this resolution the South African Customs' Union be considered as part of the territory, capable of being brought within the scope of the contemplated trade arrangements."

The Parliament of Canada has agreed to give a subsidy of $750,000 to a fast line of steamships to run 20 miles an hour, calling at Halifax and St. John, N.B. The Conference passed a resolution approving of the action of the Dominion Government in liberally subsidizing the direct Australian service, and the large subsidy which it voted for the fast mail across the Atlantic. The resolution points out that Great Britain in the past has voted large mail subsidies to steamers running to the Cape and Australia, and commends the fast Atlantic service for similar aid from the Imperial Government. The Queen sent a gracious reply to the address of greeting from the Colonial Conference. Lord Rosebery also sent a message of greeting. The central idea of the Conference was Imperial Unity, to keep the British Empire intact commercially and politically. The delegates are some of the ablest men of Australia. The Hon. F. W. Suttor from New South Wales was the giant of the Conference, the *par excellence*. A series of festivities, unparalleled in the history of Ottawa, took place during the twelve days' sitting of the great Colonial Conference, commencing at Government House with a grand dinner party by the Governor-General. In the Senate Chamber by the Dominion Government, at the Drill Hall by Sir Adolphe Caron, Minister of Militia. Dinners by Sir John Thompson, the Premier, at the Russell House, by members of the Legislature, and by the Hon. Simon Fraser from Victoria, to the Nova Scotia representatives in the Dominion Parliament. The delegates could only spend three days at Toronto; during that time they were banqueted at the Rotunda by the Board of Trade, by the City Council at the Queen's Hotel, and by the Governor of Ontario at breakfast at his official residence. After breakfast the delegates were presented with an address by the Imperial Federation League of Canada. The gentlemen who represented the league were headed by the Right Rev. A. Sweatman, Lord Bishop of Toronto.

The following is the closing part of the address:—"It is felt that the labors of those who, during the last ten years, have striven in all parts of the empire for closer union, have not been in vain, and that the policy commenced by the construction of the Canadian Pacific Railway and its use as an Imperial highway, continued in the holding in London of the Colonial Exhibition of 1886, the meeting of the Colonial Conference of 1887, and the recent completion of the Imperial Institute, has reached in this conference a stage from which magnificent and enduring results may be confidently expected.

It is our earnest hope that gatherings such as this conference will soon be crowned by the establishment of a permanent body, in which all the great questions affecting the commerce and welfare of the empire will be dealt with, so that the subjects of one sovereign, under the prestige and historic memories of a great nationality, shall be able to speak with one voice as a united empire." Sir Henry Wrixon, in replying on behalf of the colonies, in the course of his speech said : " We recognize your courtesy in waiting on us this morning, and we cordially reciprocate your sentiments and good wishes for the unity of the empire. It is an empire on which it has been truly said the sun never sets, and under whose flag is spoken every language of the earth. Nothing since our leaving home has struck us more forcibly than the men who inhabit the Dominion of Canada. We have seen wonders in nature and the wealth which your country contains. Your scenery is beyond that of any other part of the world. These things are grand, but let me say that they do not make a nation. It is not the fertility of the soil, the richness of mines, nor great waterways that make a nation. It is the people who make the nation. We have seen in your people all the elements of progress and growth. We have seen that you are thoroughly Anglo-Saxon in character, and filled with that determination that has made the motherland, and which has been exemplified in deeds commemorated by that noble statue we saw at Queenston Heights yesterday—the monument to General ·Brock." Immediately after the speech of Sir

Henry, the delegates drove to the City Hall, where the civic reception was held. After which the whole party took carriages and set out for a drive around the city. A stop was made on Queen Street to let the visitors have a view of the great Orange procession, just then passing. The party visited the Parliament House, the Toronto University, the Athletic Club and other public buildings. The delegates were afterwards taken for a sail on the lake in a steam yacht, which went around the island. Several of the Australian delegates were accompanied by their wives and daughters. Miss De Villiers and Miss Huddart praised the yacht and its commander, and said they had never met such charming people as the Canadians. Tea was served on board the yacht. The delegates visited the Falls of Niagara and surroundings. The delegates were delighted with the hospitalities, banquets and brilliant receptions given them everywhere. They left Toronto for Montreal July 13th, where a grand reception was accorded them at the Windsor Hotel. They visited the historic city of Quebec. I have, in as short a manner as possible, grouped together a few things about the visit of the Colonial Delegates to the Dominion of Canada.

The Pan=American Congress.

THE Pan-American Congress of Religion and Education met at Massey Hall, in Toronto, in July, which continued four days. The non-appearance of the Roman Catholic Archbishop Ireland, of St. Paul, Minn., who was largely advertised to deliver a lecture at the opening of the Congress, was a great disappointment to a more than three thousand audience. However, the Roman Catholics were there in full force, represented by Father Ryan, S. J., Dean Harris, of St. Catharines and Dr. Conaty, Rector of the Sacred Heart, Worcester, Mass. Father Ryan is Rector of St. Michael's Cathedral, Toronto. He is a native of Irish Town, Carbonear, Newfoundland, and one of the most eloquent and popular priests in Canada. He is a portly, jovial, good-looking, good-natured Newfoundlander. At the meeting on Sunday afternoon, at which three thousand persons of all denominations were present, the eloquent and genial Father Ryan was chairman. At the meeting on Saturday Father Ryan discoursed eloquently on the organization of charity and the Catholic Church, and hoped they all would become good Catholics. Dean Harris' paper was a tribute to the self-sacrificing lives of the martyr missionaries of the great Roman Catholic orders. Dr. Conaty spoke on the "Roman Catholic Church in the Educational movement of to-day," in which he repudiated the notion that the church of which he is a member had neglected her work as the teacher of mankind. The Anglican representatives were conspicuous by their absence, their only representative being Dr. Clark, Professor of Trinity College. He spoke briefly on the importance of cultivating the spirit of unity which expressed the predominating sentiments of those present. The enthusiasm of the audience was raised to the highest pitch by the splendid oration of the Coadjutor Bishop of Minnesota, on the "outlook for church unity," who represented the Episcopal Church in the United States. The Methodists were there with some of their leading men. President Burwash, of Victoria College, read a paper on the "Co-relation of Intelligence, Religion, and Morality." The paper by President Rogers, of the North Western University, Illinois, on Christianity and Education, was of first rate excellence. President Burns gave an address. Rev. Dr. Courtice, the new editor of the *Christian Guardian*, gave a paper on "Subjective and Objective Methods of Reform," and the eloquent address of Major Meroin,

F

editor of the *American Journal of Education*, on the "Press as an Educational Factor." The inaugural address of President Smith was admirable, whilst the excellent paper of the Hon. Mr. Bonney, on the "New Movement for the Unity and Peace of the World," was eloquently expressed. Several ladies spoke at the various meetings. Miss Jane Adams, of Chicago, gave a paper on the "Wretched and suffering, and what was being done for them." Mrs. Wood spoke with power and eloquence on "Our Girls." Mrs. Rogers read a paper on "Recent Progress in Philanthropy. Mrs. Mountford gave an eloquent and telling speech. It is not easy to select speeches from so many speakers. Persons from various parts of the United States took part in the meeting. The object of the meeting was Christian Union and the free expression of opinion on religion and education. No person or party at the meeting sought to conceal or disguise their opinions or sentiments. The tendency is towards Christian Union among all denominations. At a union public meeting, recently held at the Opera House at Bay City, Michigan, representing all communions, several Roman Catholics spoke. At the opening the entire audience rose and united in saying the Lord's Prayer. Immediately after, one of the Roman Catholic clergymen acted as precentor in leading the singing of the hymn, "Nearer, My God, to Thee." I have thus, in as brief a manner as possible, touched on a few points of the Congress.

The Secular and Religious Press.

THE press has become a rival to the pulpit. There seems to be a great falling off in pulpit force. All the great daily secular press of Great Britain and America has been adopted as the medium of communication to the public on all sorts of theological and religious subjects. The tendency of the age is to substitute newspaper literature for books. Formerly, men got their knowledge from books. They now get it mostly from newspapers. No doubt the press, by its daily and weekly sheet, has aided wonderfully in the spread of general intelligence. In this respect it has done and is doing an invaluable service. It can present facts as they occur. It can daguerreotype the living features of the age, and it can bring before us with graphic power the world's moving panorama. A reader of newspapers knows something of everything. It is a fact that in a vast number of families the books are on the shelves and the newspaper is the reading matter of the household. The great power wielded in the political world by the great dailies is apparent to all, and is largely so in the religious world as well. The potency of the press for good or evil is recognized everywhere; that it is "mightier than the sword," is fully admitted. Napoleon the First said that he would rather have three armies opposed to him than three powerful editors. In France, a ready newspaper and acute criticism are the best means of raising a man in society, and making him a political personage. Thackeray, in one of his novels, speaking of the power of newspapers, says: "There she is, she never sleeps, she has now at this moment ambassadors in kings' palaces." Sir Thomas Brown says: "Scholars are men of peace, they bear no arms, but their tongues are sharper than Actius' razor, their pens carry farther, and give a louder report than thunder. I had rather stand in the shock of a basilisk than in the fury of a merciless pen." The great Dr. Arnold founded and supported for a time a newspaper of his own, conducted in the interest of social reform. The newspaper, next to the pulpit, is the chief mode of directly influencing the people. In the time of Queen Elizabeth the powerful discourses delivered at Paul's Cross influenced public opinion. And so we find in Wales in the present day, the pulpit is the chief means for conveying information to the people. What the newspaper is to the English, the pulpit is to the Welsh. The pulpit and the press are all powerful in moulding public opinion. No one, who is a mere reader of newspapers, can be deeply versed in any department of knowledge. This kind of knowledge answers very well as the small currency of social life, but will never produce a thorough and well grounded information as derived from reading books. The author of a good book is really the silent preacher, he steals into the study of his reader's imagination and shapes his thoughts. Sir William Berkeley, Governor of the Colony of Virginia, in the reign of Charles the Second, wrote: " I thank God there are no free schools or printing, and I hope we shall not have them these hundred years; for learning has brought heresy and disobedience and sect into the world, and printing has divulged them, and libels against the government. God keep us from both." The world was more than four thousand years old before printing was discovered. When Guttenberg, in the fifteenth century, printed and published the famous *Nazarine Bible*, it was supposed that none but the devil could have done it. The press wields an immense power. There are now sent by mail over the Dominion of Canada 78,844,164 copies of newspapers annually. In some of the newspapers we see a column headed, " Crumbs of crime swept from every corner of the globe." Was there ever an age when the desire to obtain criminal news and parade it in all its disgusting particulars before the public, raged as it does now? It is the greatest crime of modern journalism, that in the demand for sensational news some newspapers are betrayed into dishing all manner of revolting gossip relating to private affairs of families. There is no "forbidden" ground. It is time that this moral gangrene be cut out of the body of the press, and it be confined to its natural, legitimate and healthy functions. Some ministers have told me they have refused to admit certain newspapers into their families because of their publishing all sorts of scandals. There are a great many morbid appetites. Some people do not want to be edified, but only to be amused. They will read a story if it is spicy, but will not read an essay, no matter how instructive. It is a question whether many ministers really appreciate the value that the religious press may be made to them in their work. The clergyman who sees that every family in his congregation is supplied with a religious newspaper has done up a large part of his pastoral work and visiting and oversight in that one matter. His families will be visited fifty-two times a year, making them more intelligent in regard to the church's life, work and benevolence, its missionary operations, and its living questions. It comes with words of advice and admonition and instruction. It has a message for every member of the family, and has as its object the making of people more desirous of seeking after Christ and more steadfast in their church. There are ministers who do not perhaps, reflect upon the value of a religious paper in the homes of their people. It supplants worldly, and often criminal and scandalous reading. It enforces the truth and persuasions of the pulpit. The religious newspaper is a constant teacher of righteousness in the home, and yet there are homes in which neither a secular or religious paper can be found.

Incineration.

The Right Rev. Dr. Howley, Roman Catholic Bishop of St. John's, Newfoundland, in his address at Belvidere Cemetery, said:

"Church discipline excluded all systems of treating the human body after death save that of interment. Cremation was utterly at variance with the spirit of Catholic Faith."

The only resident of Toronto, that I know of, who has been cremated, was Lady Macpherson, wife of Sir David Macpherson. She died in the South of France, and by her own special request was cremated. In the Spring Sir David brought the ashes of his wife to Toronto. Lady Macpherson was a member of the Church of England.

Public sentiment is growing in favor of the process of incineration as the best means of disposing of the remains of the dead. Many of the clergymen have recently preached and written in favor of cremation, giving reasons from a scientific and sanitary standpoint why it should be universally adopted. Dean Hodges, of the Cambridge, Mass., Episcopal Theological School, has recently debated in favor of cremation, saying that it makes no difference to the dead how their remains are disposed of, but it does make a good deal of difference to the living, and it is for their health and happiness that the decaying bodies should be consumed as soon as possible. There are now seventeen crematories in the United States; in 1876 the first one was started in Pennsylvania, now they are to be found in several States, ranging from Massachusetts to California. In 1885 there were 36 cremations in the United States; in 1886, 119, and these figures have yearly increased until in 18l3 we find 677 cremations, and in eleven months of 1894 there were 876. The French Cremation Society states that in Paris alone more than 20,000 bodies have been cremated since the commencement of the movement. All things are possible with God, and whether the body is consumed to ashes by fire or whether it goes to dust by decay, it will be easy for Him to reanimate the elements with living power and bring the conscious man back into physical life as a resurrected being.

> "Ask not, How can this be? Sure the same Power
> That rear'd the piece at first, and took it down,
> Can re-assemble the loose scattered parts,
> And put them as they were."

Mr. Walter S. March thus describes his visit to a cemetery in the vicinity of Boston in 1895:

"The Massachusetts Cremation Society hold that the increase of population brings with it a demand for cremation as the most simple, satisfactory and least trying method of disposing of the dead. By it the land is saved for the benefit of the living, and contagious diseases are not stored up to be a menace to life, as in the case with earth burial; but the germs of disease are destroyed and the water supply of cities need not further be contaminated by the drainage from graveyards. Sooner or later the practice adopted in some of the crowded parts of Europe, of leasing the same grave over and over again on ten year terms to a succession of tenants, would have to be adopted in the United States unless cremation becomes a universal method. Cremation, as practiced by this society, may be thus described: The body in a wooden casket is placed upon rollers on the catafalque, which is brought to the door of the retort; (a large oven-shaped apartment about three feet wide, eight feet long and three feet deep) the body is then gently placed in this retort, the doors are closed, and the heat applied. The process is so perfect that in no period of combustion can any odor be perceived. The relatives are admitted to the retort room from time to time to see the process of disintegration, if they so desire. The time needed is from one to three hours. On the following day the ashes are delivered to the relatives in an iron or metallic case, as may be preferred. I may here add that one family known to the writer had the remains of a brother in one of these cases, and this case formed part of the paraphernalia of a drawing-room mantel shelf. In cases of death in a family, if cremation is desired, the undertaker must communicate with the society, and make an appointment for the time of incineration. The proper papers are then signed, and the payment of $30.00 made. A large chapel adjoins the retort room, but until this chapel is finished the crematory will not be in suitable condition for the burial service. This cremation society is incorporated under the laws of Massachusetts, has a capital stock of fifty thousand dollars. It has disposed of 2,800 shares of stock, and in order to complete its chapel seeks to sell the remaining 2,200 shares at $10.00 per share. It has a President, Vice-President, Clerk and Treasurer, Nine Honorary Vice-Presidents, and Nine Directors residing in Boston, Cambridge and Worcester Mass."

Persons living in the country where the quick and the dead do not jostle each other for room as they do in crowded cities, and where the "God's acre" has long been set apart and used as a depository for the departed, has but a faint notion of the trouble that awaits the family in the city—especially if in moderate circumstances—when death overtakes a member of it. It is said the primary reason why our ancestors interred the dead beneath their churches, or in the churchyards immediately surrounding them was that the deceased might enjoy the benefit of the prayers of the attendants of the churches. It never occurred to them that the near vicinity of dead bodies constituted a menace to the living. When land grew scarce in London the graves were opened and used over and over again, till in some of them the surface was raised to a level with the church windows. Disgusting abuses grew up in connection with the London churchyards—such as the systematic removal of the contents of the graves to a large common pit and the appropriation of the coffin-plate, nails and handles to be sold as old metal by the sextons. The English Burial Act of 1855 led to the establishment of cemeteries. Scientific and sanitary considerations combined to cause trees and shrubbery to be planted in English cemeteries. The scientific theory on which the planting proceeded was that vegetation would absorb the carbonic acid and other gases generated by bodily decay. In London it has been proved that shallow wells in the vicinity of graveyards were polluted by the drainage from them, which caused them to be closed, and now these old, disused burial places have been converted into pleasant parks and playgrounds, until there are no less than 173 of these breathing places within the city. Mr. Haden, an experienced medical man, in a paper read before the Liverpool Medical Institution, in May last, thus defines what he and other burial reformers consider perfectly sanitary sepulture—burial in an easily perishable envelope. He says, a body buried in such a way that the earth may have access to it, does not remain in the earth, but returns to the atmosphere. Suppose a body buried three or four feet below the surface, the earth as earth affects it in no way whatever. The part played by the earth in its revolution is that of a mere porous medium between it and the air that is above it. Through this medium the air, with its dews and its rain filters, and when it reaches the body oxidizes it—that is, resolves it into new and harmless products, and then these new products passing upwards again through the same sieve-like medium re-enter the atmosphere and become the elements of its renewal, and the nourishment and growth of plants. The body, in fact, literally as well as figuratively, ascends from the dead, and fulfils the cycle of its pilgrimage by becoming again the source and renewal of life. In Woking, England, where there is a large cemetery, a coffin made of pressed pulp is used, and those who are engaged in the burial-reform movement direct their attack to the coffin, which they say it is irrational to make too strong, and bricked-up graves they consider still more opposed to sanitary sepultures and call them a reproach to intelligence. They lay down a fundamental principle "That the natural destination of all organized bodies that have lived on the earth's surface is the earth ; and that to seek to prevent the beneficent agency of the earth by enclosing the dead in imperishable coffins is in the highest degree irrational, since it engages us in vain resistance to an inevitable dispensation, and that it is far wiser to yield a timely submission to a well defined law of nature." In the United States the cemeteries are beautiful parks to which the public resort for recreation and pleasure. The same use is made of the lovely cemeteries of Toronto. So the cemeteries of St. John's could be utilized in the same way. In London, pine coffins are imported from Germany and sold at half a dollar each. And there is yet another cheaper kind made of wicker-basket work, the object being to have the body to decay as quickly as possible. But it will take some time to overcome the prejudices and preconceived notions of those who are opposed to it.

At funerals the tendency is towards extravagance and pride. The coffin is covered with tinsel and finery, in some cases totally out of place, considering the surrounddings of the deceased when alive. There should be enough show and public decorum and social respect for the dead, but as little money as possible expended for showy surroundings. A costly coffin is put into the earth to rot. What a misapplication of money expended in mere fopperies in death. To what does it go ? To silk scarfs, black crape, kid gloves, white satin, and black cloth for the worms. I remember when a few persons of taste and fine feelings tried to relieve the gloom of death by strewing a few flowers upon the coffin and the grave as symbols of life after death; but now other emblems are added—costly floral crosses, anchors and crowns, until the profusion covers the significance of the use of them. A husband will buy costly flowers for the decoration of his wife's coffin who never bought a pot flower for the lightening of her sick room; a man will spend twenty dollars for carriage hire at the funeral of his wife when he never spent a dollar on riding for her when alive. The funeral of an artisan, earning ten dollars a week, will go to fifty or a hundred dollars expenses for the burial of a member of his family. Sometime ago a man applied to me to bury his son. I went at the time appointed; the coffin was not ready, so that the funeral had to be postponed to another day owing to the undertaker not having a coffin fine enough ready made. This was a poor man; two years after he was sued for the funeral expenses. I could give several cases of this kind. For a decent interment, all that is requisite is the cheapest form of pine coffin. Sometime ago Canon Forest, of the diocese of Ontario, died. He was, according to his own instructions, buried in a plain pine coffin, no gloves, no crape given out, no hearse employed and no funeral sermon preached. In Russia the mourning color is white. At the funeral service of the late Dr. Shelton, Dean of Buffalo, U. S., the gloomy black emblems of mourning which usually are the accompaniment of funeral pomp and ceremony, were conspicuously absent. The church was fragrant with flowers, signifying that the Church never sorrows over its dead, but rejoices and is happy in the translation of its saints. Purple and white, the mourning colors of the church, prevailed, the latter strongly predominating. Some people adopt a mourning paper bordered by a black band a quarter inch in width. The use of such paper obtrudes your grief upon everybody you write to and makes a display of it. It is not necessary to proclaim it to the world. It is wholly a personal matter. I have often attended funerals years ago where there were more eating and drinking and carousing than at a wedding. Happily these things, for the most part, are now done away with. In the towns and cities of Canada women do not attend funerals, but in the villages and country places all through the country, women attend funerals. In country places the people think it is no funeral unless a sermon is preached. The funeral sermon must be given over the smallest child.

What a vast amount of money is wasted at funerals! According to a report drawn up by Sir Edwin Chadwick for the British Government, he states that upon a moderate calculation the sum annually expended in funeral expenses in England and Wales is thirty millions of dollars. It is calculated that from $300 to $500 were necessary to bury an upper tradesman; $1,250 for a gentleman, and $3,000 to $8,000 for a nobleman. In England, several societies have been organized to do away with the expenses at funerals. The Roman Catholic Synod of New York has promulgated a decree prohibiting the lavish displays that are made at funerals, and in Toronto, two years ago, a burial reform association of the Church of England was organized to lessen the expenses of funerals.

"Tradition."

THAT the church of England does not altogether reject tradition we may learn by reading her 34th article. Tradition is something which is handed down from generation to generation, either orally or in writing. First —Ecclesiastical Tradition, which has been used by the church from the beginning. Second—Hermeneutical Tradition, that is, the creeds, liturgy, etc., and third— Oral Tradition. The Roman Catholic Church asserts that the Scriptures are not perfect without Oral tradition, that is, handed down from age to age by word of mouth, which was given by our Saviour and his Apostles, and which has come down to this time. According to the Council of Trent, Apostolical Traditions have the same authority as the word of God itself. According to some of the Cardinals, tradition is the foundation of the scriptures, which cannot subsist without it, while tradition subsists very well without the Bible. Cardinal Ballermine, one of the greatest theologians of the Roman Catholic Church, asserts that the scriptures, without tradition, are neither necessary nor sufficient, and some traditions are greater than the scriptures, and more obligatory to be observed. Look at the effect of Oral tradition. It was given to man in the three different ages of the world. First, to Adam, and men became so corrupt that the truth was lost, and God was obliged to make another revelation; secondly, to Noah, which was at length almost lost, until God made Himself known again; thirdly, to Abraham. Afterward God committed the written law to Moses on the tables of stone. That Christ and his Apostles said many things which were never written cannot be doubted, but how are we to know what they were? Some would say, by tradition; there cannot be anything more uncertain than that. Why were the Jewish and Christian Scriptures committed to writing? It was to preserve them against the casualities of an Oral communication.

There is nothing more uncertain than the sending of unwritten messages. Start an oral communication eighteen centuries ago—what perversions it would encounter in the long line of descent? It would pass through so many hands, suffering from the manipulations of every one of them, so that long before it would reach our times, the alterations and mutilations practiced upon it by ignorance, superstition, and prejudice would almost destroy its identity, and put it past recognition. "The form of sound words" which the Church inculcates upon her children are, first—the Holy Scriptures; second—the Consensus and Praxis Ecclesia, gathered from the fathers, councils, and historians. The authority of Holy Scriptures is paramount and ultimate; that of the Consensus and Praxis secondary and confirmatory. What the discipline and rules of the church were we learn from the fathers. The New Testament was not written until from thirty to sixty years after the death of Christ. There were, therefore, worship, discipline, organization and a creed established before the New Testament was written. The New Testament is not at all systematized, but the doctrines taught by Christ and his Apostles are constantly referred to, and there is a recognition of them throughout the whole. The teaching and preaching of the apostles was as much the word of God before the New Testament was written as it was after. But in order to avoid corruption through tradition the New Testament was written. We have the Apostles' creed, the Nicene Creed, and St. Athanasius' Creed, which are summaries of the Gospel. The Nicene Creed was founded on the ancient creeds by the Council of Nice, A.D. 325, and was adopted as the rule of faith by the universal Church in all subsequent times. The canonicity of the New Testament was, I believe, decided by the Council of Carthage. So far as we know, the first Council to enumerate the books of the New Testament, was that of Carthage, A.D. 397. The stream of Jewish tradition is embodied in the Targums. An account of the early oral Targums and Jewish Talmudic tradition is given by different writers. As in the case of the Oral Law, and afterwards of the Oral Massora, the force of circumstances compelled the final writing down of the Targum. In the Talmuds some fine illustrations of the word of God are given. When I was quite a youth I read in some of the Talmuds, "And when the Queen of Sheba heard of the fame of Solomon, she came to prove Solomon with hard questions at Jerusalem; and

Solomon told her all her questions."—2 Chron. XCVI.—12. In the Talmud of Gemera the following beautiful illustration of the above passage is given. I quote from memory: The Queen of Sheba, attracted by the great reputation of Solomon, set out to visit this celebrated potentate at his court, with the intention of asking questions, and to realize the extent of his wisdom. The interview was in the presence of the whole court. At the foot of the throne stood Sheba's Queen; in each hand she held a garland of flowers—the one composed of natural, the other of artificial. Art emulated the lively hues and the variegated beauties of nature, so that at the distance it was held by the Queen for the inspection of Jerusalem's Monarch, it was deemed impossible for him to decide, as her question imported, which was the natural and which was the artificial wreath. The sagacious Solomon seemed posed, a solemn silence pervaded the assembly, the son of David inspects the garlands with attention. It was a time of awful suspense with the Jewish Court. At length an expedient presented itself to this highly favored king and philosopher; observing a cluster of bees hovering on the outside of one of the windows, he commanded it to be opened, and the bees rushing into the court alighted instantly on one of the wreaths, while not a single one fixed upon the other. The decision was no longer difficult—the mystery was now unfolded, the learned Rabbis shook their beards in rapture, and the wondering Sheba, the potent Empress of the South, had now an additional reason to be astonished at the wisdom of Solomon.

The Church of England in her 6th article, says: "In the name of Holy Scripture, we do understand those canonical books of the Old and New Testament, of whose authority was never any doubt in the Church. All the books of the New Testament, as they are commonly received, we do receive, and account them canonical." With regard to the Apocrypha, the article says:—"And the other books, (as Hierome saith), the Church doth read for example of life, and instruction of manners, but yet doth it not apply them to establish any doctrine." The Apocryha are books of doubtful origin and authority. They are so-called from a Greek word, which signifies hidden, because their authors were not known, nor are the proofs of their Mission upon record, for which reasons their writings were not received in the Canon of the Jewish Church. The Bible contains the revealed will of God, and is a perfect rule of faith and practice. A plain Christian, by prayer and diligent reading, may understand as much of it as is necessary, without the assistance of learned criticism.

Popularity.

THERE is the popularity of the statesman, the politician, the scientist and the lecturer, but I shall confine myself to the popularity of the preacher. Popularity is not always a sign of real merit. Some men have a way of ingratiating themselves into the favor of others, when in fact they are worthy of but little esteem. Some men, too, are popular because they say " yes, yes," to everybody. They raise no antagonism. They never resist the tide. They go as they are carried. They propose nothing, they oppose nothing. They are mere bubbles that float on the surface. These walking negatives enjoy a certain kind of popularity. They are in nobody's way. Nobody speaks ill of them. They are nobody's target. Men of pronounced character are always the object of somebody's criticism. They think for themselves, and they say what they think. Taking the world as it moves on day by day, the thoughtless crowd will not speak well of a man who rebukes their follies and checks their waywardness.

But neither popularity nor unpopularity is a test of merit. The judgment of man is not always righteous judgment. The man whose life is in accord with the word of God, ought to be popular if he is not, and he whose life is not in such accord ought *not* to be popular if he is. It sometimes happens that a man's neighbors, and those who are nearest to him and know most about him, are the most unsuitable of all persons to form an estimate of him. David, the psalmist, was a man who had enemies, and plenty of them. On one occasion he said, "I am a reproach among all mine enemies, but *especially among my neighbors.*" On another occasion he said: "Yea, mine own familiar friend in whom I trusted, hath lifted up his heel against me. The most unpopular man that ever lived in this world was our Lord Jesus Christ. "He came to his own, and his own received him not." The very people among whom he lived cried out, "Away with him, away with him." It is well to seek the good opinion of our neighbors, and so to act as to secure it, but not if it required us to deflect from the line of right. When the apostle speaks of being "all things to all men," he means, be conciliating to all, be rude to none, please everybody, if possible, but please God first. A man who will do this will be sure to have opposition. St. Paul had enemies; he was beaten with stripes five times, and stoned and left for dead. Our Lord said, "Woe unto you, when all men shall speak well of you, for so did their fathers to the false prophets." The popular preacher is not always the best preacher. People seldom like best what they need most. Some ministers are not engaged for their orthodox faith, but for their power to interest and afford entertainment. I have known excellent ministers rejected, because the people did not want the gospel pure and simple. The tendency of the modern pulpit is to round off the sharp edges of the truth so that it will be the less cutting to the conscience of fashionable and respectable sinners. It is not pleasant to tell people what they don't want to hear. It is a great deal nicer to prophesy smooth things than to cry "Repent or perish." There are preachers who drift into scientific preaching—philosophical, astronomical, geological, and such subjects as these,—*biogenesis* (begetment from a living original); *abiogenesis* (begetment from a lifeless original); and *reniogenesis*) the begetment of one sort of living creature from another living creature of a different sort). Some preachers indulge in very tall talk about "mephitic glooms of sceptical inanitions." There is an excess of sermonizing in these days. Too high a premium is put upon rhetoric and mere machinery. The taste is for sketchy, exciting sermons which tend to sensation and not to edification. An æstheticized gospel may tickle the itching ears of some, but the old-fashioned gospel still proves itself to be the power of God unto salvation. There has grown up a sentiment against preaching the old-fashioned truths of the gospel, and as a consequence some pulpits ring with sensational and startling utterances. The current events of the day are dwelt upon, while the topics of the gospel are pushed aside as threadbare and worn out. But neither the old-fashioned gospel nor old-fashioned ways of preaching it will ever be improved on.

St. Paul's faithful declaration upon leaving the Church of Ephesus was this: "I have not shunned to declare unto you the whole counsel of God." He had not shunned those parts of God's word which are most offensive to men, and preached those parts which would be most popular to the world. What a difference between St. Paul's preaching and some of the preaching of modern times! In many pulpits the preaching is altogether popular, and the most fastidious worldling could not find fault with it. Instead of giving a weekly pair of dull "dry as dust" moral and dogmatic treatises, the preacher delivers beautiful essays upon the ethics and æsthetics of religion, pronounced in the most tasteful and attractive style. The opera, the theatre, the dance, and the card-table are spoken of as innocent amusements. His mouth is closed to whatever is unpopular or unpalatable to the public taste. He proclaims a gospel of mists and rainbows, and rose-tinted clouds the production of a refined and playful fancy. There are pulpit preachers who "joke for God," who convert the sanctuary into a theatre, and the pretended preaching of God's word into a tragic comedy. The popular sermon may be rationalistic, evolutionistic, sentimental, fantastic, humanitarian, literary, anything rather than religious. It is very easy to tickle the ears of people with mere wooden, lifeless images of artistic manufacture. But just as a sensational novel unfits the mind for sober reading, so sensational preaching results in spiritual dyspepsia, by pampering the palate till it loathes all proper food. Some years ago a very extraordinary man appeared as a great light in the Presbyterian Church in Canada, a great preacher who drew crowded audiences from far and near. He was such a popular orator that he received three calls from different Presbyterian congregations at the one time. Like a meteor, he showed for a little while, and, meteor-like, he disappeared. He was a sailor and orator of high degree, an enthusiast, a sensationalist, altogether a wonderful man; he appeared for a little time to bask in the sunshine of popularity, and then mysteriously disappeared. Up to this day no one knows what became of him. Those men are not necessarily the most useful men in their generation, nor the most favored by God who make the most noise in the world. The reward of the minister does not consist in the crowded congregations that may be attracted by the eloquence of the pulpit, for the size of an audience is not always an index of ministerial success, nor is the wealth and culture of the congregation to which he ministers, for often in the midst of the great wealth there is the least piety; nor in the large salaries received, for sometimes the undeserving receives the largest pecuniary recompense. The common idea of pulpit eloquence with some is low and sensational. It means a rapid, loud, emphatic utterance, with a good deal of action, of high-sounding sentences. Some people require of the preacher that he shall arouse and excite them, and they enjoy the temporary stimulus and emotion which the preaching causes. But preaching of this kind does not inspire nor tend to practical activity ; such preaching may be popular, dramatic and entertaining, but in a large measure unspiritual. This sort of preaching may attract people on their mental and fashionable side, but is ineffective in the making of Christian character. The theories of schools and philosophies have too often displaced the pure and simple Gospel of Christ. A man may preach fervent sermons, but if he does so from emulation or love of popularity, he is yielding to a dangerous temptation. If these are motive forces his usefulness will diminish and so will his popularity. The grand theme of apostolic preaching was Christ. Amid the multitude of orators, there is only one class to whom the term "preacher" is in a sense consecrated, that class who seek to win men to the Saviour as the central orb of the system around which all other truths revolve, and from which they derive their brightness, influence and energy.

Newfoundland as a Health Resort.

Good health, we are often compelled to seek it away from home, in outdoor rambles, in the field, in the forest, or by the ever-changing sea. Nature, in her loveliest attire, offers us the rarest enticements to partake of her bounty.

> "There is a pleasure in the pathless woods,
> There is a rapture in the lonely shore,
> There is society where none intrudes,
> By the deep sea, and music in its roar."

NEWFOUNDLAND AS A HEALTH RESORT.

We read the books written by travellers in other lands, and gaze in imagination on the beautiful scenery they describe, the refreshing and invigorating air which they inhale, and wish that we too might see the sights they were able to describe, and revel in the luxuriance of nature, in her craggy mountains, her silvery streams, her golden strands, and her balmy zephyrs, thus we overlook the fact that what we seek is near at hand. There is no country with more varied and grander scenery than the coast-line of Newfoundland, now stern and rock-bound, now graceful, picturesque and romantic. If the grand scenery of the bays of Newfoundland were distant and difficult of approach—in the United States, the United Kingdom, "gay France," "sunny Italy," "romantic Switzerland," or "classic Greece," how eagerly would tourists wend their way to them. Travelling either for long or short distances, has now become a pleasant cure for many complaints, mentally and physically, and is an educator in geography, botany and history. In Newfoundland we have a bracing climate, with no trace of malaria. Sunstrokes are entirely unknown. The thermometer rarely reaches 90 deg. Fr. Sunshine without excessive heat. The flood and earthquake, tornado and cyclone, which devastate portions of the earth from time to time, are unknown here. My friend, Miss Freeman, visited Newfoundland in 1890, this is what she says of it:—

"One thing I am very sure of, Newfoundlanders do not know what hot weather is. Warm weather we have had since I came, the thermometer on one day registered 80 deg. in the shade—the highest point that is ever reached. Yet, though the sun shone hot upon the wharves, the air was soft and breezy, and upon the hill-top a cool, refreshing wind made the temperature so pleasant that I walked about with closed sunshade. Of delightfully cool warm weather (if you will permit the paradox) Newfoundland has her full share. But of sultry, intense heat—under which men droop and grow pale—she endures not even an hour."

The late Roman Catholic Bishop, Dr. Mullock, says:—
" We have all the advantages of an insular climate, a mild temperature with its disadvantages, uncertain weather. I may remark likewise what Abbe Raynal recorded already, that the climate of Newfoundland is considered the most invigorating and salubrious in the world, and that we have no indigenous disease."

Again the Bishop says:—

"What an awful climate, they will say, you have in Newfoundland; how can you live there without the sun, in a continual fog? How surprised they are when you tell them that for ten months at least in the year, all the fog and damp of the Banks goes over to their side and descends in rain there, with the south-westerly winds, while we never have the benefit of it unless when what we call out-winds blow. In fact, the geography of America is very little known, even by intelligent writers at home, and mistakes made in our leading periodicals are frequently very amusing."

According to a table, kept by Mr. Delaney, for 1859, the highest temperature was 90 deg. on the 3rd July; 8 deg. on the 3rd March, and the mean temperature of the year 44 deg.; mean max. pres. of barometer, 29.74 inch; rain 63.920 for the year; max. quan. in 24 hours, 2.098 inch; wind N.N.W. and W.N.W., 200 days; N.E. 25 days; W. and W.S.W. 38 days; S.S.W. and S.E. 102 days; rain fell on 110 days; snow 54 days; thunder and lightning 5 days. According to a register kept at St. John's, Newfoundland, in 1841, it being more exposed to bank fog than any other part of the coast, the average of thick fog and partial light fog extending a short distance inland, was 17½ days of thick fog and 19½ days of light fog and mists, making a total of only 37 days of cloudy weather throughout the year. The register kept at Citadel Hill, Fort George, Halifax, Nova Scotia, in 1859, was kindly furnished me by Mr. G. Moulds, Staff-Sergeant, Royal Artillery, there were 110 days of cloudy weather; thick fog 42 days; and light fog a portion of the day 60 days. It will thus be seen that while in Newfoundland there were only 37 days of thick and light fog, during the year 1841, there were, in 1859, in Nova Scotia 42 days of thick fog, and 60 days of light fog a portion of the day, making a total of 102 days of foggy weather, besides 110 days of cloudy weather.

In Newfoundland the sea-fog prevails mostly on the eastern and southern shores. The fog along the coast hardly ever approaches nearer than from a half to a mile of the shore. The sea-fog does not reach inland, sometimes, however, it is brought by the south winds over the narrow neck of land which separates Placentia Bay from Trinity Bay. The fog of St. John, New Brunswick, is called the "St. John doctor." Persons afflicted with lung and other diseases resort there during the summer to inhale the sea-fog. Newfoundland is admitted by all who have ever resided there to be one of the healthiest countries in the world. Not a fever of any kind is generated in the country, and that fatal disease, consumption, so common on the American continent, is hardly ever known there. Sir Richard Bonnycastle says;—"There is no colony of England which can produce a better fed, a healthier or better clothed, or a more industrious and better behaved population than the fishermen settlers and natives of Newfoundland." Perhaps the free use of fish diet may be conducive to the health of the people of Newfoundland. Fish is rich in protein, which is the food element that makes blood, muscle, bone and tendon. Fish may be more nourishing than meat, considering how, from its soft fibre, fish is more easily digested. There is in fish a substance that does not exist in the flesh of land animals, viz., iodine—a substance which may have a beneficial effect on the health, and tend to prevent the production of scrofulous and tubercular disease, and probably this is the reason why so little of pulmonary consumption is known in Newfoundland, which is so fatal in highly educated and refined society. If we give attention to classes of people, classed as to the quality of food they principally subsist on, we find that the fishing class are especially strong, healthy and prolific. In no other class than that of fishers do we find larger families, handsomer women, more robust and active men, or a greater exemption from maladies. Bayard Taylor, the great American traveller, journalist, author, and Consul in Europe, says, in his sketch of Newfoundland, that the women were the handsomest he had ever seen. And this has been remarked by all visitors—the healthiness and rosy cheeks of the inhabitants. For the last hundred and fifty years, some of the New England farmers, professional men and others, have occasionally visited Newfoundland for their health, some of the farmers have gone down in fishing schooners and spent three and four months in Newfoundland and Labrador, and returned home recuperated, with rosy faces from inhaling the refreshing and saline air of Newfoundland. Some families now take their servants with them to the northern part of Newfoundland during the summer months, which they prefer to Boston, Albany, or New York. Every facility is now afforded the tourist by steam and sailing vessels to reach St. John's. The Red Cross line, which plies between New York and St. John's, calling at Halifax. A line of steamers runs from Halifax calling at Sydney, C.B., and another line from Montreal calling at Quebec, Sydney, C. B., and Charlottetown, Prince Edward Island. The distance from Halifax to St. John's is 568 miles. St. John's, the capital of Newfoundland, is situate on the the most eastern part of the coast in the Bay of St. John, which, however, is but a slight indentation of the coast. The first authentic record of St. John's is given in a letter to King Henry VIII., by John Rut in 1527, who was at that time employed on a fishing voyage. This is recorded by Hackluyt, one of the earliest writers on Newfoundland.

On approaching St. John's from the sea, the shores present an air of grandeur and sublimity. The coast for miles consists of old red sandstone and conglomerate, from three to six hundred feet in height, presenting an almost perpendicular wall, which resists the unbroken surges of the Atlantic Ocean that incessantly thunder at its base. In the summer this wall of nature's masonry is adorned with touches of the beautiful—the interstices and crevices of these sublime cliffs are dotted with grass, wild flowers, plants and shrubs of various kinds, the green foliage of which, trailing along the red surface of the rocks, gives it a picturesque and romantic appearance. St. John's is one of the finest harbors in Newfoundland, where a vessel might in a few minutes shoot from the stormy Atlantic into a secure haven, and ride at anchor completely land-locked, in from four to ten fathoms of water on a mud bottom. St. John's is an old historic city, and has many points of interest for the invalided tourist. The entrance to St. John's is very narrow, which is therefore called the "narrows." The channel from point to point, that is from Signal Hill on the north side to Fort Amherst on the south side, is 220 fathoms across; but it widens just within the points, then again gets narrower on approaching China Rock, from which to Pancake Rock the distance is only 95 fathoms across; after which it expands into a beautiful sheet of water, one and a quarter miles long and a half mile wide. In war times a chain was thrown across, from Chain to Pancake Rocks. On each side of the Narrows are lofty cliffs, from four hundred to six hundred feet in altitude, studded with forts and batteries, while a short distance to the right is seen Cuckold's Head and Sugar Loaf, towering in solitary grandeur above all the surrounding coast. The south side of the harbor is formed by a lofty and unbroken range of hills which plunges into the water at an angle of about 70 deg., which is lined with wharves, warehouses, oil manufactorios, dwelling houses and some shops. The city of St. John's contains about 35,000 inhabitants;

it is built on a succession of hills rising from the water side, and much like the hilly part of the upper town of Quebec.

The street life of St. John's is a picturesque and striking scene in the diversified dress of the fisherman, the sealer, the Spaniard, the Portuguese, Italian, the German, French and American. Most of them only frequent the street while they are discharging and taking in cargoes, in the summer and autumn, for different parts of Europe and America.

St. John's has been terribly devastated by fires in 1816, 1817, 1846, and the last great fire of 1892; but, like the Phœnix, it always rises better, brighter, and more triumphant from its ashes. The public buildings are the Colonial Building or Parliament House, Government House, Post Office, Museum, Roman Catholic Cathedral, Church of England Cathedral, which was nearly destroyed by the late fire, but now being restored; St. Andrew's Presbyterian Church was destroyed by the fire, now rebuilding. The principal Methodist Church and the Congregational Church were destroyed by the fire, but re-building. Nearly all the public halls, hotels and other public buildings were destroyed by the recent fire.

In and around St. John's are many things and places of historical interest. It was twice destroyed by the French. Some relics of their dominion are still to be seen. The stone buildings at Fort William were erected for their commander, and some chairs, with the *fleur-de-lis*, which belonged to the commandant, are still in existence. In 1860 His Royal Highness the Prince of Wales arrived at St. John's. He was accompanied by His Grace the Duke of Newcastle and the Earl of St. Germain. They remained in St. John's three days. The city presented the Prince with a Newfoundland dog, to whom he gave the name of "Cabot," in honor of the great Italian navigator who discovered Newfoundland on the 24th June, 1497. The Hon. Francis Brady, Chief Justice, was knighted in honor of the visit of His Royal Highness.

There are many places in the neighbourhood of St. John's where persons resort for health and pleasure parties. Portugal Cove is 9 miles distant. The tourist can either walk or ride over a beautiful road. The craggy rocks and wild towering cliffs, crowned with fir trees, surrounding Portugal Cove, gives it an exceedingly romantic appearance. Three miles from St. John's is "Virginia Cottage," once the rural retreat of Sir Thomas Cochrane, the Governor. The lands are beautifully embellished with trees, and laid with gravel walks. There is also a small lake along which winds a walk. This lovely spot was adorned from the private purse of Sir Thomas Cochrane. Waterford Bridge, Topsail, Manuels and Kellygrew are places of pleasure and health resorts. Quide Vidi, three miles distant, is entered by a gut of the sea, sometimes mistaken for St. John's on account of its narrow entrance. Here we get the "sweet singing of the sea." The little village nestles under the iron-bound cliffs, protected by the gut from the great rolling breakers and the ocean blasts; inside the gut is like a mill-pond. About two miles from the village is Quidi Vidi Lake, a beautiful sheet of fresh water, which is frequented for bathing and regattas. Logie Bay, ten miles distant from St. John's, contains a chalybeate spring, that is, water containing a portion of iron in solution. It is chalybeate to rather a greater extent than the waters of the "King's Bath," in Bath, England. The King's Bath is the principal spring of the Bath waters. The water is found useful as a general bracer, and in cases of dyspepsia and chronic rheumatism. The celebrated Saratoga, New York, springs are also *chalybeate*. The waters belong to a class termed *acidulous saline chalybeate*. Other health resorts in the vicinity of St. John's are Petty Harbor, Flat Rock, Outer Cove, Pouch Cove, Broad Cove, and Torbay with its beautiful meadows and well-cultivated fields.

Some of the purest spring water is found all over Newfoundland. It bubbles up clear as crystal from slate rock, conglomerate and granite, sometimes on the surface and from a foot to ten feet deep. It is just hard enough for drinking and soft enough for washing. All natural water contains minerals, and most water animal and vegetable substances. Water is a form of food. The use of spring water had much to do with the remarkable longevity of the earlier generations of Newfoundlanders. Owing to the great bays penetrating from sixty to ninety miles, and the want of roads, five steamers are employed by the Government for carrying the mails and passengers to the various ports of the island. For those seeking health, and who love adventure, a coastal trip along the bold coastline and beautiful harbors of Newfoundland would prove novel, exciting and interesting.

Conception Bay is the most popular and best cultivated Bay in the Island. In 1501, Gasper de Cortereal, the Portuguese navigator, visited Conception Bay, and gave to it the name which it bears, after the miraculous conception of the Virgin Mary. He also gave the present names of many coves and headlands. Harbor Grace is the capital of Conception Bay, and next town in trade and population is St. John's. The population is 6,000. It is called the "Brighton of Newfoundland," on account of its beauty. The harbor is seven miles long. The town is well supplied with churches and schools. Here is situated the Roman Catholic Cathedral of the diocese of Harbor Grace. The Church of England is the first stone church ever built in Newfoundland. Several merchants are largely engaged in the fish trade. The next important place is Carbonear, with a population of five thousand. When the French fleet attacked and destroyed St. John's in 1696, the British settlers at Carbonear successfully resisted Iberville, the French commander. Again in 1706, when St. Ovide, the commander of the French fleet, destroyed every other British settlement, Carbonear and Harbor Grace defended themselves. A detachment of men were garrisoned on Carbonear Island, at the mouth of the harbor. The writer has often seen some of the cannon and the remains of the fortifications there. There are some fine drives around Harbor Grace and Carbonear, and all along the shores of Conception Bay. The Hon. Patrick Morris used to say that this Bay exceeded the celebrated Bay of Naples, in beauty and grandeur of scenery. At the Northern entrance to Conception Bay is the Island of Baccalieu, known as the breeding-place of innumerable birds, turs or murs (*Colymbus Triole*), called Baccalieu birds. These birds form no nest, and lay their eggs, which are pyriform, of a greenish color, with black spots, and of great size, on the bare rock. Great quantities of eggs are taken from the island in the month of June by the fishermen. Their eggs are obtained by letting persons down from the top of the cliffs by ropes. The daring adventurers soon lose sight of their companions, as they pass down the perpendicular walls and overhanging parts of the cliffs; when they reach the terraces, which are not often more than two feet wide, they cast off the rope, and having procured a load of eggs, they signify to their companions on the top their desire to be drawn up, by pulling the rope. This occupation is attended with great danger, and sometimes men have been killed. To one unaccustomed to visit these places, it presents almost a scene of terror, to see myriads of birds fluttering on the wing, darkening the air and screaming dreadfully.

"Who can recount what transmigrations there
 Are annual made? what nations come and go ?
 And how the living clouds on clouds arise?
 Infinite wings ! till all the plume-dark air
 And rude resounding shore are one wild cry."

The air is so pure and invigorating, and the breeze from the rolling sea so refreshing, that the Rev. Father Ryan, a young priest, had gone there with his mother to reside several months for the restoration of his health. Trinity, the capital of the district of Trinity Bay, contains a population of 3,126, the population of the whole district of Trinity Bay in 1890 was 17,290. It is distant from St. John's 68 miles by steamer, and one of the most charming places in Newfoundland to visit. It is very probable the whole of the earlier voyagers to Newfoundland visited Trinity Bay. The celebrated Captain Whitbourne, who went in a ship of his own against the Spanish Armada, in the reign of Queen Elizabeth, visited Trinity Harbor as early as 1578, where he obtained poultry and fish. Trinity Harbor is so called from being entered on Trinity Sunday. It is one of the best and largest harbors, not only of Newfoundland, but of the world. It has several arms and coves, where the whole British navy may ride land-locked, secure from wind, tide or sea. The northwest arm runs in various directions a distance of three miles. The southwest arm also flows in different branches to about the same distance, when both arms nearly meet, forming Rider's Hill, which is situated in the centre of the harbor, and at the foot of which stands the town, into a peninsula. It has very much a Swiss appearance. The first steamer which ever appeared in Trinity Bay, entered Trinity Harbor in August 1842, when numbers gratified their curiosity by going on board and inspecting the vessel. It is scarcely possible to find a place more picturesque and beautiful than Trinity. Nature has been prodigal in her treatment of the loveliest scenery from every standpoint of Trinity. The woods in some parts skirt the edge of the water, amongst which are seen the graceful birch, shining like a silvery column amid the dark evergreens and underwood. Towering piles of rocks are seen tossed into fantastic shapes, from the fissures of which the fir, birch, and mountain-ash spring. Here also are heard the roaring of several large brooks, thundering in solitude, and creating an ever varying succession of spray and foam, as they dance along their course from rock to rock in musical cascade. There are well cultivated gardens and meadows, and splendid roads in every direction. The head of the N. W. which may be called "a silent sea," for the stirring of the "ocean old" is not felt there. It is a most charming place for bathing, for which purpose it is very often used. Those who are fond of a bath in the rolling sea and the foaming undertow, can gratify themselves by going outside the heads, where the ocean waves thunder on the gravelly beach.

> "And I have loved thee, Ocean ! and my joy
> Of youthful sports was on thy breast to be
> Borne, like thy bubbles onward. From a boy
> I wantoned with thy breakers ; they to me
> Were a delight, and if the fresh'ning sea
> Made them a terror, 'twas a pleasing fear."

The air is so pure, bracing and invigorating, and the surroundings so cheerful and pleasant, that it is a saying "to live at Trinity is to renew your lease of life a hundred years." In no part of the world are the environments more favorable to longevity.

The next important places to Trinity are Old Perlican, famous for shipbuilding, and Heart's Content. Here is situated the buildings of the Atlantic Telegraph Company, where thirty-five operators are employed sending the news over the world. At Dildo Cove a fish hatchery is established, supported by the Government. Random Sound may be called an inland sea. Here was first commenced brick-making, and preserving salmon in tins in Newfoundland. Some miles inland are seen the remains of gardens, once occupied by the red Indians or Bocothicks, the aborigines of Newfoundland. The place is fast settling—lumbering, fishing, and farming are carried on to a considerable extent. No better place could an invalid visit for the restoration of his health.

Bonavista is the capital of Bonavista Bay, which contains a population of 17,124. The first land discovered by the Cabots, appears to have been Cape Bonavista, to which they gave the name of *Terra Primum Vista*—the land first seen, happy sight or view. In 1760, the celebrated navigator, Captain James Cook, visited Bonavista and surveyed the coast. The French were allowed to fish along the shores of Bonavista Bay, until the Peace of 1783, when their right to fish along this part of the coast was relinquished. Traces of the French occupancy are still to be seen, consisting of heaps of stones, which were used for curing fish on, also several rude grave stones, which marks the graves of their dead. Cape Bonavista is a narrow strip of land, jutting about three miles into the ocean. It is table land, and agricultural operations have been pursued there to some extent. Bonavista and environs are quite level, all of which are laid out in well cultivated meadows, and gardens hung round with fruits and flowers. At the head of Bonavista Bay there are numerous islands, and the scenery is interesting and beautiful. Lumbering, farming and fishing are followed. The tourist would be delighted to visit the various settlements in Bonavista Bay, which are too numerous to mention. The Bays and Districts of Newfoundland, correspond to the counties of the Dominion of Canada, and the United States.

The principal place in the District of Fogo and Twillingate, is Twillingate, it is situate on an island of the same name, and contains a population of 5,000, the whole population of the district is 20,742. The distance from St. John's is 230 miles. It is the most northern district of the island. Twillingate is divided by the sea, forming the north and south side of the harbor into two islands. It is an old settlement, the principal trade of which has long been carried on by merchants connected with the trade of Poole, England. The next important place is Fogo, which is on an island of the same name. It contains a population of 1,600. Tilton Harbor ranks next in trade and population. At Tilt Cove, an extensive copper mine is being worked. There are some very nice gardens and meadows, but fishing is the principal occupation of the inhabitants of the district. These islands have only the salt water sobbing between them. A good deal of boating and yachting are resorted to, and the sportsman with slaughtering gun, wings the goose, duck, curlew, plover and a variety of sea fowl. Seals, too, are taken.

Fogo and Twillingate islands lie at the mouth of the great Bay of Notre Dame, or, as it is generally called, Green Bay. In this capacious bay are seven smaller bays, among which are Seal Bay, Badger Bay, Gander Bay, Hall's Bay, and Bay of Exploits, in the last of which a good deal of lumbering is carried on. This part of the country during the summer season abounds with deer, and is celebrated as being the hunting-grounds of the Red Indians of Newfoundland, now extinct. The Indians had fences erected 20 miles into the interior, all of which have long since disappeared. From the Bay of Exploits a small river extends about 70 miles, which reaches Red Indian Lake, which is 40 miles long, thence a chain of lakes extend to the Grand Lake near St. George's Bay, which is 54 miles long, and empties into the ocean. An inland water communication could be effected from the north to the west of the island, both of which are agriculturally and geologically considered the most valuable portions of Newfoundland. In the Bay of Notre Dame there is some fine forest timber, consisting of birch, pine, spruce, fir or balsam. Several saw mills are in operation here. In Germany patients are kept in pine forests for the recovery of their health. In Newfoundland spruce and balsam are the principal forest trees throughout the country. The emanation from these trees, particularly the balsam, is said to be most beneficial in lung and other diseases.

Ferryland was one of the earliest settled parts of Newfoundland. It was said to be the rendezvous of one Easton, a piratical adventurer, who in 1578 commanded a fleet of ten vessels. This daring adventurer impressed a hundred sailors for his fleet, and levied a tribute from all engaged

H

in the fisheries. In 1623, James I., by letters patent, gave his principal Secretary of State, Sir George Calvert, all the south-east part of the island lying between the Bays of Placentia and Trinity, which he erected into a province under the name of Avalon. He planted a colony at Ferryland, removed there himself with his family, erected a splendid mansion, and built a strong fort. After some years he returned to England. He was now created Lord Baltimore and obtained a grant of lands in the colony of Maryland, called after Charles' Queen. He removed thither and founded the City of Baltimore, now one of the principal cities in the United States. The whole population of the district of Ferryland is 6,472, distant from St. John's 33 miles. The town of Ferryland, situated on the sea shore between Cape Race and St. John's, has now become a watering place. The "Downs" is a most delightful promenade. Civilized man is becoming more and more a migratory animal, hundreds snatch a few weeks from professional and social duties for recuperation and rest at Ferryland. There are certain qualities in the atmosphere, especially in summer, which for its enjoyability is not to be matched.

Placentia Bay is one of the largest bays in Newfoundland. It is 60 miles broad and 90 miles long, rich in minerals, fisheries and agriculture, with numerous settlements, harbors and islands, such as Odearin and Harbor Buffet. In Plaisance (beautiful place) or Placentia, the French founded a colony in 1660. It was the ancient capital of the French and is now the capital of the district. Hardly a vestige of its ancient fortifications of Fort Frederick and Castle are now to be seen. The remains of the castle on Crevecœur Hill are slowly perishing. The population of Great and Little Placentia is 2,500. The population of the district of Placentia and St. Mary's is 10,917. It is distant from St. John's 140 miles by railroad. His late Majesty, William IV., when on the Newfoundland station as Prince William Henry, visited Placentia. It is one of the historic places of the country, and is now one of the popular places of resort for health and pleasure. St. Mary's is the chief place in St. Mary's Bay. It has a population of 1,500. The whole surrounding country is a fine agricultural district. Cape St. Mary's is called the "garden of Newfoundland," not because of its agriculture, but on account of its superior fishing grounds. The cod-fish is larger and better than what is usually caught in other parts of the island. Fishing boats assemble here from remote places. No better place for health and recreation could be found.

Burin is the capital of the district of Burin, containing a population of 5,000. Burin Bay is a beautiful inlet of the sea, nine miles long, and from a quarter to a mile wide. The fishermen have some fine fields and gardens along the shores. There are many places interesting in the district, such as St. Lawrence, Lawn and Lamaline, the latter of which is only ten miles distant from the French islands of St. Pierre, Miquelon and Langley. All these places the traveller in search of health would find most enjoyable.

Fortune Bay contains a population of 10,956, distant from St. John's 280 miles. The capital of the district is Harbor Breton, with a population of 1,200. It is one of the finest harbors imaginable, having arms and inlets running in various directions. It is the seat of one of the wealthiest and oldest mercantile establishments in Newfoundland. At the head of the bay and Bay Despair, there are herds of deer numbering thousands. The scenery around Harbor Breton is grand, towering cliffs of sienite, some hundreds of feet in altitude, appear in all their wild sublimity, against which the ocean billows roll, wrapping their base in sheets of spray and foam. There are a number of settlements throughout Fortune Bay. Then there are Hermitage Bay, St. George's Bay and Bay of Islands, all of which are delightful places for the tourist and invalid to visit. This part of the country is the most valuable for agricultural and mineral purposes. There is the Humber River running 12 miles from St. George's Harbor to the Grand Lake, which is 54 miles long, Deer Lake 15 miles long, and Red Indian Lake 40 miles long, whence a small river flows 70 miles to the Bay of Exploits at the north-east part of the country. Here is every facility for boating and canoeing. This part of the country is interesting as having been the home of the Bocothicks or Aborigines of Newfoundland. The island is full of pretty fish ponds. These little lakes scattered over the country are supposed to be remnants of the glacial period. Geologists say that at the close of the glacial period a rainy season followed. The rivers worked out the valleys. There were great floods. The debris was carried down into the valleys and deposited in what is known as the river gravel. This pluvial period was followed by a slight return of the glacial, and this by another flood. These lakelets are of all sizes from an eighth to two miles long, well stocked with trout, and adorned with fragrant water lilies. The water of these lakes appears brown, which is probably owing to a muddy bottom. There is no hard water in any of the lakes of Newfoundland. Hills dot the surface of the country, enclosing a succession of the most salubrious valleys. There is an abundance of sunshine without excessive heat. The nights are cool and pleasant, nearly always requiring a good covering during summer, and sleep is both restful and invigorating, restoring to the body a vigor and strength that is unknown in countries where the nights are hot and sultry. Miasmatic troubles are unknown. It is a remarkable fact that horses never contract heaves. Newfoundland should be the paradise of the fowler, the angler, the sportsman, the botanist and the naturalist. It is true Newfoundland does not produce the wines of France and Italy, the orange groves of Spain, Portugal, Florida and California, the sugar and cocoanuts of the West Indies, nor the costly silks and aromatic odors of China and India. But she is free from those dreadful agents of destruction, earthquakes, volcanoes, tornadoes and cyclones that sometimes desolate villages and towns in those countries which are covered with a blooming vegetation. The poisonous breath of the hot Siroc and the wet Monsoon, which spreads pestilence in the luxuriant countries of the east, never reaches her. The hiss of the boa-constrictor or of any snake or reptile has never been heard in Newfoundland. Frogs, toads, lizards or snakes have never appeared in the country. There is probably no other land superior to it as a health resort for the invalid suffering from almost any of the ills flesh is heir to. A thorough fine summer day in Newfoundland is simply unmatchable. The "blue unclouded sky" of Italy, lasting for weeks together, cannot compare either for health or comfort with the changeful sky of a temperate climate. The summers in Newfoundland are comparatively short. Now cool, now warm, mind and body will be benefited by the variety. The open air, in the shape of oxygen and ozone, is probably more wholesome than is found in most countries.

Reminiscences.

THE love of home is an inherent principle of our nature. The mind is touched with a thrilling sensation of delight when we look back to the happy period when, with father and mother, brothers and sisters, we assembled around the fireside. Here, love reigned, and those dear domestic hours never wore a fringe of woe, save when affliction's breath tainted the lovely scene, else all was joy and hope, gay as the morning, and no thought of separation ever flitted across the unruffled mind. Here have we heard the familiar purring of the cat and the monotonous hum of the tea kettle, while the frost of winter drove every member around the blazing fire.

The chirping of the cricket caused by the friction of its wings, has been welcomed as a messenger of good.

The bright sparks indicating the coming of letters have occupied our attention. All these little incidents, and a thousand more, recall the happy days of early home.

> "Be it a weakness, it deserves some praise,
> We love the play-place of our early days.
> The scene is touching, and the heart is stone
> That feels not at that sight and feels at none,
> The wall on which we tried our graving skill,
> The very name we carved subsisting still.
> The bench on which we sat while deep employed,
> Though mangl'd, hack'd and hewed not yet destroyed."

We carry with us everywhere a love of home, which nothing, no, nothing, can dissipate from our minds. From the icy shores of Greenland to the sultry climes of Africa, it is balm to the bosom torn with sorrow. The dying soldier in the battlefield, amid the tears and cries of thousands, thinks of his aged parents and " home, sweet home," soothes his dying pains. The immortal Nelson, amid the roar of cannon and the groans of the dying strewn around him, and even while the scenes of mortality were fast fading from his view forever, with his expiring breath speaks of the scenes of home. To the sailor wandering over the waves amid the howling of the stormy hurricane and maddened boiling surf, the thought of seeing home again gladdens his spirit, and more than compensates for the hardships of the voyage.

When the traveller, roaming in a foreign land, thinks of home he touches a chord which starts the unbidden tear; the name of the country to which he belongs meets his eye as a gem; it adorns the object with which it is connected; it excites pleasing remembrances, and he revels in the bright dreams of " home, sweet home." The profligate who has left his home and friends, and whose conscience, seared with blackened crimes, burdens his guilty soul, is eased of his load of woes when he looks behind and thinks of his deserted home. The captive, shut up in dungeon gloom, excluded from the pure air and light of day, chained to the damp, cold wall of his dismal prison, lonely and sad, he sits till waked by recollection his spirit takes its flight and mingles once again amid the scenes of home. The beggar, wandering from door to door, poor and friendless, amid the dark and dreary winter storms, who knows not whither to rest his weary, cold and famishing body, thoughts of happier days gather round his heart—he, too, once had a home, nursed and tenderly lulled to sleep with the kiss of love on the lap of his fond parents, who now sleep in the cold and silent tomb.

The winter season gathers the scattered members of a family around the social hearth. It is a delightful scene when the parents and children are seated around the blazing winter's fire, after the shades of night have curtained the vaulted sky. It is now the domestic affections are called into active exercise, and each member of the family is employed. Here, you behold one sewing, while at the same time engaged in a profitable conversation, there, you see another reading some interesting book, while a "flower of life," a little, rosy, blue-eyed boy, is occupying the attention of the parents; and if religion throws her hallowing influence over the scene, hope bears them on her wings to that home where "sweet fields beyond the swelling flood stand dressed in living green," and they anticipate the happy period when they shall greet each others arrival at their everlasting home above, a home where "their souls shall banquet and be satisfied, fully and forever," a home "whose wide regions they shall traverse in all the might of their untired faculties, discovering and gathering fresh accumulations of intelligence, satisfaction and surprise."

"But all who loved the garden long have vanished—
The children, with their merry laugh and song,
The dainty maidens, with their mirth and gladness—
No trace is left of all the joyous throng.
Ah, some rest calmly in the quiet churchyard
That nestles in the shelter of the hill,
Where roses bloom and robins warble sweetly,
Where many a restless heart at last is still ;
And some are sleeping far from home and kindred,
Far from the scene of childhood's playful hours,
And not one voice may ever wake the echoes
Of yonder garden's leafy, shady bow'rs."

We instinctively glance backward and review the scenes of the past, listen to the voices that echo down the aisles of memory. It is pleasant retrospection, shaded by many hues of varying emotions, half sad, half sorrowful. It is not altogether profitless to dwell upon the years and scenes that lie behind us. And, as memory repeats the voices and vision, the smiles and tears, the greetings and good-byes, stirs within us the deepest emotions.

"Parents I had, but where are they?
Friends whom I knew I know no more,
Companions once that cheer'd my way,
Have dropped behind or gone before."

There are times when the mind loves to dwell on the past scenes of life, and reflect upon the happy days of youth ; but while sketching the bright picture of the joyous past, the dark future comes in to dash the vision, and the regretful feeling will arise—it is gone, it cannot come again.

"O when I was a tiny boy,
My days and nights were full of joy ;
My mates were blithe and kind,
No wonder that I sometimes sigh
And dash the tear-drop from my eye,
To cast a look behind ! "

In the hour of lonely solitude, and even amidst the busy pursuits of life, the memory of man calls from their long forgotten sleep past circumstances and men, and we view with emotions of pleasure by-gone days; but the scene soon changes, and leaves us to think of our present condition.

> "Affection still by kind remembrance led
>   Shall wander in the autumn of the past,
> And seek for days whose loveliness is fled
>   Like leaves which died and vanished in the blast."

It is now 48 years ago since I left my native country, Newfoundland. During that time I visited it twice, after an absence of 26 years I visited it for the last time. What strange feeling comes over one who revisits once familiar scenes after the lapse of more than a quarter of a century. Such a one can fully appreciate the bewilderment of poor Rip Van Winkle. How numerous were the ghosts of the past continually encountered; they met me at the corner of the street, the by-ways, the kitchen, the parlor, the wharf, the chamber, and shook the curtain at midnight " to call up shadows, in the silent hours, from the dim past, as from a wizard's cave." " Where are the Roman Cæsars and the Grecian Chiefs, the boast of story."

> "Ghost-like I paced round the haunts of my childhood,
> Earth too seemed a desert I was bound to traverse,
> Seeking to find the old, familiar faces.
> How some they have died and some they have left me,
> And some are taken from me, all are departed,
> All, all are gone, the old, familiar faces."

During my visit to Carbonear, as I rambled through the village of the dead, where my forefathers dwell—the churchyard—I thought of the words of the ancient physician, " I passed by the burying-place of my fathers, and in an agony of grief I cried—where are they ? and heard nothing but the voice of echo—where are they ?"

In and around Carbonear I found very few of my early associates living. In the grey-haired, wrinkled, old ladies, I found the once blooming and handsome belles of the place—the companions of my youth.

> "Where are you, with whom in life I started,
> Dear companions of my golden days;
> Ye are dead, estranged from me or parted,
> Flown like morning clouds a thousand ways.'

How far off these old days seem now, and how pleasant the retrospection. Nothing to me seems now to have that freshness and flavor about it which everything had then. To me these days were the spring-time of life—the first flashes of youth and hope; now they are all past and the winter of life is upon me.

> "I am growing old—'tis surely so;
> And yet how short it seems
> Since I was but a sportive child,
> Enjoying childish dreams.
> I cannot see the change that comes
> With such an even pace;
> I mark not when the wrinkles fell
> Upon my fading face.

> "I know it's folly to complain
> Of whatsoe'er the fates decree;
> Yet, were not wishes all in vain.
> I tell you what my wish should be,
> I'd wish to be a boy again,
> Back with the friends I used to know,
> For I was, O! so happy then—
> But that was very long ago."

Temperance.

By Temperance I wish you to distinctly understand that I mean total abstinence from all that intoxicates. I believe it is now generally understood that temperance and total abstinence are synonymous terms. I know of no better way of recommending temperance than by pointing out the evils of intemperance. This is a frightful monster, a hydra with many heads. The first head which presents itself on this hydra is loss of reputation and the increase of pauperism and crime. A man no sooner becomes the slave of intemperance than he begins to neglect his occupation. The consequence is, if he has no money his credit is stopped and he becomes reduced to a state of beggary, and in many instances theft has to be resorted to in order to supply the wants of his starving family. Another of these heads is the loss of health, of conscience, and of the fear of God. Look at the drunkard's swollen face; his burning eyes ready to burst from their sockets, and his quivering frame ready to sink into the jaws of death; what a host of diseases wait upon him to hurry him to his long home, "Fever, with cheek of fire; consumption, wan; palsy, half warm with life, and half a clay-cold lump, and ever-gnawing rheum, convulsive, wild, swollen dropsy, panting asthma, apoplexy, full-gorged. These, and a thousand more, horrid to tell, attentive wait."

Some of the most eminent physicians declare that the greater part of the diseases which attack the human frame, originate in the use of intoxicating liquors. Speaking of the hereditary influence of drunkenness, Dr. Trotter says : "The morbid juices of the parent are transfused into the veins of his progeny, and thus a feeble offspring is forced into existence, pregnant with its own destruction." "No person," says Sir Astley Cooper, "has a greater hostility to dram-drinking than myself, insomuch, that I never suffer any ardent spirits in my house, thinking them evil spirits. And if the poor could witness the white livers, the dropsies, the shattered nervous systems which I have seen, as the consequence of drinking, they would be aware that spirits and poisons are synonymous terms." Another medical writer says: It is "a disease far more destructive than any plague that ever raged in Christendom; more malignant than the burning typhus, the loathsome smallpox, the cholera of the East, or the yellow fever of the South; more loathsome and infectious than all of them together, with all their dread array of suffering and death united in one ghastly assemblage of horrific and appalling misery." And the following declaration is signed by thirteen physicians and fifty-three surgeons of Birmingham: "Being of opinion that the habitual use of intoxicating liquors is not only unnecessary, but pernicious, we have great satisfaction in seconding the views of the temperance society, by stating our conviction, that nothing would tend more to diminish disease and improve the health of the community, than entire abstinence from the use of intoxicating liquors, to the use of which so great a portion of the existing misery and immorality of the lower orders amongst the working classes is attributable. Conscience, which used to act as a faithful monitor, is, by the intemperate man, rocked into silence; he turns his back upon the means of grace, desecrates the Sabbath to the most unhallowed purposes, and curses the minister whose faithful ministry he was accustomed to attend, and God and religion are hardly ever more thought of than if they had never been heard of.

The next head that appears on this hydra has the face of insanity and murder. O! how intemperance prostrates the intellect! That mind which could soar on the pinions of contemplation and investigate the heavenly bodies as they roll in magnificent grandeur over the immensity of space, calculate their periodical revolutions, penetrate the secrets of nature, and inform us when there should be eclipses of the sun and of the moon; that mind which poured from the pulpit the most powerful strains of solemn eloquence, beseeching sinners to be reconciled to God; that mind which, at the bar, charmed and captivated the listening auditors; that mind which successfully directed the most complicated machinery of commerce; that mind which could write the history of its own formation, invent various machinery conducive to its happiness, and rear piles of architecture, withstanding the storms of a thousand winters. This mighty mind is ruined; these astonishing faculties are prostrated and laid in the dust by that fell monster, Intemperance. Hundreds die through *delirium tremens*, and many end their days on the scaffold through intemperance.

It has been asked, " Which is the greatest crime, drunkenness, adultery, or murder?" The reply has been:— " Drunkenness, because it leads to the perpetration of the other two.'

Dr. Crawford says, that "of the 286 patients in the Richmond Lunatic Asylum, Dublin, at least one-half became insane in consequence of the abuse of ardent spirits," and I know that the same has been observed in the other public lunatic asylums in Ireland; several of these have been driven to the perpetration of the most horrible crimes, such as the murder of a father, a wife, a child. A late American writer says: "Of two hundred murders committed annually in the United States, where has one been known but under the influence of the intoxicating cup? And the thousands of criminals who have been thrown into our penitentiaries, some for crimes whose very rehearsal makes our blood to curdle, few can be found who have not been stimulated to their ferocious deeds by alcoholic influence." It is said there can be no harm in the temperate use of liquors, but the experience of thousands prove that it is from the temperate use of them all the evils result. No individual becomes a drunkard all at once; it is by indulging in the moderate use of spirits that the pernicious habit is acquired. Intemperance steals upon us by slow and imperceptible degrees. It is a truism that requires no argument, that the individual who abstains from the temperate use of intoxicating liquors will never become a drunkard. Palliative and half-measure principles have been tried again and again, but never could succeed in reclaiming the intemperate. There is no safety, then, but in the ark of total abstinence.

A minister with whom I am well acquainted, and who for a number of years resided in Nova Scotia, informed me that whilst living there he knew a respectable man who carried on a large and profitable business as brandy merchant. In the course of a few years his eldest son became a regular and confirmed brandy drinker, until nature through its influence became exhausted, and he sank into a premature grave. The father, seeing the awful consequences of the sale of brandy in the death of his son, banished the brandy from his warehouse, and became a wine merchant. He had not long commenced this new business before his second son began to indulge freely in the use of the generous wine, until he fell a victim to its destructive tendency, and died also. The father, reflecting on the loss of his second son, resolved to do away with the sale of wine, and immediately commenced the sale of malt liquor. But, strange to say, after having been warned by the death of his two sons, he himself became addicted to the use of the last mentioned article, and advanced by degrees until drunkenness terminated his existence. His establishment was broken up, and the remainder of his family left penniless and wretched. The father and sons doubtless acted upon the principle that moderation was safe. From this instance we see that there is no remedy but in total abstinence; had these three individuals been teetotallers, such misfortunes never could have befallen them.

You, my young friends, are the material of future generations, and it depends on you, under God, whether the rum puncheon shall be banished from our shores, or the deadly poison continue to be imported. I remember a few years ago having taken passage at Bristol in a vessel bound to Newfoundland; that, after getting down to Cumberland Basin, every man left the vessel in order to indulge themselves in the use of malt liquor, though they had previously taken too much of that pernicious beverage. On his way from the vessel to the street, one man, barefooted, climbed up a large chain suspended from a wall, supposed to have been a perpendicular height of fifty feet. Knowing that he was under the influence of liquor, we expected to have seen him dashed to pieces ere he descended half way, but Providence preserved him to reach the summit, with his feet lacerated in a shocking manner. I was now solely in charge of the vessel. After waiting for several hours, the captain came on board in a state of intoxication; and, after another hour's delay, we succeeded in getting all the sailors on board; shortly after which came the pilot with his men and got the vessel out of the basin, which was no easy task amid a crew of drunken men. While passing down the river, the captain and one of the sailors fell fighting; two more were under the bowsprit, holding on to the martingale with their hands, and their feet nearly touching the water; another was hanging by a rope over the side of the vessel, while another was standing on the forecastle, uttering the most horrid oaths and imprecations on the passengers of a steam packet just then passing by. We were now obliged, with as little delay as possible, to hoist out our boat, in order to save those men from drowning who were suspended from the martingale and over the side of the vessel, which we happily succeeded in doing, and we placed them on board in safety. But this was not the worst; after getting about quarter passage the captain discovered that, through his intemperence, he had neglected putting more provisions on board than was necessary for half passage. We were now obliged to go on an allowance of one biscuit a day per man, and, to add to our calamity, about a week after it was found that three of our largest casks of water had leaked out. We were now reduced to one biscuit and a half pint of water each in twenty-four hours. The sailors began loudly to complain and threaten the captain ; and, in order to appease their anger, he broached a cask of rum, and to each man he daily apportioned three half-pints which almost produced daily intoxication. But, in justice to the captain, I feel bound to state that he did not taste a drop of any kind of intoxicating liquor after he left Clifton until we arrived in Newfoundland. The fifteenth day after being on an allowance the joyful sound of "Land ahead" echoed through the vessel, the sight of which gladdened my heart, and led me to offer up my thanksgiving to that God who brought us over the vast Atlantic in safety. But the most melancholy part of my tale is yet to be told. After arriving at our port, and after the cargo had been discharged, part of the main hatch having been left open, and three of the sailors going on board in a state of intoxication, one of them (poor unhappy man!) stumbled and fell through the open hatch to the bottom of the vessel—a lifeless corpse!

It is, however, a well-known fact to those who do not use liquors that none can stand the deck so well as those who drink coffee or tea instead of liquors. I have read an address signed by one thousand captains of vessels, stating it to be their decided conviction that intoxicating liquors administered to seamen in the smallest quantities, instead of strengthening, weaken and debilitate the human constitution, that some of them had been going to sea from twenty to upwards of thirty years, and that during the whole of that time they never saw twenty-four hours wherein a kettle of tea or coffee could not be procured.

Intemperance is the prolific source of almost every

physical and moral evil; it is deeply rooted and wide spread. Intemperance has extended to every country and marred the social, domestic, intellectual and moral enjoyments of man ; it has made its victims of the blooming youth, the man of strong-built, sinewy limbs, as well as of decrepitude and old age; its dominion is the dominion of appetite, and hence no age, no sex, no vocation, no people are strangers to its powers. It has entered every village and almost every family circle, infested the farm, the workshop, the study, the counting room, the court of justice, the hall of legislation, the pulpit, consumed its victims on land and on the ocean, in polar seas and in torrid zones, in navies and armies, and cursed nations that have never known the light of the Gospel or the way of salvation. I knew a young man who rose from the position of a shop-boy to that of a book-keeper, and thence to the position of a merchant. Afterwards he became gradually fond of the bottle, began to appear slovenly in his dress and person, then to neglect his business, until he eventually became a confirmed drunkard; his business, which was in a flourishing condition, began to decline until it became broken up; he continued the victim of intemperance until his shattered constitution could hold out no longer; he was arrested by the hand of disease, and finally by the strong arm of death. The last time I ever saw him he was suffering from excruciating disease in his side, fully conscious of the awful state to which intemperance had brought him. "Ah!" said he, "this affliction has been produced by my own evil conduct, but I hope I shall live to be a better man, and to warn others of the evil consequences of drink. About a month after this interview he breathed his last. I was intimately acquainted with another young man, bookkeeper in a mercantile establishment, who, by diligence and economy, after a servitude of seven years, was enabled to lay up the sum of two hundred pounds; he entered the marriage state, and with his wife received one

I .

hundred pounds more. Previous to this, however, he had grown fond of a glass; and now, finding himself in the possession of money to a considerable amount, he began to spend his evenings at the tavern, and to indulge freely in the use of spirits during the hours of business, until the employer he had lived with for so many years was very reluctantly compelled to dismiss him. He then threw off the mask which before had partly concealed his true character, and showed himself an open drunkard. He abandoned business of every kind, and made the tavern almost day and night his home, until the money he had been so many years accumulating, together with his wife's portion, was all spent. At length he was arrested in the course of iniquity; he fell into a consumption, and now for the first time during his profligate course, he began to think of the misery of the past, and to contemplate the future with horror. He would say, "Do you think there can be hope for one so guilty as I have been?" and when answered in the affirmative he has said, "Ah, no! God will never receive me after having sinned against so much light and knowledge as I have." He continued lingering for two months, during which he sought the pardoning mercy of God, when his spirit returned to God who gave it, leaving a mourning widow and three children.

Passing by a house early one morning I saw several individuals assembled around the door. I enquired what had happened, when a most appalling spectacle was pointed out to me. It was the cold and lifeless body of poor L———. His face presented a hideous appearance, being quite black and distorted from strangulation. This unhappy man had once moved in the most respectable circles of society until liquor made him the common associate of drunkards. He had been attending a wedding the previous night, and left in a state of intoxication at an early hour. He succeeded in reaching a vacant house a short distance away, over the steps leading to the door of which I saw him lying head downwards, a sad picture of the degradation of human nature, without a single relation in the world to drop a tear over his melancholy destiny.

But not only are sailors, clerks, merchants and others addicted to the practice of strong drink, but many ministers of the Gospel also have often been ruined by it. I was well acquainted with two most excellent men who were ensnared by this insinuating vice, and who unhappily became the victims of private tippling. Another was so much the captive slave of the fiery liquid that his expulsion from the ministry became absolutely necessary, and he has for many years been pursuing the avocation of a sober and industrious farmer in a distant land.

At this moment, says the Hon. and Rev. Baptist Noel, in a late sermon, I know a minister who was eloquent, earnest, diligent, successful, beloved. He became, how, I know not, the slave of this vice—his ministry is suspended, his reputation gone, himself the prey of deadly anguish. I know another, eminently endowed, who brought many souls to God, but is now an outcast from his friends, and has probably ended his ministry forever.

In the life of the celebrated Rev. Robert Hall, page 49, the following circumstances are recorded:

"'You remember Mr. ——, sir?' 'Yes, very well.' 'Were you aware of his fondness for brandy-and-water?' 'No.' It was a sad habit, but it grew out of his love of story-telling, and that is a bad habit for a minister of the Gospel. As he grew old, his animal spirit flagged, and his stories became defective in vivacity; he, therefore took to brandy-and-water, weak enough, it is true, at first; but soon, nearly half-and-half. Ere long he indulged the habit in a morning, and when he came to Cambridge he would call upon me, and before he had been with me five minutes, ask for a little brandy-and water, which was of course to give him artificial spirits, to render him agreeable in his visits to others. I felt great difficulty, for he, you know, sir, was much older than I was; yet being persuaded that the ruin of his character, if not of his peace, was inevitable, unless something was done, I resolved upon one strong effort for his rescue. So the next time he called, and as usual, said, 'Friend Hall, I will thank you for a glass of brandy-and-water,' I replied, 'Call things by their right names, and you shall have as much as you please.'"

"'Why; don't I employ the right name? I ask for a glass of brandy-and-water.' 'That is the current, but not the appropriate name; ask for a glass of liquid fire and distilled damnation, and you shall have a gallon.' Poor man, he turned pale, and for a moment seemed struggling with anger; but, knowing I did not mean to insult him, he stretched out his hand and said: 'Bro. Hall, I thank you from the bottom of my heart.' From that time he ceased to take brandy-and-water."

Temperance societies are now the order of the day; yes, and of the the night, too. If, on the wings of imagination, we traverse the Atlantic and Pacific Oceans, we shall find Temperance Societies studding the shores of these vast oceans, resembling so many stars treading upon the shades of the evening, illuminating the countries in which they are, and shedding all around them an atmosphere of blessings.

In Ireland, through the exertions of Father Matthew, millions have burst the bonds which bound them to the car of drunkenness, and have become teetotalers; and England, Ireland and Scotland have their hundreds of thousands identified with the cause.

In Russia, Prussia, Sweden, Germany and America, the cause of total abstinence is flourishing in a most astonishing manner.

This great movement has exerted a beneficial influence on trade and commerce, by creating new wants, forming new habits.

It has awakened the dormant energies of intellectual existence and given a taste for literature. It has excited new hopes, new fears, and new desires of religion and the glory of God.

Let total abstinence be diffused throughout the length and breadth of the world.

What a host of evils intemperance carries in its train! No picture can sufficiently portray the horrors of this evil and vicious propensity. It has torn from the heart the kindliest sensibilities and dearest affections; it has caused the aged and widowed mother to mourn through nights of anguish for the ungrateful conduct of her profligate son, worked up to madness by the influence of the fiery alcohol; the arm of the midnight assassin has been nerved to wreak his vengeance in the blood of his fellow man.

There is an old Hebrew proverb which says that wine makes a man first a lamb (gullible), then a lion (ferocious), then a surine (sensual), then a monkey (silly), as well as conceited.

The subject of temperance is an old one, and it still occupies the attention of the public. We all know the misery that has followed intemperate habits. I am glad to know that there is not now the drinking among sailors and fishermen which formerly prevailed. Proofs are not necessary to show that both property and human life on the sea are safest under the care of minds never clouded by the fumes of alcohol and muscles never unstrung by its magic power. The Church of England Temperance Society was formed on a double basis, that is, one pledge for total abstainers and another pledge for moderate drinkers. This has been done to enlist the support and sympathy of all persons, and therefore we are glad to have those who do not feel it their duty to become total abstainers, and yet aid in the work. Some of the greatest supporters of churches, missionary societies, and all other benevolent institutions, throughont the world are moderate drinkers. Total abstinence, without the grace of God and the restraining influence of the Holy Spirit, will not make people religious. The New York Methodist paper says:—" There are 500 hypocrites, impostors and cranks, of one sex or the other, getting a living as temperance lecturers, evangelists, etc., in the United States and Canada. And the people listen to them and pay them as willingly as if they were spotless." One of the most horrible deaths I ever read of was of a total abstainer, he had been a cold water drinker for fifty years. When he was dying he said: " Water, water, give me water, for in five minutes it will be denied me. O that I could take some of it with me to hell." He was a gambler, and while his associates were bereft of their senses with drink, he robbed them by thousands. Take a company of coiners, forgers, or an organized gang of thieves and burglars, they don't want a man addicted to drink, but a sober man, one whom they can trust as master of their plans and purposes. So that, although we may be total abstainers, yet without the power of the Holy Spirit restraining and ruling the heart, we may be led into all manner of crime.

Temperance flourishes, and intemperance is not only more infrequent than in former years, but more disreputable. Let us go back a hundred years or more. Writers tell us that within that time sobriety was the exception, intemperance, to the point of intoxication, more or less the rule. A man who had not been drunk was a very rare exception. It is said condiments were used to create thirst, glasses were made so they would not stand, but must be held until emptied, and a man's worth was estimated by the number of bottles he could drink. Coming down to times within the memory of men not yet very old, it will be found that strong drink was bought and kept in every household as regularly as tea and sugar, and that it was in daily use. The farmer took it with him to the field, the fisherman carried it in his boat, the carpenter had it under his bench, the merchant kept it in his office, the shopkeeper kept the jar under his counter, which he freely handed out to some of his customers to drink from, the tailor, cooper and blacksmith slaked their thirst with rum and water and strong beer. Every occasion of the least importance was marked by its liberal use. If the clergyman called, not to offer drink was a great want of respect. Did a dealer call to pay his bill he considered himself but shabbily treated, if the black bottle was not produced. Not to get drunk at a wedding was all but an insult to the bride, and not to drink liberally at a funeral was a reflection on the memory of the deceased. Ship captains about to sail were expected to drink so many parting glasses with friends, that they sometimes went to sea in a muddle-headed condition. If I were to give an account of deaths by drowning and shipwrecks through drink, it would fill a volume. No fisherman would think of going along the coast, fishing, without having a keg of rum in the cuddy of his boat. No seal hunter would go to the ice without taking one, two, or more gallons of rum to drink during the voyage.

When I was a boy I used to serve out two gallons of grog at a time at eleven o'clock and at four o'clock to the working men; my father had a number of men employed about the wharf and vessels, so that it took a considerable quantity of liquor to serve them all. Nearly all the ministers of those days drank moderately. Three miles from where I was born, a preacher used to keep a keg of rum in the pulpit as the most unlikely place his friends would go to look for it. He used to go there and drink to excess. I knew a minister that when he had taken too much liquor used to go to the church and lock himself in until he got sober. I was travelling with a preacher in Conception Bay, Newfoundland, when we came to a brook, he took a cocoa-nut shell out of his pocket, filled with rum, from which he took a good "horn." He told me he was obliged to carry rum with him, at he could not preach without a stimulant. I knew a man who could not engage in the exercise of prayer without the stimulating influence of spirits. He was warned, time after time, of the dangerous and fatal tendency of such a practice, but the baneful habit had become so deeply rooted, that he labored under the strong delusion as to argue, "that whatever entered the body would never defile the soul." I have met with several clergymen, some of them graduates of Trinity College, Dublin, ordained by the Bishop of Chester and the Archbishop of Canterbury, addicted to drunkenness, their clothes ragged, and their Letters of Orders in tatters, worn from carrying them about in their pockets. I might give a number of cases of drinking clergymen which came under my own personal observation. I was once dining with an Irish Dean, who had a large party of military officers. After we had retired to the smoking room, he said to me: "Do you know what we call a good fellow in Ireland? A man who can smoke like a chimney, sit like a hen, and drink like a fish." Many years ago, in Canada, one of my outstations where I occasionally officiated was at a tavern that had a hall in connection with it. On these occasions a number of persons from the surrounding country used to come to the tavern. But most of them, instead of coming to church, remained at the tavern fire, to warm themselves, and obtain "spiritual" refreshment. Tumblers, decanters and toddy-sticks were the text books. I was personally acquainted with several tavern keepers who were total abstainers, one of them would not employ a man about his premises who was not a total abstainer. Some years ago I was riding by stage from Worcester to West Boylston, Mass., where John Goff, the great temperance lecturer, then resided. On the roadside were assembled a number of men, women and children. I asked the driver what they were doing. He said, "They have just pulled down a rum hole. A man sold liquor there; he had been warned a number of times not to do so, as his business was doing great injury in the community; but he paid no heed to the warnings he received, so to-day, in order to get rid of liquor-selling among them, the people assembled and pulled down his house with the ropes you see there." In the county of Yarmouth, Nova Scotia, during my residence there of nine years, no liquor was allowed to be sold in any part of the county, and I believe the law is still in force. In the village of Tusket, in the same county, a man sold liquor secretly. He was warned by the women not to let their husbands have liquor, but he disregarded them, so one day, as he was riding from Yarmouth to Tusket, a company of men met him, took him out of his buggy, tarred and feathered him, bid him desist from selling liquor or quit the village. In a short time he removed to Boston.

How great the change from those old times, when nothing could be done without the jovial glass! What ship-owner would now send liquor as ship's stores, or who would tolerate a habitually intemperate captain? Eating and drinking have both been banished from funerals, and excessive drinking at weddings or at any social gatherings would be an insult to the host and the guests. The mechanics, farmers, planters and fishermen have learned to temper their water with oatmeal, molasses, lemon, etc., rather than with rum. The minister now preaches temperance from the pulpit. Taking the masses through, intemperance, habitual or even occasional, is considered injurious to reputation, to credit, to social standing, a hindrance to prosperity, becomes a bar to confidence and to reputable employment. A drunken captain might be a jovial fellow, but, from a business point, a sober captain was much to be preferred. For the same reasons in mercantile affairs and in professional employments, men of sober habits are sought after. A tipsy doctor, however skilled, was not likely to be sent for to attend a sick child. I have heard of a doctor who got hold of the bed-post, instead of the arm of the patient, when he called out : "Dead, dead—not a single pulsation."

The Rev. Dr. Dunham says of America:—"This Gospel has been in the world for more than eighteen hundred years; it has been proclaimed in this country weekly for more than one hundred years; all over our land churches have been reared. Sunday schools instituted, means of grace conducted with open doors, sermons preached and religious literature scattered; and yet the great evils which infest human society have not been abated; nay, they have gone steadily marching on with increasing force and sway. They seem to have thriven luxuriously in the very atmosphere of the Gospel of Christ.

Let us take an illustration : The amount of intoxicating liquors drank per capita has increased four hundred per cent. in this country during the past fifty years; the cost to the people of the liquor traffic has increased $300,000,000 in the past twenty-five years; the consumption of strong drink has increased one hundred and fifty per cent. faster than the increase of population; and the increase of the consequent evils, pauperism, wretchedness and crime, has been proportionate. Nor is this all. Mark how the liquor traffic controls political parties, corrupts municipal affairs, retards the church, tramples unrestrainedly upon law, breaks down all regard for the sanctity of the Sabbath, begets a spirit of lawlessness and immorality, opens wide the floodgates of sin and of all kinds of iniquity, and thus is undermining the very foundation upon which the security of our republican institutions rest. And mark you further; during all this time there has been no let up in the proclamation of the Gospel.'

Expedients for Raising Money.

I HAVE never attended a bazaar. The Society for the Propagation of the Gospel in London has given notice that it will not receive money for the support of missions that has been derived from bazaars, concerts, etc. If a person who is not religious should bring a gift, it is not to be rejected. "The money is not heretical," as the begging friar said to the American tourist, when he told him he was a heretic. Mr. Spurgeon has spoken out strongly against church entertainments. He says: "We do not hesitate to assert that the characters of many hopeful young people have been shipwrecked, not by the avowed haunts of vice, but by the influence of the questionable entertainments in connection with their religious relationships. Pleasant lectures and wholesome singing were all very well when used for higher ends; but there has been a gradual coming down, till, in some cases, the school-room has endured what the theatre would have refused as too absurd." The *Presbyterian Banner* says: "Occasionally, when the church authorities make arrangements for a series of religious meetings, they are coolly informed that it will be best to postpone it for at least a time, as the young people have made ready for entertainments during the period selected. Indeed, not long since we were told of a church session that felt itself compelled to postpone a communion for two weeks, that it might not interfere with arrangements and entertainments of various kinds projected by 'the young people.'" The *Independent*, the organ of the Congregationalists in Canada, says: "The support of the Church should always be sought on the ground of unselfish and Christian benevolence. But, many Churches have departed from this ground, and seek their money from concerts, lectures, suppers, fairs, neck-tie parties, maple-sugar socials, and even dances and theatrical exhibitions. There is no telling where a Church, which once takes up with shifts and expedients for raising money, will stop. The temptation will come to provide the most worldly amusements in return for the financial aid it seeks. It is not the slender purse, but the lean spiritual life of the Church members which makes their treasury lean. Improve the spiritual life of the Church, and one of the first results of that will be to fill up the exhausted treasury of the Church. In many of our Canadian churches, the social meetings in the week go very far towards nullifying all the preaching of the Lord's day. It is simply a disgrace to any Christian Church to allow on its social programmes slangy or coarse songs or readings. In such cases there is no thought as to whether the exercises are demoralizing or stimulating. The sole thought is, will they draw a house? We have heard programmes which were so simply disgusting that the only fit place to carry them out would seem to be a saloon. We believe in socials, in a good laugh, in a warm handshake, and every other thing that recreates us without defiling us. But we protest against bringing the spirit of the world into our churches, even though the treasury may be low." A noted member of the English Wesleyan Conference ascribes the decline of their churches "to the acceptance of four gospels, the gospel of fun, the gospel of bazaars, the gospel of music, and the gospel of fiction." This is "an age of progress." The Church has gone into the amusement business largely; she has entered the market, and is in competition with those great caterers. It is thought that the Church, in order to hold its young people to its altars, must provide for the natural craving for amusements; to keep them from the theatre and opera, churches must be made into semi-theatres and semi-operas So far from preventing attendance upon a full-grown theatre and opera, by these efforts the appetite is whetted for them. Can there be any doubt as to the inconsistency of this indirect method of trying to raise money for the support of the church in contrast with straightforward, honest appeals to men to give of their substance to Him on whom they depended for all things. It would greatly promote the spirituality and usefulness of the church, if much of the showy extravagances were curtailed, and so carry out the vow of baptism in renouncing " the world, the flesh, and the devil." It is evident that the world is in the Church, from the manner in which money is sought through concerts, suppers, bazaars and theatrical exhibitions. It is idle for a man to claim that when he gives twenty-five cents for admission to a church concert, he is giving it to the cause of God, for he is only passing it away for " value received" in the shape of eatables, music and speeches.

Giving is worship. It is certainly as much a duty to give as it is to pray, or the performance of any other devotion, for giving is worship. Our praying for the coming of the Kingdom is incomplete without the giving to aid the coming of the Kingdom : that the asking is amiss that is not accompanied by the gift. Money is the sinews of war in religion as well as in political or military campaigns. Our Lord left behind Him no mode of advancing His Kingdom which dispenses with the use of money. It may seem strange that His Kingdom should rest on such a material *substratum*. Yet without money the Church's enterprise would be paralyzed. Ignorance of the need and the duty to give, a spirit of covetousness, a lack of interest and indifference, cause the neglect of giving. Selfishness is so ingrained in our nature that appeals have to be made over and over again. It is impossible to invent any process which will do that which is clearly a personal and responsible duty devolving upon all. People who have to be periodically whipped up to give, will soon be beyond the reach of such a process. If every member of the Church would comply with the divine will, as indicated to the Jews—requiring one-tenth of their all—the aggressive work of the Church would be easily accomplished. Let this method of systematic benevolence be adopted, then there will be no crippling for want of funds for missionary and other purposes. Our giving should not be stationary, or stereotyped in its amount, any more than our getting is—giving "as God hath prospered us." We must think as much about giving as getting. The rule laid down by the apostle is, "Upon the first day of the week let every one of you lay by him in store, as God hath prospered him." They were once a week to think how much they ought to give, and they were to put that by. There is an old saying, "Riches take to themselves wings and fly away," and he who would keep them must clip their wings by giving. To give makes a man more like God, who is always giving to our bodies and souls. God never answers to the asking of his creatures, I have nothing to give. This law of frequent and stated appropriation, cuts up by the roots the common practice of giving large sums, and then for a long time nothing, and also that of giving only or chiefly at death. It also repudiates the practise of "waiting to be solicited." A rich man said: "I feel that, as to my prosperity, I am but God's steward, and I am afraid to die rich." Another said: "What I gave away remains to me, what I have retained I have lost." "Quick! quick!" said a woman who came into the possession of a thousand pounds which she did not expect, "let me give the tenth part before my heart grows hard." She knew that riches had a tendency to harden the heart. Another woman of limited means who came into the possession of a fortune, said: "Ah! when day by day I looked to God for my bread I had enough and to spare; now I have to look to my ample income, and I am all the time haunted with the fear of losing it and coming to want. I had the guinea heart when I had the shilling means; now I have the guinea means and the shilling heart." Wilson, Bishop of Sodor and Man, said: "To be rich is a great misfortune." He gave away annually all his income. John Fletcher, Vicar of Madely, when offered the parish of

Dunham, worth four hundred pounds a year, said "Dunham will not suit me; there is too much money and too little labor." He took Madely, not worth half so much, and one of the wickedest places in England. He was never happier than when he had given away the last penny in the house. John Wesley for a number of years lived on twenty-eight pounds a year, and gave away all the rest of his income. Selwyn, late bishop of Lichfield, said on the opening of the Keble College, Oxford: "These words of John Wesley ought to be inscribed on the portals of every college, 'Gain all you can, save all you can, and give all you can.'" Many people are willing to trust their souls in the hands of God, but not their money. Permanent giving for religious purposes should not be dependent on occasional enthusiasm, but upon intelligent conviction, upon an abiding sense of responsibility, and upon that zeal which is awakened by the constantly constraining love of Christ. Honoring God by our substance is one of the surest ways by which poor human nature can manifest its love. Some people with pious exterior break down when it comes to making a financial sacrifice for the cause of Christ. They find it comparatively easy to worship God by singing and praying, but an exceedingly difficult problem to give the worship which calls for dollars and cents. We are told that religion costs nothing, "Come without money and without price," and that is the reason that some people seem to have so much of it.

These so-called sacred concerts are purely and simply secular entertainments. The pretence of sacredness is too apparent to deceive any one who does not wish to be deceived. The whole service is a mere secular entertainment on the Lord's day. And the pretence to sacredness is an aggravation of the evil of it.

Obtaining money for the aid of the Church through a resort to lotteries, church fairs, and festivals destroys the true spirit of philanthropy and self-sacrifice which is the very essence, the very foundation, of all practical Christianity

First General Synod of the Church of England in the Dominion of Canada, 1893.

THE first General Synod for the consolidation of the Church in Canada, met in the city of Toronto on the 13th of September, 1893. The assembly of this General Synod of the Church marks an important historical event in the history of the Church of England in British North America. For over a hundred years the Church in the Dominion has been extending and growing and the time has now arrived for the consolidation of the Church for the whole of British North America. The Provincial Synods of Canada and Rupert's Land are unable to handle the large questions of Church life which are now pressing on the Canadian Church. The Anglican communion throughout the world will feel the deepest interest in this first meeting of the General Synod.

The first department of Church work which claims the attention of the General Synod is the General Mission work. The parish regulates its own missions. The ordinary diocese attends to its local mission work, but such missionary districts as the diocese of the great Northwest and Algoma, with the Domestic and Foreign Missionary Society, the filling of vacant missions and opening new ones. Second, the increase of the Episcopate and the organization of nine new dioceses.

Where new dioceses have been formed in England, in New Zealand, in Australia, in Canada and in the United States, the Church in her missionary work is in a much more vigorous and aggressive condition than before, and a fresh impulse given to all kinds of church work. Multiplied dioceses have always resulted in multiplied co-workers. We have bishops, but the Church burdens them with vast fields of labor, which they must constantly travel over, and it is difficult for them to undertake what the Apostles and primitive bishops regarded as one of the first duties of a Christian bishop—the fellowship of the ministering to the saints, the care of the poor of Christ, of His widows and orphans, the sick, etc. The present cumbersome episcopal jurisdiction should be divided. According to the census of 1891, during the past ten years the new church edifices erected in the Dominion of Canada have been, Anglican 416; Presbyterian 411; Baptists 324; Methodists 322; Roman Catholic 299. The Church of England population has been estimated one third of the total population of the city of Toronto. There are 40 congregations of the Church of England, and over 60 clergymen of the Church of England resident in Toronto. Toronto is the premier Anglican Church city of the Dominion. It is considered a high honor to Toronto to be selected as the scene of the first meeting of the General Synod of the church in the Dominion of Canada.

On the 13th September the delegates met to organize the first General Synod of the Church for the consolidation of the Church of England in the Dominion of Canada including the whole of British North America. Fourteen Bishops were present out of twenty dioceses. The only absentees were the Bishop of Montreal, who was too ill to attend, and the Bishops of Selkirk, Moosone, Mackenzie River, Caledonia and the Bishop of Newfoundland; some of them, no doubt were prevented from attending owing to the long distance to be travelled on so short a notice. The clerical delegates numbered forty-one and the same number of lay delegates. These delegates comprised some of the greatest and most prominent men in the Dominion, renowned as statesmen, lawyers, merchants, and the most eloquent and lettered theologians in the Church of England in the Dominion. There are 1,062 clergymen in the Dominion of Canada. The proceedings opened at 11 o'clock a.m., with a choral service in St. Alban's Cathedral, in which the whole of the Bishops and the clerical and lay delegates took part.

Toronto, like Dublin, has two cathedrals, St. Alban's

J

and St. James', belonging to the English Church. The Metropolitan Bishop of Rupert's Land preached the sermon. In the afternoon, at 3 o'clock, the delegates met in the Convocation Hall of Trinity College and adopted a constitution which involved no change in the existing system of provincial or diocesan synods. The Synod to consist of two houses, the Bishops constituting the upper, and the clergy and laity together, the lower house. The dioceses have been brought into one organic whole from ocean to ocean, which will lead to the development of the Church in British North America and increase her influence in forming and quickening the religious, moral and educational character of the people. The consolidation of the Church is an event of the highest importance to the Anglican Church in Canada. Bishop Mackray, Metropolitan of Rupert's Land, has been elected by the House of Bishops as Primate of the Dominion of Canada and Archbishop of Rupert's Land. Bishop Lewis of Ontario, has been styled Metropolitan and Archbishop of Ontario. Dean Carmichael, of Montreal, was elected by the Lower House as Prolocutor. Bishop Mackray is a Scotchman, and has had literary honors conferred upon him by various universities in England and Scotland, and last year the Queen conferred the unique position of Prelate of the Order of St. Michael and St. George, thus singling him out as the foremost of the Colonial Bishops. Bishop Lewis is an Irishman, an LL.D. of Trinity College, Dublin. The Metropolitan of each ecclesiastical province now in existence or hereafter created to be designated Archbishop of his see, as well as Metropolitan of his province. All agencies employed in the general carrying out of the work of the Church, will come under the control of the General Synod, such as the general mission and educational work—the relations between the dioceses in respect to widows and orphans and superannuation funds—regulations affecting the transfer of clergy from one diocese to another. Education and training of candidates for holy orders. A motion was made to consecrate five missionary bishops for the North West, but was referred to the next meeting of the Synod. It is in contemplation to appoint nine more bishops to fill the new sees to be erected. There is no more comprehensive description of the Church than that it is a great missionary organization. The commission originally given by the Saviour was, "Go ye into all the world and preach the Gospel to every creature." Bishops should be sent into the field as an act of faith, and seek the necessary endowment after. The dignity of the office is sought to be kept up by a large stipend. The Church's work is hampered on all sides by the present inadequate number of bishops. Public opinion is against large endowments for new sees. The American Church has shown us that her Bishops lose none of their dignity because their salaries are small. Why should there be five or six thousand dollar bishops over seven or eight hundred dollar priests? The present endowment funds of the various sees could be divided so that as each bishop dies, the four or five thousand dollars he gets may be used for two successors instead of one. I believe the late Metropolitan of Canada, Bishop Medley, during the last eleven years of his life, gave half of his stipend to his coadjutor. And the late Bishop Field of Newfoundland offered to give the half, or if necessary the whole of his salary for an assistant bishop. He strongly urged the sub-division of his diocese. In 1851, a fund was raised in England, Ireland and Scotland, the interest of which, together with annual subscriptions, went to the salaries of the seven Scottish bishops, each of whom received from $550 to $900. The bishopric of Argyle is endowed by a separate fund. Each of the seven bishops in Scotland now receive a salary of $2,000 per annum. It is said the reason why no delegate appeared from Newfoundland was because they would seem to enter into confederation with Canada and that while Newfoundland was outside the Dominion, the Church in the Island would not approach the question of union with the Church in Canada.

The General Synod is not to interfere with the rights, powers, or jurisdiction of any diocesan synod as now held. I hope at the next meeting of the General Synod, Newfoundland will be duly represented. Without coming into political confederation, the Presbyterians of Newfoundland are in connection with the general assembly of the Presbyterian Church of Canada. For a number of years the Methodist Conference of Newfoundland has been affiliated with the General Conference of the Dominion of Canada, from which it receives an annual grant of $13,000 for the support of its missions. Last year the grant was:—

Newfoundland	$ 11,772
Labrador	1,465
Removal Expenses	553
	$13,790

Without the aid of the General Conference of the Dominion, the Methodists in Newfoundland could not support their missions. By joining the General Synod of the Church of England, the Church in Newfoundland would no doubt receive a grant for the support of missions, and thus be enabled to re-open old Missions at Labrador and establish new ones at Newfoundland. The Roman Catholics, with a population of 75,254 in Newfoundland, have three bishops. while the Church of England, with a population of 69,210 at the present time has but one bishop. The Church of England ought to have two more bishops—missionary bishops, one for the northern part of the Island and Labrador, the other for the West Coast. The General Synod of the Dominion would help to support these Missionary Bishops. The General Synod closed on Wednesday, the 20th of September, after a session of eight days. The next meeting is to be held at Winnipeg, in September, 1896.

Extempore Preaching.

THE history of the Church of England is identified, not with read, but unread discourses, and *that* has been a source of its power, previous to and after the Reformation. The powerful unread discourses delivered at Paul's Cross had a wonderful effect on the people. Discourses, really extempore, are probably but rarely delivered. More or less preparation is not only general, but necessary. There are congregations which prefer sermons to be read, others to have them unread. Some years ago a congregation requested me not to use a MS., as the people preferred preaching without it. Another congregation asked me not to speak without a written discourse, as it was more "Church like," and the people did not like extempore preaching. The late Bishop Wilberforce, in his charge to his clergy, directed that at least one extempore discourse out of their two Sunday sermons should be delivered. It is significant to note that whilst the habit of reading sermons has been argued against by some ministers of the Church of England, it has been on the increase by various denominations. A Baptist minister told me he always read his discourses, "and I say by the time we get into it, the Episcopal Church will get out of it." A venerable dame, who, on being asked on her return from Church what the great Divine from the city had been saying, resolutely asserted that she " could not mind," giving as her reason that "he read," and on being asked how that prevented her "minding," replied, "If the man could not mind his own sermon, how could he expect me to mind it." A young man from the city, visiting the country, argued in favor of *reading*, as being more favorable to correctness of diction. His chief opponent was a miller, who closed his argument by saying, " Oh, yes, you folks in the town are great grammar critics, but in the country we like best to have it hot and hashy." Neither written nor extempore preaching will avail much to bring men to the knowledge of Christ, unless the soul of the preacher is saturated with the influences of the Holy Ghost, unless he feels the love of God shed abroad in his heart by the Holy Ghost given unto him; and just in proportion as he feels the love of God pervading his own heart, will he wish to communicate it to others. It is largely the power of God in us that He employs to lead others to Christ. Flowers of rhetoric or witcheries of elocution, "the well-tuned period and the well-tuned voice, the strength of action and the flow of words," will not bring the guilty to cry, "God be merciful to me a sinner." The grand theme of Apostolic preaching was *Christ*. To-day the theme is divinely appropriate as ever. *To-day the world needs Christ* as it needed him them. Let men preach Christ, and their preaching will bring life to dead souls. The Bishop of Salisbury having a young man of promising abilities to preach before George III., the bishop, in conversation afterwards, wishing to get the King's opinion, said: "Does not Your Majesty think that the young man who had the honor to preach before Your Majesty, is likely to make a good clergyman, and has this morning delivered a good sermon?" To which the King, in his usual blunt manner, hastily replied: "It might have been a good sermon, my Lord, for aught I know, but I consider no sermon good that has nothing of *Christ* in it." There are two ways of knowing divine truth—experimentally and theoretically. The tone of the pulpit has been fearfully lowered by the introduction of essays on science and philosophy, and sometimes church politics. Effective preaching must be faithful, affectionate and earnest, all three combined. It must be fearless, crushing through the prejudices and secret sins of the hearer. "Masillon, you have offended me," said Louis XIV., the Grand Monarch, to the great preacher. "That is what I wished to do, sire," said he. Effective preaching is "not by might, nor by power, but by my spirit, saith the Lord of Hosts." In a preacher nothing can be a substitute for *earnestness*. "How is it,' said a bishop to a player, "that your performances, which are but pictures of the imagination, produce so much more effect than our sermons, which are all realities?" "Because," said the player. " we represent our fictions as though they were realities, and you preach your realities as though they were fictions." A good deal of the preaching of the present day is from the head. It is prevailingly intellectual; it is from the head. There are brains in it, but not much soul. Such preaching is, perhaps, adapted to the wants of many, but to the needs of few. There never was a time at which more interest was shown in the externals of religion. We want more of the old style of preaching—the kind they had before railroads and steamboats, telegraphs and telephones, the kind that did not tickle the ear and starve the soul. It is a question whether the work of the pulpit or the pastorate is the more important. There have been men who had no great gift as preachers, who by reason of their kindliness, common sense, and diligence as pastors, have succeeded in building, or in keeping up good congregations, whilst there have been men gifted with no small power of pulpit eloquence, who, by reason of their failure as pastors, have succeeded in reducing a once flourishing congregation to zero. There are clerical " deadheads' who push better men from the gospel car. That the pulpit thus manned, should be powerless, is a natural sequence.

Plagiarism in the Pulpit.

WE sometimes hear of clergymen giving sermons to their hearers which are not their own. Do we not frequently read advertisements in the London papers offering to supply clergymen with lithographed sermons in all styles of eloquence, and at all prices? I believe that most clergymen try to give us the best of their own, although cases do come to light now and again where a "brother," who would do very well as a mere barn-door fowl, arrays himself in the gorgeous plumage of a bird of paradise, without the slightest acknowledgment. Some sermons are a singular piece of patchwork. They consist of a paragraph from one author, a scrap from another, a section from a third, portions from several. They shine in all the colors of the rainbow. It is a patchwork; every patch has been filched. We have heard from the pulpit some of the masterpieces of great French preachers, and from the sermons of Paley, Barrow, South, Hooker, Taylor, and other great English divines without acknowledgment. Of the late Daniel Wilson, Bishop of Calcutta, it has been said six or seven of his discourses, taken at random, contain extracts from or references to fifty-nine different authorities. There can be no objection to clergymen taking as much as they please from the writings of others, provided they do it honestly and judiciously; and we are satisfied that no compositions are so much benefited by the process as sermons. As to Rev. Dr. Vaughan, who succeeded the celebrated Robertson at Brighton, fifteen hundred of his sermons were reported and published; it is said hundreds of these sermons were given from various pulpits by different clergymen in England and America without acknowledgment. We do not discuss the moral questions; but as to the strength of the temptation there can be no doubt. A young minister was lately told by an old lady, after hearing him preach, that he "would doubtless improve as he grew older." This greatly discouraged him, for the sermon he had used was one of four "crack" sermons preached by the late Bishop Wilberforce before the Queen. This sermon did not sound from him as it sounded from the Bishop. No sermon can be stolen without losing some of its pith and power in the process. Sermons are often judged, not upon their own intrinsic merits, but by the reputation of the man who preaches them. We know a distinguished minister whose written sermons, when young, were regarded as giving promise that "if he lived, and improved, he would make a fairly good preacher in the course of time." In later years, these same sermons, preached without revision or modification, were pronounced by those same judges as his ablest efforts for logic and eloquence. So slight is the worth and weight of the popular verdict on pulpit performances! Canon Lytton's sermons are frequently given from pulpits not of the Church of England. Jabez Bunting, a giant in Methodism, used to take the sermons of the old divines, grind them up, and make them his own. And of Robert Newton, one of the most popular preachers, his congregation used to complain of his having the same sermons so often. The same sermon, by the injection of some new thoughts, grows better with every delivery. George Whitefield said that he never felt perfect master of a sermon until he had preached it the hundredth time. Oliver Wendell Holmes, in his "Autocrat of the Breakfast Table," says: "Old lectures are a man's best; commonly, they improve by age."

Some preachers imagine if they throw in a Latin word now and then they improve their composition, and this reminds us of the pulpit of a country congregation becoming vacant, a preacher was advised by his friends to apply for the vacancy, and to be sure, in his trial sermon, to throw in some scraps of Latin. The candidate knew nothing of Greek or Latin. He was a Welshman and interlarded his discourse with Welsh words. The preacher, looking towards the door, saw a man cracking his sides laughing. He was a Welshman and understood the words the preacher was using. So the preacher said to him in Welsh (which passed off as Latin) "For God's sake say nothing of this, I will see you after I get through." The preacher, being such a learned man, succeeded in getting employed by the congregation as their new pastor. Some sermons have taken their authors a week and even a month to write them. It is said it took Melville and Moore a year to write their "Golden Lectures." There are men of peculiar mental habits who can write a sermon in a very short time, having previously well digested the matter of it. But ordinarily, to write one good sermon a week is as much as any man can do. We should not value a sermon by the length of time it occupies. The danger of short sermons is that of producing no impression. The danger of long sermons is that of creating a bad one. Dr. MacLaren, the present Archbishop of York, who stands to-day a prince among preachers, says: "Burn all your manuscripts, and never write any more to be read in a pulpit. Whatever else you may do with your pen, I believe the worst thing you can do with it is to write sermons with it." It is only "thoughts that breathe and words that burn" that will have any real effect under the influence of God's spirit upon the life and conduct of the hearer. You never knew a burning flame of missionary zeal in a congregation whose pastor was cold and indifferent. He is generally the vestal whose hand lights and keeps burning the sacred fire. Too often sermons present nothing but a few vague generalities, noticeable for nothing except their failing to arouse the sleepy conscience—a few common-place truisms, and delivered with a dull monotony. Hooker, speaking of the effects of lukewarmness upon a congregation, says: "How should there but be in *them* frozen coldness when his affections seem benumbed from whom theirs should fire? Congregations are like the fluids, they are sure not to rise above the level of the zeal of their teachers."

Plagiarism is not confined to the pulpit. Politicians, statesmen, lawyers, physicians, and lecturers have indulged in it. A minister is expected to come to the pulpit Sunday after Sunday, with two new discourses in his pocket, each occupying from twenty to thirty minutes in delivery. How can we expect him to be always original! It is simply a mental impossibility and unreasonable to expect of poor clerical human nature. Suppose a young man to begin preaching at the age of twenty-five, and to continue preaching till he attains seventy, and that he delivers two discourses every Sunday. His 104 discourses would fill six octavo volumes, which being multiplied by 45—the term of his preaching life—would give a product of 270 volumes. Just think of it! Therefore, we are not disposed to join in the hue and cry against the preacher, who finding elsewhere materials better than he can supply himself, works them into his own compositions and so benefits his hearers.

"Music as Religion and Religion Music."

Music has a power which is peculiarly its own; it can find its way where nothing else can penetrate; can excite thoughts and feelings which are impassive to every other touch; it will outlive all other art, and is perhaps the only one which is essentially eternal. The music of heaven revealed to St. John in the Book of Revelation when on the Isle of Patmos, is represented in a vision: "And I heard the voice of a great multitude, and as the voice of many waters, and as the voice of mighty thunderings, saying, Alleluia, for the Lord God omnipotent reigneth."

The story is told of an Asiatic prince, who was invited to an elaborate musical performance, with the expectation that he would be overwhelmed with grandeur and beauty; but to the astonishment of his friends, the most delightful of the entertainment to his ear was the discordant tuning of the instruments. This he desired to have repeated. The Rev. Dr. Horace Bushnell, one of the greatest Congregationalists in the United States, says:—"Entering one day the great Church of Jesus in Rome, when all the vast area of the pavement was covered with worshippers on their knees, chanting in fervent voice, led by the organ, their confession of penitence and praise to God, I was impressed as never before with the essential sublimity of the rite of worship, and I could not but wish that our people were trained to a similar exercise." Ambrose, Bishop of Milan, introduced a high style of music; St. Augustine himself listened to it in the Church of Milan, where he represents himself as being melted to tears. The soul of man has affiance with this Divine power of music. Henry Ward Beecher, when attending the Church of England at Stratford-on-Avon, England, when he heard the Amen sung for the first time with the organ, seemed lifted into the third heaven. He says:— "I never had such a trance of worship, and I shall never have such another view of heaven until I gain the gate. I never dreamed before of what heart there was in that Amen." In the Scriptures natural objects are often personified, represented as possessing life and action and as addressing themselves to man. We read of the hills breaking forth into singing, the floods lifting up their voice, the desert rejoicing, and the trees clapping their hands. There is an affinity between the soul and nature. If man will shut his ears and his heart to the voice of inspiration, he cannot always be deaf to the voice of material things. The sailor, while listening to the music of the midnight wave, and surveying the sparkling worlds over his head rolling along their courses, jewelling the concave of the firmament, resolving the universe into one great instrument of music,

"Forever singing as they shine,
The hand that made us is divine."

feels the indescribable emotions that nature produces in his soul. Man has a sympathy with the natural objects around him. A pirate while visiting the coast of Florida, was awakened to repentance by the music of the dove, the soft and melancholy cooing of the doves, the only soothing sounds he heard during his life of horrors. He effected his escape from the vessel and became a better man. Thus God spoke by the music of the doves to the soul of the pirate, reminding him of truths learned in days of innocence. "There lives and moves a soul in all things, and that soul is God." Mr. Alfred Parsons, now a resident of St. John's, was one of the greatest musicians of his day. I remember when he was so young and small that he used to stand upon the table to play the fiddle for the young ladies at their social evening parties at Carbonear, Newfoundland. These evening parties were held in rotation at the residences of the different belles, through the entire winter, and little Alfred Parsons invariably played the violin for them. He had the true musical instinct. Many years after when I met him at St. John's, he used to say, " Come, let us go and hear the organ ; that swell thrills through me and elevates my soul." The organ referred to was in the old Roman Catholic Chapel, and the only one in Newfoundland. Mr. Parsons at the present time is one of the greatest violinists in Newfoundland, and equally as good a singer. Thirty years ago, on my second visit to Newfoundland, I spent an evening with him on Cochrane Street. John Bemister, his brother-in-law, and wife were some of the party. Mr. Bemister was a first-class violinist and singer. So with the two fiddles and the splendid voices of their wives and daughters, we had a grand musical festival.

In the long ago there were no concerts, lectures or bazaars held in Newfoundland, no sources of recreation, so that the young fishermen had to resort to fiddling and dancing to while away the winter evenings. Norman McLeod, who was chaplain to the Queen, tells of his father being minister of a kirk in the Highlands of Scotland. On Saturday evenings he assembled all the servants at the manse, where they had a dance, his father playing the fiddle for them. And he adds that the fiddle has now been nearly banished from the Highlands, but that there was more religion and more open-hearted hospitality among the people then than there is now.

Personal Recollections of Kossuth.

I MET him in the city of Hartford, Conn., U.S., in 1851. He was of middle stature, fine presence, and full of life and energy. He wore a high red feather in his cap, spoke broken English, but so as to be clearly and distinctly understood. His speeches showed him a man of genius, some of them wonderful efforts. He showed surprising information, readiness, fertility in the resources of thought and eloquence of expression. Daniel Webster said of them that they were the most eloquent speeches ever uttered by any man in America. Referring to money he called it "material aid." Since then, these words of Kossuth have been used in speeches, books and newspapers almost throughout Europe and America. As to the Hungarian struggle, it was not for liberty of the masses. It was a contest between the Emperor of Austria and the nobility of Hungary. The Magyar nobility had no idea of liberty for the masses of the population who tilled their broad acres. It was for the independence of Hungary as a kingdom, in which the Magyar aristocracy should be the ruling element that they were contending. In the course of the struggle, the nobles quailed before the combined powers of despotism. Kossuth then appealed to the middle classes and finally liberated the serfs. The common tenure of a peasant's holding 60 acres of land, was that he gave to the landlord one day's labor in the week, with a waggon and two horses, or two days at hard labor alone. In 1839, Kossuth was prosecuted for high treason, and sentenced to four years' imprisonment. After a year and a half of confinement he was liberated under an act of amnesty. The great effort to gain freedom for the masses failed. The battle for Hungarian independence was fought and lost. During the revolution in 1848 which agitated Europe, Hungary was involved in civil war. The name of Kossuth had a talismanic power. He became the representative of freedom. As such he was almost adored by the masses. Naturally and originally he was the head of a high-spirited aristocracy, contending for independence of imperial control of Austria. Being defeated, the great leader passed into exile, under the constraining protection of Turkey. Austria and Russia wished to have him given up, but France and England interfered, and he was allowed to remain in Turkey. He placed himself under the protection of the United States. An American man-of-war brought him to America. On his arrival in New York in December, 1851, a brilliant reception was given to him. He was honored with the most enthusiastic and magnificent reception ever accorded in America to any individual when he became the guest of the Empire State. After his return from America, he has resided in Turin, earning his living by literary labor. I have just read in one of the newspaper that he is dying at Turin.—*Memento mori.*

Incidents of a Visit to New York.

I LEFT Toronto the first week in October, 1893, for the City of Gotham. On my arrival at the Grand Central Depot at New York, I found a number of relatives and friends waiting to receive me. We immediately entered the street cars and drove to Hunter's Point Ferry. After crossing the river we took the train for Woodside, four miles distant, where I took up my quarters in a beautiful cottage surrounded with lawn, fruit trees and flowers. Four years ago, Woodside was only an embryo settlement; now it is a flourishing village, embellished with churches, schools, hotels, stores, etc., a beautiful suburb of Brooklyn. I took a drive to West Bay, formerly called Bowery Bay, a place of resort for pleasure-seekers. Never before has the importance of rest and recreation been so clearly recognized, and in no previous age has such broad and costly provision for healthy pleasure-seeking been made. I called to see my old friend, Bishop Southgate, who resides at Astoria, a few miles distant from Woodside. The Bishop has a large and elegant mansion facing the sea, on which is seen steamers, sailing vessels, barges and all sorts of craft, passing and repassing. Nearly opposite the Bishop's residence is Ward's Island, on which stands a large Asylum for the insane. The Bishop is now in his 81st year, and retired from active duties. The Bishop said: "I can hardly think it possible that forty-one years have come and gone since you left me at Boston to go into the diocese of Nova Scotia. Everything that was then said and done is as fresh in my memory as if it was done an hour ago." The Bishop said that the building of the great Protestant Cathedral is retarded a little. After making excavations, it was found that the ground was not solid enough to commence building; it is expected another site will have to be chosen. I said it is going to cost an immense sum of money—twelve million dollars.

The Bishop said, "We have men who could give the whole cost of the building and not feel it; but most of our millionaires are worldlings, white-washed with a form of religion." The Bishop was once Bishop of Constantinople and Missionary Bishop of the East. He has told me many interesting incidents of his residence at Constantinople. It was quite invigorating to inhale once more the saline air as we paced the shores of Long Island, down by the sounding sea.

> There is a pleasure in the pathless woods,
> There is a rapture in the lonely shore;
> There is society where none intrudes
> By the deep sea, and music in its roar."

The water between Brooklyn and New York, which is a continuation of the sea of Long Island Sound, is crowded with sailing crafts of every shape and size, with barges of every imaginable construction and form; steamers, from the smallest yacht up to the steamship of thousands of tons. The wonder is that they so seldom come in collision. More than forty years ago, when I was here, New York and Brooklyn presented a forest of masts of sailing vessels. But most of the sailing vessels have now been superseded in the carrying and passenger trade by colossal ocean steamships, designated "floating palaces" Speaking of these changes to a friend, he said, "When you visit New York fifty years from now you will be able to come in an air ship," which prophecy about the air ship may be fulfilled. During the first week of my visit, rain and the most dense fog, far exceeding anything of the kind ever seen in Canada, prevailed, and so thick you could "cut it with a knife." The young lady who was my escort said we should be lost, for we could hardly see anything around us; streets and shops were lit up, but the lights were scarcely perceptible in the streets through the fog, which hung like a dark curtain. It must have been like the London fog of which we read. When I was at St. John, New Brunswick, the fog whistle and bell were continually kept going.

Wandering through Central Park we proceed to Madison Avenue, to pay our respects to the President-elect, but found that Mr. Cleveland had removed from Madison Avenue, the place of his residence when I saw him two years ago, to West fifty-first street. We next wended our way through Broadway, the great commercial artery. Here we called on several friends and relatives, and rested for the toils of to-morrow. I visited St. Bartholomew's, one of the "open churches" of the city. It is open daily for private prayer, and is much used. During the year over 7,000 persons availed themselves of this privilege. This is the church where Cornelius Vanderbilt, Chauncey M. Depew, and other notabilities attend. It is fitted up in the most ornate and costly style of architecture. St. Thomas is a beautiful, spacious church edifice, and one of the most prosperous in the city, with numerous missionary and charitable organizations in connection with it. Among its rectors were several bishops and among its assistant ministers was the Rev. F. Courtney, now Bishop of Nova Scotia. The new Episcopal Cathedral will be the largest and most magnificent ecclesiastical structure in America, estimated to cost over ten million dollars. The church is making wonderful progress in the U.S., and seems to be rapidly absorbing the denominations around her. A priest of the Diocese of Albany said to me: "In two of the Episcopal Churches of Brooklyn, on Sunday last, low mass was celebrated; the Episcopalians are fast coming over to us, and in a few years the whole body of them will cast their anchor on the rock of Peter." In reply to this, I said quite a number of priests in Europe and America have joined the Episcopal Church, and just now, in Spain, "the garden of the Lord," a church has been opened by the Archbishop of Dublin, the congregation attending which had belonged to the Roman Catholic Church. Not long ago I heard

Father McIlvane announce to his congregation that from time to time ten million of persons had been lost to the Church. The *Tablet*, New York, says: "Five hundred lost, to one convert from Protestantism." The *Irish World* said: "The loss to Catholics in this republic has been 18,000,000." J. O'Kane Murray, in his History of the Catholic Church in the United States, says: 'It may safely be said that more Catholics have fallen away from the faith in this country, during the last two centuries and a half, than there are in it living to-day." The editor of the *Celt*, lecturing in Ireland, said: "The Roman Catholic Church loses sixty per cent. of the children born to Catholic parents in the States."

The Linotype machine is not a type-setting machine in the ordinary sense of the word. On the contrary, it is a machine which, being operated by finger-keys, like the type-writer, produces type matter ready for use on the press or stereotying machine. The various type-setting machines invented have failed to successfully set type. About twelve years ago a fairly satisfactory machine was invented, from which is developed the present wonderful Linotype. The machine operates at the amazing speed of from four thousand to nine thousand ems per hour. One operator's work, by great effort, was found to be 61,300 ems, corrected matter, in eight hours. There are now four immense factories engaged turning out Linotypes, in England, Brooklyn, Baltimore and other cities.

New York is getting into a terrible state. Wealthly men and moral reformers seem not to be safe, freqently cranks threaten to take their lives, unless they give up so much of their money to them. So also, the lives of moral reformers are threatened. The leader of the crusade against vice, the Rev. Dr. Parkhurst, a popular Presbyterian minister of New York, has determined to take steps to protect himself against violence—he received a letter which said he would be killed if he persisted in his social crusade. Robberies, murders and suicides are on every hand.

Most of the candidates for municipal and legislative honors are either saloon keepers or their tools; 7,783 saloons are pledged to support them. New York appears to be misruled by an olegarchy of liquor sellers. Nearly all the men in municipal politics were poor a few years ago. They have now grown wealthly, and live in a state far beyond their visible means. The total of the salaries paid in Washington by the United States government amounts to $13,364 196; the total of salaries by New York's city government amounted to $16,000,000. The present Mayor Gilroy of New York is very popular; he was born in Ireland six years before coming to New York; he belongs to the Roman Catholic Church. A religious political meeting was held in the Opera House which was crowded with people of every denomination and politics. Among the audience was the Women's Christian Temperance Union who marched from their rooms in a body, wearing the white ribbon. Sitting on the platform were the clergy of different denominations, some of whom appealed to voters to shake their party shackles off and vote for men who will represent the moral interest of the State. 100,000 women are registered voters in the State of New York. Great destitution prevails in all the cities of the United States. It is estimated that throughout the country 800,000 persons are unemployed. It is expected that the repeal of the silver law and the reduction of duties on imported goods will give a fresh start to trade. The reduction of duties on horses, eggs, iron, etc., will benefit Canada as well as the United States. Some of the papers say: "Hard Times. No. Dry goods men's business never better. Some lines 200 per cent. over 1892," I spent some time with friends at Harlem. So far as the beauty of the coming New York is concerned, Harlem is destined to be the most beautiful part of the city. The streets are boulevards for spaciousness, and the footways are promenades. Harlem and the annexed district present many miles of beautiful reaches, which in a short time will be one of the notable features of the commercial metropolis. The municipal consolidation of Brooklyn and New York will make New York one of the three or four largest cities in the world.

It is estimated that in the whole population of the United States 930,000 were born in the British Provinces. The exodus from the Province of Quebec cannot be stopped; it has been going on every since Quebec became a British province. The exodus of the French Canadians is largely owing to the want of farms. The French Canadians are a prolific people. They have large families. The head of the family had originally perhaps fifty acres of land; this has been divided five or six times. They cannot find land in the old and thickly settled parishes, so they emigrate to Lowell, Manchester and other manufacturing towns of the New England States. Many of the encumbered and mortgaged farms of the descendants of the Puritans now belong to French Canadians. Hundreds of farmers of the New England States have sold out their farms and emigrated west. A number of those deserted farms have come into the possession of the French Canadians. Last year over 1,000 persons returned to the Province of Quebec from the United States, and there is a constant exodus of American farmers from various parts of the United States to the Canadian North West. Year after year the United States is losing its character as a land of opportunity and plenty. Causes identical with those which impoverish the many in older lands are already strongly in operation in the Great Republic. The United States is a land of comfort and luxury for the wealthy few, but of hard fare for the toiling millions. What was once a nation of freeholders is fast becoming a nation of tenants. In 1890 half the population of Georgia were tenants, while in Maine the percentage of tenants almost doubled in the decade. Nor is the proportion of freeholders larger in the cities— the proportion of tenants ranges from 77.24 to 81.57.

With the average of comfort, prosperity is no higher, if it is as high, in the United States as in the British Colonies. The Republic is no land of milk and honey for tenants, but every year becoming more and more the landlord's paradise, when he can get his rent. In New York alone last year there were 28,000 evictions, which put nearly 100,000 people homeless on the streets. We sometimes hear complaints that evictions are numerous in Ireland. In the same year that there were 28,000 evictions in New York there were only 5,000 in Ireland. It is therefore evident that the United States is no longer a land of Goshen to the tenant.

The New York *Sun* says: Trinity, St. Paul's and Grace Church defy the advance of business interests. Three landmarks on Broadway occupy sites so valuable that their retention confounds every calculation of real estate speculators. They are the only three churches on Broadway below Forty-second street, and each has come to be part of the popular distinction of that thoroughfare. They are Trinity, St. Paul's and Grace. All three have high claims to architecture eminence, and all three are of one denomination—the Protestant Episcopal.

The site of Trinity Church, on Broadway at the head of Wall street, is appraised officially at $4,000,000; that of St. Paul's Church, at Broadway and Fulton street, at $1,750,000, and that of Grace Church, Broadway, opposite Eleventh street, at $350,000. The frontage of Trinity Church, including the church-yard, is 406 feet, of St. Paul's Church, 167 feet, and of Grace Church, 150 feet. The gross valuation of these three churches is $6,100,000, and as the usual rate of assessment on real estate is about 60 per cent. the actual market value of these three Broadway plots is in excess of $10,000,000. In European cities it is no strange thing for public thoroughfares to be dotted with venerable edifices erected for ecclesiastical, military or governmental purposes, but in New York, where there is no material partnership between church and state, and where, perhaps, more utilitarian views prevail than abroad, the steady enhancement of real estate values has been such that few religious corporatians have been strong enough or felt themselves strong enough to withstand the temptation to sell. On the present site of Tiffany's, for instance, Broadway and Fifteenth street, formerly a church stood. There was a chapel opposite the site of the old New York hotel. But with the advance of business interests the congregations reluctantly moved away. These three landmarks named have stood their ground, and it seems probable that they will continue to do so.

St. Paul's church is the oldest religious edifice in this city. It was built in 1764, and it was the church which George Washington and his associates attended immediately following the inauguration ceremonies in 1789. Trinity Church is the third of that name on the present site, and was erected in 1846. Grace Church was erected in 1845, one year before Trinity, and the site, at the head of Broadway where it turns an angle at Tenth street, was carefully chosen. All three buildings enjoy the advantage of being kept in excellent repair, and are improved from time to time by the liberal contributions of benefactors. This is especially true of Trinity and Grace Church, which may almost be said to improve year by year. It is a peculiarity of these three landmarks of New York that those who attend them come, in nearly every case, from sections of the city far up town, so that they are, if such an expression may be used, the three churches to be reached by carriage. Very few persons who attend either Trinity or St. Paul's reside in their vicinity, and the number of such parishioners decreases each year. Grace Church retains its high rank architecturally, notwithstanding the number of new church buildings in New York, and it has the additional distinction of being popular for fashionable weddings.

Education for the Church.

At a meeting of the Nova Scotia Synod, Bishop Binney said :—" We cannot deny the great and valuable services to the church by men who had not taken the arts course, men in some cases much more fitted and able for the work of the ministry than some who could boast of a B.A. degree." Not long ago, mentioning the name of a bishop, a clergyman said to me that he could not read a chapter in the Greek Testament, yet he made an excellent bishop. Dr. Chalmers, in one of his four celebrated lectures, in the University of Edinburgh, says :—" Give me a band of men, who never walked, as you have done, the halls of a university, whose only library is the inspired oracles of God; whose only tutor is the Holy Ghost sent down from heaven, and let them loose on some wild moral territory, and they will do more, ten to one, than our college-trained ministry, who must utter every truth and shape every Gospel enunciation according to the rule and square of a rigid orthodoxy." Some of our greatest orators never received a classical education of dead languages, but rose to distinction entirely by the study of the English classics. John Bright, who was one of Mr. Gladstone's Cabinet, and the greatest orator in the House of Commons, said in one of his speeches at Birmingham, " When I was young I knew nothing of classics and mathematics, and I have not learned anything about them since. I regard what are called classics, that is the ancient languages of Greece and Rome, as rather luxuries than anything else. I think a man may be as great a man and as good a man and as wise a man knowing only his own language and the wisdom that is enshrined in it, as if he knew all the Latin and Greek books that have been written. Let no man think himself stupid because he is not a classical scholar." The name of a minister was mentioned, and it was added that his congregation was not in a very prosperous state, although he was a very able and scholarly man. "Oh," was the reply of an excellent lady, "I don't like those able and learned men as preachers; they are dry sticks." "Yes," said another lady, "there seems to be an idea that the two are not usually combined. I have heard of a popular preacher whom it was proposed to make a professor, and when the matter was mentioned to him he said laughingly, "Oh, I haven't emptied my church yet.'" The English Methodists complain that since their preachers have received a collegiate education they have gone into scientific preaching, gone into speculative theories of the unthinkable, the insoluble, or unknown. At the meeting of the General Conference of the Methodist Episcopal Church in the United States, one of the speakers said:—" One of the perils to which Methodism is subject to-day is the prevailing idea, the prevailing taste, it may be, and the opinion among the people, and especially among those of the cities, that this nineteenth century is one of progress, and that it is one of culture and one of esthetics, and, therefore, the efforts, the thoughts, the manners and customs of the Methodist Church must be subordinated to the fashionable idea of culture and estheticism. This church has extended its dominion far and wide, not only over this continent, but over the lands of other continents: and it has been done under the system that was adopted by our fathers. It may be a fashionable church; it may be a church that shall show to the world at large and the hypercritical that we dress as well, move as well, talk as well, that in all that enters into the elements of fashionable life we are among the very foremost. But when that becomes the prevailing idea of the Methodist Church, it is lost to its integrity, to its love of the Methodism of early years —which is the boast of the Methodism to propagate Christianity. One of the effects is this: That the power of preaching is hardly what it used to be. And why?

Because we need less of the idea that we must be just as refined as any other church ; that we must say just as many good things as we can get into a sermon before the people, while there are brothers who are famishing for the bread of life, and talk about political economy and evolution. I would restore our people, and especially our preachers, back to the old days of simplicity in this and the impassioned appeals; although we might see very many superfine people leaving our doors. Yet it is the way to reach the heart of the sinner. It is not to please the world ; it is not to have eloquent articles; to have compliments paid to our preachers, that are about as well educated, or as logical as any other preachers." The Roman Catholic Bishop, Spalding, of Peoria, U.S., says :—" The early zeal of the Wesleyans has already cooled. They no longer shout, fall into ecstacy, see visions, as in the good old days that are gone. It is not sufficient now that a preacher should hear the call of heaven ; he must be educated. The simplicity of dress and peculiar manners which the Methodist once affected are forgotten; the religion of tradesmen and backwoods farmers is clothed in broadcloth. Methodism is respectable, and henceforth harmless." It is well known that some of the greatest men the world has produced in science, in literature and in theology never graduated at a university. A knowledge of Hebrew, Greek and Latin is not indispensable to the preaching of the gospel. A good Hebrew and Greek scholar may be very deficient in some other respects. A preacher who may be altogether wanting in classical attainments may yet be educated, polished, deeply versed in all Biblical knowledge, and an accomplished speaker. There are subjects, political, literary, scientific, philosophical, that would be quite out of place in the pulpit. A preacher of the Gospel is expected to confine himself to the Gospel. The preacher comes not into the pulpit in the garb of a philosopher or scholar. His business is not to display his learning, to excite the admiration and call forth the applause of his audience. "Jesus Christ and Him crucified," must be the grand theme of his preaching—the golden thread running through all his discourses. The late Bishop Samuel Wilberforce says :—" Should not our preaching be rough enough, so to speak, to make itself felt through their dull skin of ignorance and inattention ; should it not startle the careless, should it not positively jog the drowsy man, ere his slumber is sound ? Should it not avoid the easy uniformity of a man applying a nostrum, and with the living earnestness of one who believes he has all important truths to convey, declares the curse of sin, and the blessed remedy provided for it in the sacrifices and perpetual offerings of Our Lord, and in the working of God the Holy Ghost ? Should you not dwell on and proclaim Christ in His Church, Christ in His Sacraments, Christ crucified, Christ risen, Christ meditating, and Christ saving."

For the most part it is not the men of extensive learning and of superior literary talents who are wanted, as men of simplicity and sincerity, men of prayer, men who so love Christ as to be willing to spend and be spent for Christ's sake. Christ did not call His disciples from the school of learning, but from the seaside, the receipt of custom, and other places of human toil. " Please your majesty," said John Howe one day to the King, who asked him why so learned a man as he went to hear so coarse and illiterate a man as Bunyan, " please your majesty, could I possess that tinker's abilities for preaching, I would gladly part with all my learning." Archdeacon Farrar, who was thirteen years a classical teacher at Harrow School, says :—" Classical education rejects all the powers of some minds, and some of the powers of all minds; in the case of a few it has a value, which being partial is unsatisfactory, while in the case of the vast multitude it ends in utter and irremediable waste."

German and French would not only be more useful,

but would afford quite as good mental training as either or both of the classic languages. The bulk of students no longer aim to achieve distinction in dead languages. Everything worth knowing in the ancient literature of Greece or Rome has been rendered into English (particularly the works of the Fathers), by the ablest scholars and linguists, giving a better translation than most of the graduates of our colleges could hope to do for themselves.

It is contended that the time spent upon Greek and Hebrew is practically wasted, because so very few master them, and the time spent on them ought to be given to more valuable acquisitions. That this is so hundreds who have studied the dead languages at college, and forgotten all about them can testify. Some say that unless a man is acquainted with the original tongues in which the Scriptures were given he cannot know that he is preaching the Word of God. It is true also with every person who is not acquainted with the Hebrew and Greek tongues, for it is just as impossible for me as another, being ignorant of these tongues, to know that our English Bible is the Word of God, and not the word of men. They are compelled to trust entirely to a translation. And, therefore, the millions who are unacquainted with these tongues can never know but they are believing and trusting in the word of men, and not the Word of God, but, alas! for his hearers, who are not acquainted with these tongues, for the preacher has no power to impart this knowledge to them. For they are compelled to trust entirely to a translation either the preacher's translation, or then the preacher must give them a translation made to his own hands. The preacher, though he may be able to read Hebrew and Greek, may be notwithstanding an incompetent translator of these languages into English. Perhaps not more than one out of five hundred who pass for learned is qualified to make anything like a correct translation from the Hebrew and Greek Bible. Our present translation of the English Bible was made by forty-six men chosen especially for the work because of their superior knowledge of these original tongues. If these forty-six men of acknowledged piety, of deep reverence for the Word of God, and profoundly learned in those tongues, could not and did not give us a right translation, why was it? Then have we any ground to hope for a better? Can any man who is acquainted with tongues give us anything more reliable than either the old or the new translation of the Word of God?

It is not indispensable that one must be trained in a college before he can preach the Gospel. Men are not taught to preach the Gospel by men, but by God. Men become Gospel preachers just as trees bear fruit—by an internal and divinely imparted energy, and not by artificial process. "Cut, and made to order," is a good advertisement for a merchant tailor, but not for a church in quest of a living ministry, inasmuch as "manufactured preachers" are like the figure-head of a ship—ornamental but not very useful. In the Universities of Oxford and Cambridge fellowships were held. It was a scholastic sinecure, requiring little labor and some distinguished merit to obtain it. John Wesley after his brother Charles' marriage, transferred to him his Oxford Fellowship to enable him to support his family.

Spiritual self culture is largely the power of God in us that He employs to lead others to Christ. The Word of God is the source of all ministerial power. He, who is so familiar with all its parts that it becomes its own interpreter, can afford to forego much that is popularly known as theological learning. We do not undervalue a broad culture. Thought is the force of forcers, Thinkers rule the world. But culture can never supply the place of the Holy Spirit. The word that cuts deepest is sharpened by the Holy Ghost. No man, however talented or otherwise gifted he may be, can hope for success in this most holy calling without placing himself under the pupilage of the Spirit of God. Nor does he graduate from this until the silver cord is loosened and the golden bowl is broken."

Professor Goldwin Smith says:—"The study of the classics is I fear an exhausted theme. There is really not very much to be added to what Milton said two hundred and fifty years ago: "Those who did not read for Honors, the pass men, as they were called at Oxford, the poll men, as they were called at Cambridge, got nothing but a miserable smattering of Greek and Latin, which could not possibly have had any value either by way of knowledge or by way of training, and which they lost as soon as their backs were turned on the university. The time of many, perhaps of most of them was worse than wasted, since they contracted not only habits of idleness and expenditure, but distaste for reading."

A Summer Holiday on the Mediterranean of the Province of Quebec.

A FEW years ago the Baie des Chaleurs was a *terra incognita*—the *Ultima Thule* of Canada, so little was this part of Canada known to the majority of readers. It is nearly 1,000 miles from Toronto, and 500 miles below Quebec. Point Maquereau on the Quebec side, and the island of Miscou—distant about fifteen miles, on the New Brunswick side, form the entrance to the beautiful Bay of Chaleurs, now designated the Mediterranean of the Province of Quebec. It is 90 miles long, and from 10 to 21 miles wide. It has no shoals, reefs, or other impediments to navigation on the Quebec side. It has, usually, a clear, bracing atmosphere, seldom visited by fog, and is celebrated as one of the greatest fishing stations on the American coast.

The placid waters of this bay are, perhaps, less ruffled by the storm than any bay on the sea coast of America which is owing to the islands of Newfoundland, Cape Breton, St. Paul, Prince Edward, and Magdalene, stretching across the mouth of the Gulf of St. Lawrence, forming a great natural breakwater which resists the swelling surges of the Atlantic waves, making it an inland sea, and the Mediterranean of Canada. Here it was the great French navigator, Jacques Cartier, in 1535, first landed and gave to it the name which it bears, Baie des Chaleurs, "Bay of Heat." Its ancient Indian name "Ecketuam Nemaacke," signifying a " Sea of Fish," well denotes its character. It abounds with every variety of fish known on the coast of British North America.

I left Toronto in July. After visiting a few friends at Montreal and Quebec, I pushed on over the Intercolonial Railroad for Dalhousie, at the head of the Bay of Chaleurs, on the New Brunswick side,' at the mouth of the River Restigouche, a place noted for its salmon fishery, and fast becoming a fashionable watering place. The run from Dalhousie to Port Daniel, the place of my destination, is eighty miles. The steamer called at a number of stopping places. The records of the old Roman Catholic Church of Carlton stretch back into the past for over two hundred years. Here some of the Acadians found shelter, who were expatriated from Nova Scotia by the British Government. The coast line is glorious —here rugged and frowning cliffs and crags, and fretted rocks, and fantastic fringes, and festoons of sea-weeds— there, smiling fields sloping to the pebbly, sandy beach, or little woody thickets skirting the sea. The valleys decked with verdure, and clothed with ripening grain, picturesque and romantic enough for the admiration of the most ardent lover of nature. The whole shore is indescribably beautiful. The Bay of Port Daniel is very beautiful. Here the scenery is grand, diversified with green fertile valleys, craggy cliffs and hills. There are glens sloping down to the sea, and each has a beauty of its own, from many points there are exquisite little sea pictures. The charm of a summer day with the bright invigorating air of these shores is something inexpressible. The lofty headland, called Port Daniel Mountain, is a mass of limestone. At its base nature sleeps in her primeval state, giving back the roar of the ocean that is eternally echoing in its wave-worn caves—whose silence is distinguished only by the solemn thunder of the great ocean waves, or occasionally by the fisherman's song. The brow of the mountain is well wooded and partly cultivated. It commands an extensive prospect over sea and shore, and a splendid and varied panorama of the beautiful Bay of Port Daniel meets the eye. From here there is a large export of limestone to Prince Edward Island. In the limestone there is a vein of sulphate of barytes, nine inches in breadth, containing small portions of copper pyrites, and of green carbonate of copper. At Malbay fossil plants have been met with, and a small seam of coal, with carbonaceous shale, measuring together three inches. Petroleum has been discovered at Douglastown, Silver Brook, and other places. At Gaspé's Basin, two wells were sunk, but oil was not found in sufficient quantity to pay the working. All sorts of excellent building stone is found, in the conglomerates we found green jasper and agates. More than thirty years ago, I took a geological ramble along the coast, the result of my observations on that occasion was published in the Quebec *Chronicle*.

The distance from Port Daniel to New Carlisle in the township of Cox, is thirty miles. Everywhere lovely scenery. Carlisle, which is the county town, was first settled by American loyalists, and some of the disbanded Newfoundland regiment. The township is called after Lieutenant-Governor Cox, Major of the 47th Regiment. He was appointed Governor of the district of Gaspé in 1774. At Hopetown the first settlers were Scotch, some of them very highly connected. At Port Daniel, Shagawake and L'Auxce Gascon, French, Jersey, English, Irish and Scotch. I resided here five years, got four churches built and a parsonage. I also procured burial grounds with a glebe of 34 acres. Got the Government to establish post-offices, and open colonization roads, etc.

At Paspebiac (its Indian name), which means "Point of Rest," is a beautiful curved beach, about three miles in length, forming a breakwater during easterly gales against the "stirring of the ocean old." Indeed the whole Bay of Chaleurs may be said to be one great harbor full of coves and beaches where vessels may ride at anchor. Paspebiac is the seat of two of the largest mercantile establishments engaged in the fish business of Canada. Here is situated the well-known firm of Charles Robin & Co., of St. Heliers, island of Jersey, which was first started in 1768. The business has been conducted in the same systematic manner as the large houses in Newfoundland in the olden times. They have branch establishments at various places along the coast. They used to export from 40,000 to 50,000 quintals of dried codfish, of the value of $200,000 to $300,000, in their own vessels, to the markets of Spain, Portugal, Italy, Brazil, West Indies and Mediterranean ports, besides 30,000 gallons of oil, herring, salmon, etc.; and oats, potatoes, shingles, etc., to the West Indies. Here also was the large firm of Le Boutellier Bros., who had also branch establishments. They used to export 28,000 quintals of dried codfish. I was personally acquainted with all the members of the firm, some of whom resided in Jersey. New partners have been added to the firm of Charles Robin & Co., and Le Boutellier Bros. have failed; most of the partners are dead, but the concern is still carried on; most of the company reside in Quebec. The present manager is Mr. Fouvell, who is M.P. in the Dominion Parliament, and with whom I have some personal acquaintance. Last year they collected over 12,000 quintals of dried codfish. A number of small traders or merchants have taken away a good deal of the

L

business of the large houses. The Gaspé codfish is small compared with the Newfoundland codfish, and neither so firm nor so fat, and the reason of the Gaspé fish commanding a higher price in the foreign markets, is because it is taken and cured in smaller quantities, and less salted than the Newfoundland fish. Paspebiac is the depot for the goods the merchants import to supply their other establishments, and also for shipping the produce of the fisheries to the various markets. These establishments are well supplied with goods imported from England, Jersey, France, Italy, Germany and the United States—dry goods, provisions of every kind, groceries, wines, spirits, etc. Numbers leave the Bay of Chaleurs to prosecute the cod fishery on the north shore of the St. Lawrence; they usually leave on the first of June, and return by the last of August. The most common mode of employing fishermen by the merchants is by the draft. A fixed price is paid per draft for the fish as it comes from the knife of the splitter, the fisherman paying for his hooks, lines, provisions, etc. On the draft of 224 pounds weight, fourteen pounds over are allowed for offal, etc. Another way of engaging fishermen is to give them half their lines, that is, they get half the fish they catch when cured, out of which they pay for their provisions. Some also fish on wages, the owner of the boat bearing the loss or gain. The fishing period is divided into two seasons, summer and autumn. The summer fishery finishes the 15th of August. The fall fish is either dry-salted or pickled in flour barrels, the greater part of which is sent to the Quebec and Montreal markets. The quantity of fish taken annually within the Bay of Chaleurs, which includes the whole of the county of Bonaventure, and part of the county of Gaspé, is as follows:—

    Dry Codfish .... 295,653 quintals.
    Herring .... 109,691 barrels.
    Mackerel.................... 9,687 barrels.
    Salmon..................... 1,131 barrels.

Halibut...................200 quintals.
Other kinds of fish..........20,000 quintals.
Cod Oil....................98,000 gallons.
Lobsters, canned ....517,783 pounds.

The lobsters are sold to the lobster canneries. The live lobster is sold at 50 cents per cwt. A fisherman will take 500 lbs. per day. The total value of the Gulf fisheries may be fairly estimated at $1,000,000 per annum. These fisheries extend along a line of coast of over 900 miles. The number of seals taken in nets on the north shore of the Gulf of St. Lawrence annually, is from 2,000 to 3,000; shot with guns by white men and Indians, 2,000; number taken by schooners on the north shore of the St. Lawrence, 13,195; number of seals taken by Magdalen Island schooners, 9,194.

The first fish that makes its appearance in the Bay of Chaleurs is the "spring herring." Besides what are salted and packed in barrels, great numbers are laid over the ground as manure. The beaches are sometimes covered with herring spawn more than two feet thick, which is frequently mixed with kelp and used as manure. After the herring comes the codfish, when all who can, leave their farms to engage in this fishery. The capelin school usually appears in June, sometimes in May. They are found along the shores of the Gulf of St. Lawrence, none are found west of the Gulf. They are not found even along the gulf shores of Nova Scotia. Millions of them are taken and laid over the ground as manure. Some are also put in barrels, pickled and dried for eating. They are also used as bait for catching the codfish. Other bait used is herring, mackerel, squid, smelt, lance and clams. The New Brunswick side of the bay abounds in oysters, large quantities are shipped to the Quebec and Montreal markets. The first salmon is taken about the middle of May, the largest of them weighing from twenty to forty pounds. The Princess Louise caught one in the Matepedia weighing thirty-four pounds, which she sent to her mother, the Queen. Gaspé consists of two countries—Gaspé and Bonaventure—each sending a member to the Local Legislature of Quebec, and each sending a member to the Dominion House of Commons at Ottawa. The following is the number belonging to each religious denomination in the Bay of Chaleurs:

County of Bonaventure.
Roman Catholics... 14,240
Church of England. 2,746
Presbyterian....... 2,870
Methodists........ 147
Other Sects....... 58

County of Gaspé.
Roman Catholic..... 17,760
Church of England.. 2,667
Presbyterian....... 57
Methodists........ 389
Other Sects....... 37

Clergymen.
Roman Catholic....... 22
Church of England..... 8
Presbyterians......... 3
Methodists........... 2

Places of Worship.
Roman Catholic....... 26
Church of England..... 13
Presbyterians......... 4
Methodists........... 2

There are 105 Roman Catholic schools and 35 Protestant. The school fund comes from three sources: the taxes, the monthly fees, and the Government grant. The inhabitants pay five cents a head in the County of Gaspé, and 69 cents in the County of Bonaventure. The Roman Catholic clergy receive tithes, which consists of the twenty-sixth part of all grain, and also potatoes in some places. The Roman Catholic church is the most conspicuous object which meets the eye everywhere.

At the head of the Bay of Chaleurs, at Mission Point, which is on the River Restigouche, there is an Indian settlement of 500 Micmacs, who profess the Roman Catholic religion. They have a church, and a priest is stationed among them who speaks their language. Here there is an Indian reserve. Some of them have cultivated the land [to some extent. Peter Basket, their great chief, visited England in 1850, and was presented to the Queen and Prince Albert, from whom he received several valuable presents. The whole population of the Gulf of St. Lawrence is estimated at 80,000 persons. The Roman Catholics are Canadian French, Acadian French, Irish and Indians. The French cling to the old *patois*, the old faith and the old habits. The Protestants are Jerseymen; English, Irish, Scotch, and their descendants, with descendants of American Loyalists. The soil produces good crops of wheat, oats, barley, potatoes, turnips, hay, etc. Farming and fishing are followed together, those, however, who follow farming exclusively, are the best off. Sea-weed and fish offal are extensively used as manure. In many respects there is a similarity in the mode of conducting business in the Bay of Chaleurs and Newfoundland in the olden times, such as the extent of the fisheries the way of carrying them on, the export of dry codfish to foreign countries, absentee merchants, the principals residing in Jersey, and their business carried on through agents, who have great influence over the inhabitants; the extent of the establishments, composing wharves, stores, shops, cooper and carpenter's shops, sail loft, rigging loft, blacksmith's forge, cookrooms, etc., the whole appearing like a hamlet. Like as in Newfoundland, these establishments are called "rooms" by the inhabitants. When I took up my quarters at the "Big House," as the agent's residence is called, I imagined myself once more revelling at one of the old rooms in Newfoundland, there is the agent presiding at the head of the table surrounded by eight or ten clerks, four or five captains, and the guests, indulging in all the luxuries of life, while the big jug of home-brewed, good spruce beer circulated. How it reminded me of the glorious old days of Newfoundland. It resembles Newfoundland, too, in its isolation, and the absence of railroads. In 1886 a company was chartered to build a railroad, 100 miles, from Matapedia to Paspebiac, in the Bay or Chaleurs, but owing to some difficulties, only a part of the road has, as yet, been constructed.

Bonaventure River abounds with salmon and trout.

It is the resort in spring of immense shoals of smelt, which enter it to spawn, thousands of barrels are taken for manuring the land. The inhabitants drive their carts to the water's edge and there load by scooping the fish from the sea with a dip net. The Earl of Derby had a summer residence near New Richmond on the Bay of Chaleurs, where he spent a few weeks on a fishing excursion. In 1892 the Governor-General with Lady Derby with suit, were on a fishing excursion there. His Royal Highness, Prince George of Wales, in command of H.M.S. *Thrush*, was the guest of the vice-regal party there. The Restigouche, the Nouvelle, the Grand Caspediac, the Little Caspediac, the Bonaventure and other rivers, all abounding with fish, the angler finds hundreds of salmon in the pools of these rivers. There are club-houses along the Restigouche and Matapedia Rivers, which are inhabited during the fishing season, by the wives, daughters and friends of the club-men from all parts of the United States. I spent some time with Mr. Bond, who with his family came here from Savannah, Georgia. They sometimes remove from the club-houses and camp out, taking their boats, canoes, etc., with them. When it rains all remain in the house, when reading, dancing, games theatricals and other diversions are resorted to. A considerable portion of the wild territory along the Restigouche and Matapedia rivers, which is the best hunting and fishing grounds in the Province of Quebec, is either owned or held under lease by Americans, as the Restigouche Salmon Club, nearly all of whom are New York millionaires. The largest catch of salmon made by the club in any season is said to be 811 fish weighing 14,283 pounds. Some years ago, the Hon. Dr. Rabitelle, ex-Governor of Quebec, built a fine residence between Paspebiac and Carlisle, where he now resides with his family during the summer months. Being an old acquaintance of thirty years standing, I called to see him, discussed the signs of times, etc.

One of the most charming drives of Canada is along the lake shore of Ontario, from Port Hope to Toronto, but not half so romantic and picturesque as the Quebec side of the Bay of Chaleurs. It is one of the most delightful parts of Canada for a summer tour. I know of no place so beautiful except the Annapolis Valley and the Basin of Mines, in Nova Scotia. There are two lines of steamers, one running from Quebec to Gaspé Basin, thence to New Brunswick and Nova Scotia: the other from Gaspé Basin touching at all the ports along the Quebec side of the Bay of Chaleurs to Dalhousie, thus affording every facility to tourists. Here there is every attraction for the fowler, angler, hunter, and those seeking a healthy climate, sea air, sea bathing and boating. Here every man can stand at his door and see "life on the ocean wave"—see the flux and reflux of its tides, giving life to the various finny tribes that gambol and frolic in their ocean home—see the ships that come and go—the numerous fishing craft, merchant ships and steamers with their revolving wings fretting the bosom of this beautiful bay. Here, too, we can revel in the luxuriance of nature, in her craggy mountains and ravines, her rich and beautiful plains, her flowing rivers and her forests, with their wilderness of foliage, or their variegated autumnal tints. Such is the Bay of Chaleurs—the Mediterranean of the Province of Quebec.

The Phocas of Terre Neuve.

THE seal fishery of Newfoundland has assumed a degree of importance far surpassing the most sanguine expectations of those who first embarked in the enterprise, and has now become one of the greatest sources of wealth to the country. In the commencement the seal fishery was prosecuted in large boats, which sailed for the ice about the middle of April, and as its importance began to be developed, schooners of from 30 to 50 tons were employed, which sailed on the 11th of March. In 1845 the number of sailing vessels employed was 350, from 60 to 150 tons, burden, manned by 12,000 men. The time spent on the voyage was from two to six weeks. The sailing vessels have now nearly all been superseded by steamers, from 300 to 600 tons, carrying from 150 to 280 men each. In 1892, 21 steamers, with a few sailing vessels, were engaged in the seal fishery. In 1880, one steamer brought in 8,000 young harps the first trip, and 18,000 old seals the second trip. The total value of both trips $132,000. Some of the steamers have brought in from 20,000 to 40,000 seals. Captain Blanford, of the steamer Neptune, with a crew of 255 men, killed 25,000 in one day, and in eight days had taken 42,250. Last year, the steamer Esquimaux, under command of Captain Phillips, was fitted out in Dundee, Scotland, leaving that port on the 7th February for St. John's, Newfoundland, from whence she sailed for the sealing ice on the 10th of March. After two weeks absence the steamer returned to St. John's, with 19,000 young seals, yielding about 190 tuns of oil. On the second trip greater success was met with, she brought in 3,700 young and 12,400 old seals, equal to 350 tuns of oil. The two trips producing 540 tuns of oil of the value of about $60,000. Naturalists describe no less than fifteen species of seals. The kind most plentiful and which pass along the coasts of Terra Neuve, or Newfoundland, with the field ice, are the harps or half-moon seals (*Phoca Greenlandica*), which is the technical or scientific name. About the last of the month of February these seals whelp, and in the northern seas deposit millions of their young on the glassy surface of the frozen deep, At this period they are covered with a coat of white fur, slightly tinged with yellow. I have seen these "white coats" lying six and eight on a pan of ice, resembling so many lambs enjoying the solar rays. They grow very rapidly and in about three weeks after their birth begin to cast their white coat. They are now easily captured, being killed by a stroke across the head with a bat, gaff or boathook. At this time they are in prime condition, the fat being in greater quantity, and containing purer oil than at a later period of their growth. It appears to be necessary to their existence that they should pass a considerable time in repose on the ice. During this state of helplessness we see the goodness of Providence in providing these amphibious creatures with a thick coat of fur, and superabundant supply of fat as a defence from the intense cold of the ice and the northern blasts. Sometimes numbers of them are found frozen in the ice. These "cats" are highly prized by the seal-hunters, as the skin when dressed make excellent caps for them to wear while engaged in this perilous and dangerous voyage.

When one year old these seals are called "bedlamers." The female is without the dark spots on the back, which form the harp or half moon, and the male does not show this mark until two years old. The voice of the seal resembles that of the dog, and when a vessel is in the midst of myriads of these creatures, their barking and howling sounds like that of so many dogs, literally driving away sleep during the night. The general appearance of the seal is not unlike that of the dog, whence some have called it sea-dog, sea-wolf, etc. These seals seldom bring forth more than one, and never more than two at a litter. They are said to live to a great age. Sometimes a stray one is caught in a net, reduced to a mere skeleton, very grey, with teeth all gone, which is attributed to old age. Buffon, the great French naturalist, says: "The time that intervenes between their birth and their full growth being many years, they, of course must live very long. I am of opinion that these animals live upward of a hundred years, for we know that cetaceous animals in general live longer than quadrupeds, and, as the seal fills up the chasm between the one and the other, it must participate of the nature of the former, and consequently live much longer than the latter."

The Newfoundland seals probably visit the Irish coast, A number of seals were killed on the west coast of Ireland in 1856, among them the old harp. Sir William Logan gives an account of the skeleton of this kind of seal having been found embedded in the clay around Montreal 40 feet deep, Seals frequent the river St. Lawrence.

The (*Phoca Christata*), or hooded seals, are so called from a piece of loose skin on the head, which can be inflated at pleasure. When menaced or attacked the hood is drawn over the face and eyes as a defence from injury, at which time the nostrils become distended, appearing like bladders. The female is not provided with a hood. An old dog-hood is a very formidable animal. The male and female are generally found together, and if the female happens to be killed first, the male becomes furious. Sometimes eight or ten men have been upwards of an hour in despatching one of them. I have known a half dozen handspikes to be broken by endeavoring to kill one of them. They frequently attack their assailants, and snap off the gaffs by which they are attacked as if they were cabbage stumps. When they inflate their hoods it is very difficult to kill them. Shot does not penetrate the hood. Unless the animal can be hit somewhere about the side of the head it is almost a hopeless case to attempt to kill him. They are very large, some of their pelts which I measured being from 14 to 18 feet in length. The young hoods are called "blue backs." Their fat is not so thick nor so pure as that of the harps, but their skins are of more value. They also breed further to the north than the harps and are generally found in great numbers on the outer edge of the ice. They are said not to be so plentiful and to cast their young a week or two later than the harps.

The harbor seal (*Phoca Vitulina*) frequent the harbors of Newfoundland summer and winter. Numbers are taken during the winter and spring in seal nets. The Square Flipper, which is perhaps the great seal of Greenland (*Phoca Barbata*), is now seldom seen. The walrus (*Trichecus Rosmaaus*), sometimes called sea-horse, sea-cow and the morse, is now seldom met with, formerly this species of seal was frequently captured on the ice. This animal resembled the seal in its body and limbs, though different in the form of its head, which is armed with two tusks, sometimes 24 inches long, consisting of coarse ivory, in this respect much like an elephant. The under jaw is not provided with any cutting or canine teeth, and is compressed to afford room for the tusks, projecting downward from the upper jaw. It is a very large animal, sometimes measuring 20 feet long, and weighing from 500 to 1,000 pounds. Its skin is said to be an inch thick and covered with short yellowish brown hairs.

In some years 150,000 seals have been taken to the shore by persons who had walked on the ice from one to three miles from the shore in some of the northern bays of the island. Some years ago the ice was packed and jammed so tight in some of the bays for several weeks that the seals on it could find no opening to go down to the water, when numbers of them crawled upon an island. Some people happened to land upon the island and discovered them. One thousand five hundred seals were slaughtered among the bushes. Seals have been known to crawl several miles over land to reach the water. The maternal instinct of the female seal is very strong. The young seals are cradled on the ice. The mother remains in the neighborhood, going off in the mornings to fish and returning at intervals to nurse and suckle them. The old seals manage to keep holes in the ice, and to prevent them from freezing over so that they may reach the water. On returning from hunting fish she manages to find the hole by which she went down, although the ice during her absence may have moved ten or twenty miles, and to pick out her own cub from thousands around her. The number of seals taken yearly on the coast of Newfoundland is from 400,000 to over 600,000, producing commercially, no less a sum than $1,500,000. The seals are sold by weight. The young are sold at from $4 to $6, and the old from $4 to $5 per cwt. The price, however, is regulated by the value of the oil in the British market. A young seal will weigh from 30 to 60 pounds, and an old seal from 80 to 200 pounds. It is calculated that the fat of 80 young harp seals will produce a tun of oil. What is called the seal is the skin with the fat or blubber attached, the carcase being left on the ice where it is killed. The flesh of the seal is frequently eaten, the heart and kidneys are like the pigs and taste like them. In the olden times some of the fishermen used to have seal flesh salted in barrels, and it constituted their principal meat for the year. The seal fishery is a constant scene of bloodshed and slaughter. Here you behold a heap of seals writhing and crimsoning the ice with their blood, rolling from side to side in dying agony. There you see another lot, while the last spark of life is not yet extinguished, being stripped of their skins and fat, their writhings and heavings making the unpractised hand shrink with horror to touch them.

The first thing which occurs in Newfoundland to break the winter's torpor is the bustle and activity attending the outfitting of vessels for the seal fishery. During the first week in March persons are seen coming in from the surrounding settlements, some by land with their bats, sealing guns, and bundles of clothing over their shoulders, others coming in skiffs, loaded with boxes, bags of clothes, guns and gaffs. From the 1st to the 10th of March the streets used to be crowded with groups of hardy sealhunters. Some were employed bending sails and fixing the rigging of the vessel, some dressing oars and preparing the sealing punts, others collecting stones for ballast, filling the water casks and cleaving firewood, while others were engaged cooking pork and duff, and others putting on board the provisions necessary for the voyage. The shouting, whistling, laughter, cracking of jokes and clatter of tongues presented a scene of babel. And then the return of the seal-hunter. The merchant climbs the distant hill or paces his wharf, with spy-glass in hand, sweeping ever and anon the distant horizon for the first view of his returning argosy. The women standing at their doors watching for their schooner's return. So familiar were they with the hull and rigging of the vessel they could tell what schooner was coming miles distant, and when she entered the harbor with flags flying and guns firing what a time of hilarity and rejoicing when the crew step ashore and find all well. The return of the seal hunter reminds one of Southey's beautiful poems, "Madoc," and "Roderic, the last of the Goths."

> * * * "This man shakes
> His comrade's hand, and bids him welcome home,
> And blesses God, and then he weeps aloud;
> Here stands another, who, in secret prayer,
> Calls on the Virgin and his patron Saint,
> Renewing his old vows, and gifts and alms,
> And pilgrimage, so he may find all well."

The seal fishery being prosecuted during the vernal equinox is rendered particularly dangerous. It is a voyage of hopes and fears, trials and disappointments, and the prosecution of it causes more anxiety, excitement and solitude than any other business in the island. Sometimes the seals are sought after at a distance of from two to four miles from the vessel, over huge masses of ice, and during this toilsome journey the men have to jump from one pan of ice to another, across horrid chasms, where yawns the dark blue water ready to engulf them. Sometimes "slob," or ice ground up by the action of the waves, and covered with snow, is mistaken for hard ice, and the poor sealers leaping upon it are at once buried in the ocean. Not unfrequently, when the sealers are at a distance from the vessel in search of their prey, a freezing snowdrift or a thick fog comes on, when no object around can be descried, and the distant ship is lost. The bewildered sealers gather together. They try one course, then another, but in vain, no vessel appears. The lights shown from the vessel cannot be seen, the guns fired and the horns blown cannot be heard. Night comes on, and the wretched sealers perish through fatigue, cold and hunger on the glittering surface of the frozen deep. Scarcely a fishing season passes but the widow's veil and the orphan's cry tell of the dreary, the dreadful death of the seal hunters. Sometimes vessels are crushed between large masses of ice called "rollers," when all on board are consigned to one common destruction. The islands of ice or icebergs are dreadful engines of destruction. Some of the iron-bound ships sometimes come in contact with them, when vessel and crew perish together.

> " Ill fares the bark, with trembling wretches charg'd,
> That, toss 'mid the floating fragments, moors
> Beneath the shelter of an ice isle,
> While night o'erwhelms the sea, and horror looks
> More horrible. Can human force endure
> Th' assembled mischiefs that besiege them round?
> Heart-gnawing hunger, fainting weariness,
> The roar of wind and waves, the crush of ice,
> Now ceasing, now renew'd with louder rage,
> And in dire echoes bellowing round the main."

Feeling a great desire to gratify a youthful curiosity, in 1832 I went on board one of my father's vessels going to the seal fishery, and hid in the state-room until the vessel got in the offing, and then appeared on deck. I was then a youth of seventeen, and wanted to see the *modus operandi* of the seal fishing. It was my first and last voyage to the Phocas. During that voyage we met with one of the most terrific hurricanes ever known in the prosecution of the seal fishery. In that storm fourteen schooners were lost, with all their crews—not a vestige of them was ever seen or heard of from that day to this. Over three hundred persons perished. The Newfoundland seal is different from the Behring sea seal. The Newfoundland seal is what is called the hair or bearded seal. They are sought after for the value of their fat instead of their fur. The Newfoundland seal skins are worth not more than 50 or 60 cents apiece, whereas the fur seal skin when dressed is worth $60 apiece in first hands. All the Newfoundland seals are whelped on the ice, and not on the land as the fur seal.

THE WHALE FISHERY.

The whale fishery was carried on by the Americans in Hermitage Bay, Bay of Despair, and Fortune Bay, during the years 1796, 1797, 1798, and 1799. During the three first years twelve vessels were employed by them, manned by fifteen men each; all these vessels returned nearly loaded. They carried on the whale fishery in this part of the country until about the year 1807, when it was discontinued, owing to some dispute arising between Great Britain and the United States. Three years after this a schooner was fitted out by the Americans, and arrived at Burin, but on account of a man-of-war being stationed there, the schooner proceeded to St. Mary's Bay, where she remained until the month of August, and had nearly completed her load when she was taken by a British sloop-of-war, and ordered to St. John's ; but the crew being too strong for the prize-master, the schooner shaped her course for America. and arrived in safety at Cape Cod.

With this ended the American whale fishery on the western shores of Newfoundland. A whale fishery commenced in Hermitage Bay, but only continued four years. In 1840 an act was passed by the Local Government, offering $800 bounty to each of the first three vessels landing not less than ten tuns of whale oil, between the first day of May and the tenth day of November. Encouraged by the bounty afforded by the passing of this act, two vessels were sent from St. John's to the western shore of the island, of about 120 tuns each, manned by nineteen men each. In 1841, twenty-five whales were captured, producing $37\frac{1}{2}$ tuns of oil. In 1842, eight whales, producing 14 tuns of oil. In 1843, five whales, producing $8\frac{1}{2}$ tuns, and in 1844, six whales, producing 13 tuns of oil. During the above years 40 or 50 whales were taken about Fortune Bay. The greatest quantity of whale oil manufactured in Newfoundland in any one year was 150 tuns. In 1866, a vessel was sent from Newfoundland to the Greenland whale fishery. She returned in September with 50 tuns of oil. The whale fishery on the Newfoundland coast is not important. The whale tribe, though called fishes, are true *mammalia*, producing from one to two cubs at a time, which are suckled in the same manner as land animals. The kind appearing on the Newfoundland coast, is the sharp-nosed whale (*Balæna Acuto Rostra.*) Pike-headed species (*Balæna Boops.*) The kind most plentiful is the fin-backed whale (*Balænoptera Jabartes*), which live on capelin, lance, etc. Fifty of these are sometimes seen spouting at one time. On those occasions fishing boats, lying at anchor on the fishing grounds, have been injured by them. The usual remedy for driving them away is to throw overboard a few buckets of bilge water. The great Greenland whale (*Balæna Mysticetas*) is occasionally seen on the coast. Probably the whole tribe of whales frequenting the Greenland seas sometimes visit the Newfoundland coast. There are a number of porpoise, from which a quantity of oil could be obtained, but this kind of fishery has not been developed.

The Hudson's Bay Company carried on porpoise fishing for a number of years; 7,749 porpoise were taken. giving an aggregate of 193,869 gallons, or 768½ tuns of oil, worth $140,000.

Extempore Listening.

DID you ever think of the value and power of sermons upon extempore *listening?* There can be no doubt that the listening of the present day is largely extemporaneous. Listening, in order to be worth much, needs preparing for, as much as speaking; there are a great many persons who listen extempore, who never think upon the subject upon which they expect the preacher to speak. A great deal has been written and said about *how* to preach. In the days of Christ and his apostles *what* to preach seemed to be of vast importance. How to listen, what preparation of mind and heart is needful, what appreciation of the truth—these are more important questions than extempore or written preaching. "Take heed how ye hear," is a divine injunction. When the sower went forth to sow, he was as faithful to one kind of soil as to another. The soil needs preparation as much as the sower and the seed. The spiritual poverty of a congregation is a fruitful source of extempore hearing. Mind acts on mind. The preaching may be spiritual and searching, but the moral sensibilities of extempore hearers, have been benumbed by their worldlings. They are too insensible to divine things to discern the value of the ministrations they enjoy. They don t like the minister; perhaps he himself may be thoroughly convinced that there is need of some change in his make up. But how to bring it about is the question. He must

M

not speak too long, nor too low, nor too loud—there must not be either wearying verbosity or flustering noise. It must be confessed that sermons are sometimes too long, making all the hearers sin against the grace of patience, and so make extempore listeners. The time has passed when the remark should be made of a preacher, "he's a regular ear-splitter," very seldom is an ear-splitter, a heart opener. Some extempore hearers come to church lingering and late, as if it were a drudgery to come to church at all. Some seek the most comfortable place in pews studiously accomodated for repose, and in the very eyes of the preacher, take their leave of him in the total unconsciousness of deep sleep. Some examine with curious eyes every visible object but the speaker, and show vast interest in the dress of every new comer.

If anything should remove a minister of a certain stamp, they would at once leave the church, and go in search of another minister who might suit them; even then their presence at divine service cannot be counted on, for if some advertised preacher, male or female, come to a hall in their vicinity, they must be there to taste the new wine, as though it must be better than the old. There is divine service in the church on week days, but they can seldom find time for it, though they can go a mile to hear a sensational and unspiritual lecture by a self-appointed teacher. Some extempore hearers think that the differences between churches are purely' speculative and theoretical, and do not involve questions of principle—that it matters little or nothing whether one follows a spiritual or a mere formal worship, whether he submits to Episcopacy or to Presbytery, and so he considers it of no consequence whether he trains his children under one class of views or the opposite. The father or mother may be nominally of the Church of England, but the family, as such, is Godless, knows no religion. They are ready to go in one direction as another. They are wholly unsettled and adrift, "tossed to and fro with every wind of doctrine," and finally land where association or mere taste or convenience may lead them. They wander into different sects. The church is in want of funds for necessary expenses or for missions at home or abroad, the extempore hearers will give but a trifle to regular work and a large sum on exceptional effort under individual control, for the future conduct and issue of which there is no security whatever. Extempore hearers say, preach the gospel and let money alone. But the preaching of the gospel has a great deal to do with money. It is as necessary to give as it is to pray. Our Saviour said to the young man in the gospel who kept all the commandments from his youth up. " One thing thou lackest, sell all thou hast and give to the poor." " Many of the wisest and best of men are of opinion that there is no sin so prevalent among professors of the Gospel as the *love of money*. It will, in all probability, prove the eternal overthrow of more characters among professing people than any other sin, because it is almost the only crime which can be indulged, and a profession of religion at the same time supported." On the fact of our stewardship: Deny it, forget it, disregard it though we may, it is still forever true that we are not owners but stewards of all we possess. On our time, talents, influence, property, on all that we have and are—the finger of God hath written " Occupy till I come." If they were not extempore listeners, less would be spent on self, and fashion, and appetite, and the world in its many forms. It is a melancholy fact that many of our churches must have a tea meeting, bazaar, or concert to raise funds, not because it would do good, but because the extempore hearers would not give a cent *directly*. They must have *quid pro quo* for their money.

Our Mother's Chair.

*Lines in Memory of Mrs. Eliza T. Tocque, by her Daughter
Annie S. W. Tocque.*

We have within our home,
   A sacred vacant chair.
One little year ago, we looked
   On mother sitting there.

A mother more than words
   Or pen can tell was once
Calling then ; scattering in our path
   The fairest fragrant flowers.

This chair we cherish now,
   And by its side oft pray,
And think of all the tenderness
   Which from it passed away.

O precious empty chair,
   We weep that 'tis unfilled
With one so learned in love's pure love,
   In sympathy well skilled.

Ah ! 'tis no common love,
   Bestowed on Mother's chair,
'Twas there she whispered her last words,
   And left us to God's care.

Twas there she calmly went
   Away to rest on high
Just as the sun in glory sank
   Down in the western sky.

We linger 'round it oft,
   When suffering grief or pain,
It seems when there we call for her,
   And never call in vain.

For in the bygone days,
   She always called us near
When sorrow came and trouble brought
   No wonderment and fear.

And by this chair our hearts'
　　Last pain and sighs would cease,
　　Her cheerful words—caress or kiss,
　　Were messengers of peace.

In this dear chair she passed
　　Through trial, years most keen,
　　And learned to know and sweetly trust
　　The Comforter unseen.

Then may we not believe
　　It once had heavenly care,
　　And that Our Lord Himself has s'ood
　　Sometimes by mother's chair.

Preachers and Preaching.

THE greatest theologians and preachers in the early ages of the Church, among the Greek and Latin fathers, were St. Augustine and St. Chrysostom, called the "golden mouthed," because of his beautiful illustrations. St. Augustine was Bishop of Hippo, in the fourth century, who is the pride of the Universal Church. The Protestant vies with Roman Catholics in paying him honor. He was a preacher of the highest order, and is said to be the source of much of the flavor of the early Puritans. The whole of the Reformers were followers of St. Augustine on the subject of Predestinarianism. Any moderate Calvanist would be content with the statements of the seventeenth article of the Church of England on this subject. Men like Ambrose, Bishop of Milan, Augustine, and Chrosostom, built up a Colossal fabric of scriptural knowledge. Some centuries after these great men, came Wyckliffe, called the "morning star" of the Reformation, next came Luther Melancthon and Calven, then came Knox, Cranmer, Ridley, Latimer, Hooper, Rogers, and others. Then came the great preachers and theologians of the sixteenth and seventeenth centuries, such as South, Barrow, and Owen. Of Barrow, it has been said "he wrote divinity like a philosopher, and philosophy like a divine." The great Jeremy Taylor, is said to be "A Bernard and St. Chrysostom combined, the honey of the one and the gold of the other." He has been styled the "Shakespeare of theology." There were the great French preachers, Bossuet, Massillon, and Bourdaloue, Bishop Warburton says, "Burdaloue, though a member of the worst Society, the Jesuits, produced the best sermons which ever were written."

Among Roman Catholic divines we have Fenelon, Pascal, Bourdaloue, Massillon, Bossuet. Among Protestants, Saurin, Claude, Daille, Superville. The sermons of Massillon and Bourdaloue are finished, and masterly specimens of pulpit oratory. The funeral orations of Bossuet are the highest and finest specimens of French pulpit oratory. Indeed, they are unsurpassed. They are perhaps unequalled by any human compositions. It is related of Robert Hall that after reading the funeral orations on Henrietta Maria, Queen of England, and daughter of Henry IV. of France, and on Louis of Bourbon, Prince of Conde, "I never expect to hear language like this till I hear it from the lips of seraphs round the throne of God."

If we were to single out the men who had done most to extend the Kingdom of Christ, for the last two centuries, we should name John Wesley, the saintly Fletcher, later on Dr. Coke and Joseph Benson, grandfather of the present Archbishop of Canterbury. Here I make a little digression to say, that some years ago, I visited Newburyport, Mass., U. S., where I saw the remains of the "Prince of Preachers," Whitefield. They are deposited beneath the floor of the first Presbyterian Church. I cannot describe my feelings, as I lifted the skull and some of the bones as they lay in the coffin of this eminent man. I visited the house where Mr. Whitefield resided, and sat in the chair in which he died of asthma, Sept. 30th, 1770.

These were all highly educated men. It is a significant fact, that the individuals who have most profoundly influenced the Christian Church at the great epochs of her career were educated men—men who had received such a mental culture and discipline of their faculties as the circumstances of their time permitted. Preaching has been regarded as an ordinance of divine appointment, and of the highest dignity by the most eminent divines. Hooker saith, "sermons are the keys of the Kingdom of Heaven, wings to the diseased minds," and says Bishop Horne, " To preach practical sermons on virtues and vices without inculcating redemption and grace, which alone enable men to forsake sin and practice virtue, were to put together the wheels of a clock or watch, and set the watch, losing sight of the main spring." Cranmer saith, "The chief labor of a Christian should be to believe, and of a minister to *preach* Christ crucified." What Bishop Lavingston said in his day, is true now, " We have long been undertaking the reformation of the people, by moral preaching—with what success? None at all. Only we have dexterously preached the people into downright infidelity. We must change our voice, and preach Jesus Christ and Him crucified." It is asserted that there is a renaissance of theology in the present age, based upon the results of modern Biblical and Historical Criticism, and of modern philosophy and science. Ministers might have much scientific knowledge, and yet be inefficient for lack of theological knowledge. Astronomy has been called a beautiful science, but it pours no light into the midnight of the sinful soul; botany has been called a sweet science, but it gives out no balm for the wounded heart. In some quarters there is a tendency to depreciate preaching of the old-fashioned type. It is asserted that the preaching which in Apostolic times bore down all opposition and converted the Roman world,—the preaching which roused the Church from the sleep of ages, and brought about the Reformation of the sixteenth century, the preaching which prepared confessors and Martyrs for the persecution they endured, and sustained them on the scaffold and by the stake, the preaching which, in our own and other ages, has prompted so many to deeds of heroic and general self-denial, has become in this advanced and cultured age altogether absolute and effete. That the pulpit must discard many of the old doctrines and methods, and adapt itself to the æsthetic and intellectual requirements of the age, preaching more refined, and elevated in tone, preaching in which the old fashioned doctrine of the Cross is ignored. The preaching of St. Paul and his fellow Apostles "was to the Jews a stumbling block, and to the Greeks foolishness." It was found that the preaching of the Apostles met the necessities of that age. Human nature and human needs are essentially the same in every age, and among all orders of Society. The grand theme of Apostolic preaching was *Christ*. Their preaching proved to be the power of God, and the wisdom of God to every one who believed it. The preaching of the Apostles eighteen hundred years ago, proved itself a sovereign balm for the world's woe. *To-day the world needs Christ*, as it needed Him then. Let men preach Christ, and now, as in these olden times, their preaching will bring rest and peace, and courage and strength, and hope and joy to weary, restless, fearful hearts. I have heard some of the greatest preachers in my day. But there are divers kind of men in the ministry. There are those who go about seeking fat pastures for the Shepherd, who follow religion when in her "silver slippers," who speculate in something beside metaphysics, who show the people through their theological kaleidoscope, many short cuts to truth, which they parade as glorious discoveries; but when weighed in the balance are found wanting. Most professions get their share of men who fall below the standard of their calling. Speaking of the discarded pulpit, Bishop Coxe says : " Young preachers now run to a sort of music-stand, or read their inflated verbiage from the lectern. The lectern was not designed to hold the preachers' manuscripts, much less to bear the flimsy performances which are substituted for preaching in some places. Good honest pulpits may be abused as well; and one hears out of them occasionally a fustian preachment. It yet remains a mystery how a Church, which retains such a stimulating and inspiring liturgy, could have such drowsy preaching." Some of the preaching of to-day is finer, more scholarly and more brilliant than it ever was. Some of the men who occupy our pulpits, are the peers of intellect and education of any other class of men. The trouble is Christ it not the grand theme of their preaching. The emotion of the sermons is not equal to their information. The logic is good, the theology is sound. Yet it would appear that either the preacher had no heart, or he preached to hearers who had none. If there be one truth more than another which needs to be stamped upon the heart of every minister of Christ, it is, that the Holy Ghost is the Lord and giver of life, and that without His influences, no power of organization, no learning however profound, no eloquence however fervid, is ought else than sounding brass and tinkling cymbal. As Bishop Hall says : " There is not so much need of learning as of grace to apprehend those things which concern our everlasting peace. Neither is it our brain that must be set to work, but our heart." Bishop Jewell says, " As the scriptures are written by the Spirit, so must they be explained by the Spirit, for without the Spirit we have neither ears to hear, nor eyes to see." And Bishop Sanderson says : "It is a kind of simony to expect to make spiritual gifts by hard study, independently of the Holy Ghost." We want more preaching of the Holy Ghost type. If the efficacious power of the Holy Ghost was expedient for the Apostles in an increased degree, it is indispensable to ministers now. Here we have the key to open and explain one great cause of the unfruitfulness of the pulpit of the present day.

The Fur Seal.

I HAVE been asked if the Behring sea seal is like the Newfoundland seal. The Newfoundland seal is what is called the bearded or hair seal. They do not breed on the land as the fur seal, but whelp on the ice and seldom bring forth more than one, and never more than two at a litter. They are sought after, not for their skin, but for their fat and blubber, which, after being taken from the skin, is thrown into vats and rendered into oil by the heat of the sun. The skins are worth about fifty cents apiece, and when salted are packed in bundles and shipped to England, where they are manufactered into shoes, caps, etc., and dressed to imitate leopard skins. The number of these seals taken annually on the Newfoundland coast is estimated at 500,000, of the value of $1,700,000.

According to the returns, the total number of fur seals caught by British Columbia vessels in 1889 was 33,570, valued at $349,825, while 7,428 seals, valued at $74,280 caught by foreign vessels, were disposed of in Victoria, B. C.

There were 213 vessels and 1,520 men employed in the British Columbia seal fishery. The number of American sea bear of the northern country killed on Behring island is said to be 500,000. The raw skin of the fur seal, salted, is worth $25. The largest is about three by six feet. The very finest seal skins do not come from Alaska, but from South Shetlands and other islands in the

Sealing Steamer in the Ice taking on board Seals.

Antarctic ocean. They are worth $60 a skin in first hands. New York gets the bulk of the American skins, and from there they are shipped to London, and Leipsic in Germany. The fur seal pelts are shipped in salt. After the furs are made up the clippings are all sent to certain places and made into hats of various kinds; nothing is lost. Most of the seal skins sold in Canada come from Alaska, but only after being plucked, dressed and dyed in London. The beautiful velvets-like coats, which are so much valued, are the under fur of the *Otariæ*, which in untechnical language are described sometimes as eared seals and sometimes as sea bears. In addition, however, to their dense soft under fur, the eared seals have a quantity of long, loose exterior hair, which has to be carefully removed. Fancy furs bring fancy prices.

The finest skins of the sea otter, caught on the north Pacific shores, bring about $625 apiece and garments made from them have sold from $1,250 upwards. The common otter is a very different animal; the skin is only worth, at best, $6. These are some of the habits of the Alaska fur seals: From the middle of April to the middle of June the male seals resort to the breeding places and are followed by the females, who give birth to one pup each, after which the pairing season begins. The younger male seals are prevented from landing by the older, and have either to remain in the water or go to the uplands, where they are captured by the hunters. The adult males fight furiously, the aggregate sound of their roaring being compared to that of a railway train. During the pairing season, which lasts three or four months, the breeding males take no food and are often reduced to half their weight, which, when they are 8 years old and in full flesh, ranges from 500 to 700 pounds. The females are much smaller. They weigh from 80 to 100 pounds. No females and no adult males are supposed to be killed for their fur, the hunters taking only a portion of the young male seals, whose skins are of a superior quality.

Capt. Thomas Alcock, of Newfoundland, who has lately established himself in Vancouver, British Columbia, master of a sealing schooner, has returned to Vancouver from a voyage to Behring sea. When within a few miles of the shore his vessel was boarded by the officers of the United States revenue cutter Rush, and told of the agreement between her majesty's Government and the United States and that arrangements had been made to close the sea until the 1st of May, 1892. The steamer took the schooner in tow and towed her to St. Paul's island, 25 miles distant, where she was searched, and as no skins were found on board the schooner was allowed to go.

Capt. Alcock, writes: "Whilst lying there I saw what few men have ever seen or ever will see. From a northeast point of the island to a point in a westerly direction the shore forms a deep curve, almost a cove. For about three miles there is a fine sandy beach from 50 to 150 yards deep and reaching up to the grass above. On this beach was a sight worth seeing—food for a sealer to feast on. To attempt to give any estimate of the seals would be folly, old and young, male and female. Suffice it to say, I have seen a field of ice on the Newfoundland coast off which were taken 240,000 young hair seals, and at another time I saw 25,000 taken off about six acres, but they were not one-eighth so plentiful as the fur seals on and near St. Paul's island, whilst the water all around us was actually alive with seals. It is quite impossible to give anything like a correct number, for look where you would it was alive with seals. Up the hill sides, as far as the eye could see, they formed one moving mass. There is one thing, however, that will effect the seals, and that is the fearful state of the air; so many seals slaughtered and their dead bodies left to rot has so tainted the air that one can scarcely breathe. You can smell the stench for miles away from the island. There is no doubt the smell of the rotten seals does more injury to the seals than all the sealers that go to Behring sea. I took one long, last sorrowful look at the wealth on St. Paul's island, protected by nothing but an American cutter. But what about the protection the English Government was going to give her people? What about the big gun Lord Salisbury fired, the report of which came booming to British Columbia, and caused and encouraged the men of Victoria and Vancouver, the loyal subjects of B.C., to build and equip schooners to hunt in the waters of Behring ocean?"

The seal fishery of Newfoundland has been pursued for 300 years, with no diminution.

Church Union.

THE Catholic or Universal Church is all the persons in the universe who are "one body," united by "one spirit," having "one faith, one hope, one baptism, one God and Father of all, who is above all, and through all, and in them all." The Church of England in her Nineteenth Article tells us: "The visible Church of Christ is a congregation of faithful men, in the which the pure word of God is preached, and the sacraments be duly ministered according to Christ's ordinance in all those things that of necessity are requisite to the same." Nothing but the truth of God, carried home to the hearts of believing people by the Holy Spirit, ever can resist and overcome the divisions of Christendom.

We often overlook the great body of truth in which all Christians agree. The Church of Rome, mighty in numbers, strong in learning and thoroughly disciplined, which makes it a great power—this great colossal Church holds to the great cardinal truths of Christianity.

It is true that universal temporal supremacy is one of

the prerogatives the Church of Rome asserts for herself. Pius IX. said: " I acknowledge no civil power, I am the subject of no prince, I claim to be the supreme judge and director of the consciences of men. I am the sole last supreme judge of what is right and wrong. I am the successor of the Apostles and the vicar of Christ. I have the mission to conduct and direct the barque of St. Peter." Yet, notwithstanding these assumptions of the Church of Rome, Pope Pius IV. offered to recognize the reforms made in the English Church in the time of Queen Elizabeth.

For some years after the Reformation in England, under Elizabeth, there was no absolute separation from the Reformed Church; all communicated together as the members of one body, and there was no separate modes or forms of public worship. All used the Liturgy. The first separation took place in the eleventh year of the reign of Queen Elizabeth. All Protestants were united, and so continued until the twenty-first year of Elizabeth, when Brown, in the Diocese of Norwich, formed the first congregation which absolutely separated from the Church. Brown himself afterwards confessed his error.

The offer of Rome to recognize the reforms made in the English Church, on the one condition that the Bishop of Rome's supremacy should be recognized, is so old an affair, and so often adverted to and substantiated, that it is almost unnecessary to go over the ground again at this late day. But the following letter, from the pen of the Rev. Mr. Little, is so excellently to the point that we cannot refrain from giving it entire. Says he:

" I have received so many enquiries in regard to my assertion in Article XXIV. that the Bishop of Rome, Pius IV. 'agreed to recognize all the reforms under Elizabeth, if only she would recognize his supremacy,' that it seems best to turn aside from the general argument in order to give a few authorities for the statement.

" It is asserted in almost every history of the Anglican

Church that Pius IV. agreed to recognize the English Reformation, provided that his own supremacy should be acknowledged. This concession on his part is valuable, as showing that our Church had lost nothing which, even in the estimation of Rome, is essential to a true Church.

"Here, in his 'Eighteen Centuries of the Church of England' (page 348) says: 'Pope Paul IV., having died on August 18th, 1559, was succeeded by Pius IV. The new Pope sent his nuncio with a letter to the Queen, announcing his approval and willingness to accept the new Prayer Book, as well as the Communion in both kinds, if only the Queen would acknowledge his supremacy.'

"Jennings, in his excellent '*Ecclesia Anglicana*' (page 319) says: 'A new Pope, Pius IV., in 1560 addressed to her (Elizabeth) a letter of very different tenor, making overtures for a reconciliation. He offered that, on condition of her adhesion to the See of Rome, the Pope would approve of the Book of Common Prayer, including the Liturgy or Communion Service, and the Ordinal. Although his Holiness complained that many things were omitted from the Prayer Book which ought to be there, he admitted that the book nevertheless contained nothing contrary to truth, while it certainly comprehended all that is necessary for salvation. He was therefore prepared to authorize the book if the Queen would receive it from him and on his authority.'

"Blunt in his historical introduction to the Prayer Book (page 35) says: 'It is worth notice, however, that the Book of Common Prayer, as thus revised in 1558, was quietly accepted by the great body of Romanist laity; and also, that the Pope himself saw so little to object to in it that he offered to give the book his full sanction if his authority were recognized by the Queen and the kingdom.' And he quotes Sir Edward Coke as saying that the Pope, Pius IV., 'before the time of his excommunication against Queen Elizabeth denounced, sent his letter unto Her Majesty, in which he did allow the Bible and Book of Divine Service, as it is now used among us, to be authentic and not repugnant to truth. But that therein was contained enough necessary to salvation, though there was not in it so much as might conveniently be, and that he would also allow it unto us without changing any part, so as Her Majesty would acknowledge to receive it from the Pope, and by his allowance, which Her Majesty denying to do so, she was then presently by the same Pope excommunicated. And this is the truth concerning Pope Pius Quartus, as I have faith with God and men. I have oftentimes heard avowed by the late Queen her own words, and I have conferred with some Lords that were of greatest reckoning in the State, who had seen and read the letter which the Pope sent to that effect, as have been by me specified. And this upon my credit, as I am an honest man, is most true.' Blunt, moreover, gives a list of authorities, viz.: 'The Lord Coke, his speech and charge, London, 1607. See also Camden, Ann, Elizabeth, page 50, edition 1615. Twysden's Historical Vindications of the Church of England, page 175. Validity of the Orders of the Church of England, by Humphrey Prideaux, D.D.. 1688. Bramhall's works, ii., 85, edition, 1845. Bishop Babington's Notes on the Pentateuch; on numbers vii., Courayer's Defence of the Dissertation on the Validity of English Ordinations, ii., 360, 378. Harrington's Pius IV. and the Book of Common Prayer, 1856.'

"Our own Van Antwerp, in his very readable and comprehensive Church History, volume iii., pages 144-5, gives the same story. The reader will also find it in Hardwicke's Reformation, and in scores of other reliable works. I have never seen the story controverted or even questioned.

"Since writing the above, my attention has been called to an additional authority for the fact that Pius IV. made the above mentioned overtures for the reconciliation of the English Church, viz.: Butler in his Memoirs of the

Catholics, volume i., pages 152-3. The testimony is especially valuable, as coming from a learned Roman Catholic."

When you take the Bible and place it in the hands of any number of men selected from the different denominations into which Christendom is divided, you find that each one of these men will interpret it in accordance with the system of faith which he has adopted, or which prevails in his denomination. One makes it to sustain his Calvinism, another his Armenianism, another his Romanism, another his Unitarianism, another his Universalism, and another his Immersionism, etc. Shall we conclude that the Bible teaches all these different and opposing and conflicting systems of religion? That conclusion would at once destroy its authority as a divine revelation, for it is impossible that the God of truth can have revealed a multitude of discordant and clashing systems of faith as essential to salvation. George Whitfield said, "the Spirit of God had expressly taught him the doctrine of election." John Wesley declared that he " was called of God to publish to the world that Mr. Whitfield's doctrine of election was highly injurious to Christ." Both of these good men could not be right, and the probability is that both were mistaken, and that the Spirit of God had never given any other instruction to either than that which He has given to us all in the Scriptures. Good Christian men are misled in the mazes of endless divisions. One body will make me accept the "Westminster Confession," another requires me to profess my faith in the "Immaculate Conception." One makes me declare "I believe in my own assurance of salvation." another will have nothing to do with me unless I believe "baptize means dip." It is admitted that denominationalism is a man-made thing, but it exists, and we cannot cleanse the Church of schisms by ignoring their existence. The only way to purge the Church of schisms is to purify the various denominations of error, and this must be done by its members sifting their doctrines and practices, casting out the chaff and retaining the wheat. There are those who believe in the Bible, who accept the Church of Christ as the Church of God, who call themselves Christians, and yet make their own fallible reason the infallible interpreter of Holy Scripture. There is but one Church recognized in the Scripture, to which all bearing the Christian name belonged in the apostolic age. St. Paul writes to the Christian believers, " We are all baptized into *one body.*" He tells us in many passages of his epistles that "*the Church is the Body of Christ.*" The evil of divided Christianity is crowding home to the hearts of earnest, thoughtful men everywhere; people feel the crushing evil, they see the endless hair-splittings that originate new churches. Much has been said and written on the subject of Christian Union—not enough to accomplish it, but enough to show that the minds of Christians are open to the dangers of sectarian divisions, and that their hearts are longing for some closer and happier communion than is allowed by the present divided state of Christendom. The Church is the Body of Christ, to be filled with His dispositions and governed by His Spirit; it is the representative of Christ on earth; it is to receive and deal with men, precisely as the Lord Jesus Himself would do if He were on earth. On every side are brethren who might be one with us, but we are all separated by artificial walls—barriers of merely human construction, kept high and strong. There is a mighty bond of sympathy telegraphing through the sea of ages and linking us with the Apostolic Church—the family of faith. Those first bearers of the cross had every reason to expect a united Church. Christ had prayed that they might be one as He and the Father were one. Uniformity was not necessarily unity. The kingdom of nature teaches us that endless variety consists with perfect harmony, when all is obedience to positive law and order. Perhaps the strength of the apostolic unity lay in the division of labor. The Church had been organized as the human body, every member having its own functions. The head cannot say to the feet, I have no need of you. The principle is the same in the family, the State and the Church. The success of the Church of Rome has been the result in the main of the adoption of this principle. Every man in his place, and a place for every man. "All these working that one and the self-same spirit, dividing to every man severally as he will." The Kingdom of God and the Church of God are both one. The prophecy is there shall be but "one fold and one shepherd." Order and truth are the foundation of unity. But in discipline and forms of worship, diversity of operation was perfectly consistent with fidelity to the faith. In some manner the communion of saints must be realized. In attempting to bring the different denominations to conform to the Catholic Church, there must be compromise in comparatively unimportant particulars, but which are not really and indispensably important to the grand objects of the Church. There must be conformity by all upon those points which are generally held important to the character and constitution of the Church. Compromise in matters acknowledged by all to be relatively non-essential, conformity in matters received by each to be essential. Thus both liberty and law can be secured, and universality and unity together be effected. If the Roman, the Greek, the Armenian, the Lutheran, the Church of England, and all Protestant denominations were brought into one Church, what a glorious consummation. If all Christians were in a united Church, and all the clergymen of the various denominations were its ministers, we should have a full supply for home and abroad. If all the money which is paid by the different denominations in support of their preachers and institutions were collected into one sum, there would be enough for the liberal support of all the ministers of the united Church, and millions of dollars for the heathen. How shall the unity of the Church be restored? It is the Spirit of Christ within us must do it, springing from the love of God, or it will never be accomplished. "We pray for the good estate of the Catholic Church, that it may be so guided and governed by thy good Spirit, that all who profess and call themselves Christians may be led into the way of truth, and hold the faith, in the unity of spirit, in the bond of peace, and in righteousness of life."

There are two great difficulties to the union of the Church of England with the Church of Rome, to say nothing of doctrines; the Roman condemnation of Anglican orders as invalid, and clerical celibacy. Many years ago, in consideration of a large body of the Greek Church joining the Church of Rome, married priests of the Greek Church were received, and unmarried deacons were allowed to marry before being admitted to the priesthood, but not after. The Roman correspondent of the London *Globe* states that "Pope Leo XIII. is devoting considerable time daily to the study of the literature bearing upon the question of Anglican orders, and that the works of the principal authors who have written in their defence are being carefully examined by the officials of the holy office with a view to giving full consideration to the claims of the High Church party. The Pope is said to be disposed to abolish the law of compulsory celibacy for the secular clergy, confining the obligation of celibacy to members of religious orders who take vows of poverty, chastity and obedience."

The Archbishop of Canterbury says: "Any corporate union with the Church of Rome, while she retains her distinctive erroneous doctrines and advances her present unprimitive and unscriptural claims, is absolutely visionary and impossible."

Mr. Gladstone says: "An attempt of a handful of priests and ritualists to Romanize the Church and people of England is hopeless and visionary. At no time since the bloody reign of Mary has such a scheme been possible. But if it had been possible in the seventeenth and eighteenth centuries, it would still have been impossible in the nineteenth."

At a union public meeting, recently held in the opera house at Bay City, Michigan, representing all communions, several Roman Catholics spoke. At the opening the entire audience rose and united in saying the Lord's Prayer. Immediately after one of the Roman Catholic Clergymen acted as precentor in leading the singing of the hymn, "Nearer, My God, to Thee."

The New York *Herald* has gathered the views of prominent clergymen upon the possibility of a harmonious union of the Roman Catholic and Protestant faiths. Here are some of their views:

Satolli thinks it not only possible, but that it will surely be accomplished some day, but, of course, says that the church would require a complete submission of all others to the Pope.

Bishop Potter, of New York, however, says: "As is the case with most Christian people, I presume I am a friend to Christian unity. The absence of it as an organic fact is an immense evil, and the source of an enormous waste of men, means, and energy. But it will not come by conformity to any one communion, as several communions now exist, and to bring it to pass no communion will have to make larger sacrifices than that to which especially you refer—the Church of Rome. Happily, the influence of American ideas and institutions is daily producing in this direction a very interesting and hopeful revolution, which, however, is as yet far from complete."

Rev. T. C. Williams (Unitarian) says it seems to him impractical, and rejects the Roman Catholic doctrine, closing with: "If the present enlightened pontiff fails to reunite two churches so similar as the Roman and Greek, how can the Guild of St. James look for a reunion of all? I should be glad to learn the particulars of your plan."

The Rev. Morgan Dix, rector of Trinity Church, New York : " My views on the question of Christian unity are well known, and have been published in the form of sermons, etc. I will simply say that I do not think there is any value in Christian Union apart from Christian unity. In other words, I care nothing for an alliance or confederacy of separate sects, as I think the point to aim at is unity in belief, organization, and worship."

The Rev. Sydney Strong, Walnut Hills Congregational Church, Cincinnati, Ohio : " You ask me a question about church unity. Organic church unity is a dream of the future. Spiritual unity is possible now, at once, and is in a measure realized. Between the best Roman Catholics, Congregationalists, and Episcopalians, there is already spiritual unity. As the years go on this will increase, until there is complete spiritual unity. Would the Christian world accept the Roman Catholic idea ? No. Let me tell you why. Because the evolution of religious life is certainly away from traditionalism, human authority and monarchism. You are asking the churches to do what might be asked of the nations of the earth— to unite under one government. It would not be possible nor wise, because the same kind of government would not do for the Russian, the American and the African. The republic would answer for one, but be a farce for another. But suppose such a thing could be done. Would it be an absolute monarchy—Papacy in religion ? Would you, living under democratic institutions, agree to become subject to an absolute monarch ? ' No,' you'd say, ' that would be going back to the dark ages. The sweep of the world's life is irresistibly towards democracy, I do not propose to try to reverse the decision of history. Besides, it is futile.' You ask me, as a Congregationalist, to become subject to the Pope, or to accept the Roman Catholic idea. I must reply ' No.' I must go forward, not backward. The irresistible sweep of the soul life of the race is away from traditionalism and absolutism, and toward freedom and independence. Do I make myself clear? The basis of the future organic unity of the church—if ever it come—will be democratic, not monarchical. The religious world is becoming democratized, not papacized. Meanwhile, let brotherly love abound. Yet, through many decades to come, it will be true that many souls will best find God through the way announced by the Roman Catholic Church, while many more—and, with the years, I think an increasing many—will best find God through the freer ways of Protestantism. At present push spiritual unity. Emphasize realities, not names.

Evangelists.

SOMETIMES an evangelist visits a place and influences people in a way that makes them think and say they "never knew what religion was before," and starts them off with a zeal that years of regular teaching could not accomplish. But in a little while they are back again in the old place. Then, again, an evangelist, or a set of them, stops in a city and preach, and the immediate effect is to stir the people that they see, as they express it, for the first time, the proper effect of the Gospel. Henceforth, they believe, the religious life of their denominations will be unspeakably better. But in a few weeks this same religious life has fallen down to zero. These things are talked of as among current experiences and observations.

Evangelists of the right kind, such as the Scriptures speak of, are greatly needed. We want more men to go to destitute places and preach the Gospel. But the so-called evangelist who goes where he is not needed—to a city full of churches and preachers, and having raised "a great arousement," goes away with his pockets full of money, to another city where he plays the same game, with the same result.

The modern evangelist elbows the pastor aside. The Scriptural evangelist goes where there are no pastors. It is wonderful how men will allow themselves to be led astray so as to employ "A pulpit punch to joke for God." The address, for the most part, savours of the most silly talk, akin to the clown in the circus, to make fun and laughter. There is a good deal of "hymn tinkering," and the music in many cases is "song tinkering." The performance on some occasions is nothing short of pantomimic. There is a good deal of noisy, jocose talk, called preaching, going on, which attracts many people, and sometimes makes them laugh and sometimes makes them cry, and which is thought by some to be "doing a great deal of good." Of course, those who think so are entitled to their opinion, but we are also entitled to our opinion, and our opinion is, that this coarseness and flippancy of speech, called preaching, is doing a great deal of harm, by teaching irreverence, and making light of serious things. The preacher ought to learn and appreciate the difference between sound and sense—learn that it is not he who speaks the loudest, nor he who makes people laugh or cry the most, nor yet he who in the common way pleases them best, but he that causes them to think, and learn the most of Christ—by denying themselves and taking up their cross daily—does the most good.

The worst sign of the times is seen in the fact, that the larger half of our population is growing up with no interest in the sanctuary, and no church-going habits. It is the universal, good-natured indifference to religious teaching and Sunday services that marks our spiritual peril. Thoughtful men in the pulpit are growing uneasy at this state of things. Hence the feverish competition to secure the presence of noted evangelists. But these are only expedients of temporary significance. The church can rely in the main only on herself, and on those influences to attract and retain her hold on men, which are generated by the regular administration of her ordinances. "Tidal waves" in religion, as in politics, cannot be depended on, its reaction is sure to follow every exaggerated and fictitious impulse.

The remedy for this is very simple. It is for the pulpit not to be "coldly correct and critically dull." Preach less of literature and science—less of abstract ethical theorizing—less of new themes on which the preacher may show his knowledge or exhibit his skill in thought and style, with scarcely any reference to the life and power of true godliness in the soul. He must come back to the simple Gospel of Christ, plain, unembellished Christianity. No wonder that a person sometimes longs to hear one of the old time trumpet blasts, "Awake thou that sleepest, arise from the dead and Christ shall give thee light." Our Lord made no mistake in instituting the Church, and setting apart men to administer her ordinances, and in providing the Holy Ghost to make those ordinances edifying. What is needed is not this new-fangled evangelism, in which there is so much of human device, and which implies that the church in the "old paths" is not adequate to the work, but simple, real, expectant faith in the promises of God, and prayer for the Holy Spirit.

The Church needs a change in quality as well as quantity of membership. One half the professed Christians amount to nothing. They are in fact worldly people, varnished over with a form of religion and that is all. They are made up of two parts, a dead and a living—the living part is the world—the dead is religion.

One gets bewildered with the number of organizations of this progressive age. We have the "Christain Faith Society," "Iron Cross Society," "White Cross Army," "Red Cross Army," "Church Army," "Salvation Army,"

Saved Army," "Gospel Purity Association," "Independent Mission Rooms,' "Young Men's Christian Association," "Gospel Temperance Society," "Girls Friendly Society," "Association for Befriending Young Persons," "Lay Preachers," "Bible Readings in Halls," "Inquiry Meetings," "Railway Missions," "Prisoners' Aid Society," "Gate Mission," "Roughs' Bible Class," "Fathers' Meetings," "Mothers' Meetings," and other more secular agencies, with a number of Guilds, etc.

A very marked feature of Christian and benevolent work in the present day is the multitude and variety of agencies organized outside the Church. The great majority of those doing extra ecclesiastical work, but for some reason they seem to prefer to do work outside rather than inside the Church. It is a very significant fact that so many persons are going outside the Church to edify one another to serve Christ. The Sunday service of many of these societies is held usually at the hour of public worship, the consequence being that many persons are absent from the ordinary service. There is no easy and natural passage from mission halls to churches, such as is desirable, and in too many cases people are content to remain in the mission hall. To avoid the appearance of denominationalism they prefer to do all their work in halls, tents, rooms, or in the open air rather than in churches. The crusade of the Salvation Army, is more completely outside the Church than most of the others mentioned. Nowhere does the army seek co-operation with the Church, though it does appeal to her ministers and people for help in money. The Army has developed into a sect with ordinances and something like sacraments. A great deal of work is done outside the Church for special classes. It does not, indeed, as a rule, seem advisable to deal with special classes of men, wherever it is possible, the "common salvation" should be offered to all without regard to class distinctions. Many persons connected with some of the organizations referred to, are beginning to think there is no need of churches or ministers—that they can do the work themselves. But the church is not the offspring of the human brain, but a divine institution appointed by God for the conversion of the world. The Gospel offered through the Church reaches all the maladies of the human soul, makes the drunkard sober, the impure, pure, reclaims man from all the vices renovates the whole man, and makes him a new creature in Christ Jesus.

Permutation of the Clergy.

CLERICAL changes are now occurring all the time. The voluntary system which prevails in this country, no doubt entails some hardships on the clergy. But we must not forget that it was with the voluntary system that Christianity subdued the world and enthroned herself in the person of Constantine over the Empire of the Cæsars. There is no doubt a restless spirit abroad. We live in an age which demands excitement, novelty, change. Very many changes occur where there is no fault on the part of the parish or the clergyman, and where there is every wish and effort to retain the clergyman. Many of these changes result from the principle of adaptation. A young man begins his ministry on a mission. Enlarged experience, ripened judgment, developed powers of composition and delivery, gradually fit him for a wider sphere of usefulness. Other cases occur where either with or without the fault of the minister, a state of things has arisen where all interests will be promoted by a removal. Other cases again spring from mere restless and vague desire on the part of the clergymen to better their condition. But there is yet another cause of the instability of pastoral relations. Certain persons find fault with the clergyman because he does not visit them, his calls are not spiritually profitable, then these calls are partial—some are overlooked and others are regarded too much. Some, notorious for evil speaking, lying and kindred vices, complain that the minister is not pious enough for them. Another cause of ministers frequently changing is inadequacy of salary; either it is too little or not punctually paid, and the constant meddling in the spiritual affairs of the parish. A young clergyman is told by his theological professor, "Now, when you are settled, if you find a crooked stick in your parish in the shape of an unruly member, don't hope to get rid of the trouble by running away; you will find one everywhere."

A clergyman is appointed to a parish, all give their new clergyman a cordial welcome. He is to them "the legate of the skies." The minister enjoys an income sufficient for comfort and respectability—not enough for luxury and display. It is a fixed sum depending on no donation parties, bazaars or concerts. In the pulpit he declares the whole counsel of God, which springs from the love of Christ—not with the tinsel rhetoric which circle round the head, but do not reach the heart. He is invited to a rectorship of one of the great city churches, but declines both the honor and the responsibility. We could adduce many instances of a fat city parish and a bishopric declined by men who preferred the humbler sphere of duty. Not every minister who is contented with a humble station has occasion to thank God on the ground of his humility, for there is a contentment of sloth as well as of grace.

The man who enters the ministry as a profession, a trade or calling, has no love for the work. And when the novelty of preaching is past, when he has grown accustomed to the power which a preacher has, in virtue of his position, there comes upon him a sense of drudgery, of weariness, and even of aversion to his work, that turns what is a perpetual joy to others into a source of trouble to him. In a large body of clergy there is just such impracticable material which goes floating over the surface of the Church from diocese to diocese. There is an old story told of Bishop Strachan, that when asked to remove a clergyman from a parish because he was "ruining the Church," said: "What! would you have me send him to ruin another parish? One church is enough for him to ruin."

It is not denied by the Methodists that the itinerancy has its advantages and hardships; but its advocates claim that these are much more than compensated by its advantages. It is a principle strictly adhered to in all departments of Methodism that changes of men should be regularly made. It may be observed that some of the wisest heads among the Methodists believe that without these changes the whole system of organic Methodists would fall into ruins. It is also preferred to all other methods of ministerial arrangements, because of its better adaptation for aggressive action. It is also claimed in favor of the itinerancy, that it secures a better distribution of the ministerial talents of the denomination than could otherwise be effected. They think the denomination is not generally profited by having a few pulpit celebrities shut up in certain rich and fashionable churches, rather than scattered by frequent removals over a much wider area. The itinerancy gives a field of labor to every minister. No local church can claim the service of any particular minister, for he belongs alike to all; nor can any minister choose for himself his place of service. And for the free working of the system, it seems needful that the ministers should be movable at all times.

Hades, or the Intermediate State.

THE present is an age of profound religious enquiry. What a mine of speculation this subject opens up to query. Liberty of opinion, however, is recognized on such points as the intermediate state, and the possibility of a dispensation of mercy for sinners beyond the grave. Wheatley, late Archbishop of Dublin, supposed that the soul at death goes into a state of sleep or unconsciousness until the resurrection. He embodied these views in his book, for which he was taken to task by the critics; but in the next edition of his work, he came out still stronger on the point. There are certain principles of interpretation of scripture which could be made to teach anything which the interpreter sought to find in it. How vain are most of the descriptions and speculations concerning the future world. Nothing can be said on the subject of the intermediate state which has not often been said before. To say nothing of essays and sermons, treatises on systematic theology have discussed the subject. Books are not accessible to everybody, and if they were there are many who would read a short article who would not read a treatise in a book. Besides this, each generation, while it uses the thought of its predecessor, is not satisfied with distilling that thought through the alembic of its own mind. What is called the intermediate state is the intervening period between death and the resurrection, when the soul is separated from the body. The faith of the Church generally received with regard to the intermediate state is briefly this : At death the soul enters the place of departed spirits, called in Greek, Hades, and in the Hebrew, Sheol. The righteous go to that part of Hades called Paradise, called by the Jews Abraham's bosom, where they are in joy and felicity, but not at once admitted to the full rewards of God's heavenly kingdom. Those who are truly united to Christ are in a state of peaceful rest and enjoyment on their departure hence in paradise; but paradise is not heaven, but is, as John Wesley calls it, the "Outer Porch of Heaven." A far higher degree of glory and happiness awaits them at the general resurrection at the last day, when they will have "their perfect consummation and bliss both in body and soul in God's eternal and everlasting glory." This distinction is maintained in all the formularies of the Church of England. The wicked goes to that part of Hades called Tartarus, where they will be in a state of misery, but not in so great a state of suffering as when the soul is united to the body. The Roman Catholic doctrine is, that the saints go direct to heaven; but those dying in venial sin, that is, not very good or very bad, go to purgatory, which is a place of punishment, in which persons who have not fully satisfied the justice of God on account of their sins, suffer for a time. They are assisted by the prayers and merits of the faithful, and are purified before entering heaven. But that the very bad, or those dying in mortal sin, go direct to Gehenna—the hell of the lost properly.

Some of the most learned men of all denominations have written on the intermediate state.

For centuries the predominant notions of Christendom as to the nature of future punishment was that it chiefly consisted of bodily sufferings. Painters expressed their ideas on this subject by representing hideous demons in flames of fire. There is no idea of mental suffering embodied in the paintings of the great masters. Some have given horrible descriptions of the lost. David Stoner, one of the most popular of the Methodist ministers, says: "On the lost soul entering the stormy ocean of eternity, hurricanes of fire and brimstone sweep across the infernal deep, every blast howls eternity, every demon you meet with will hiss eternity, upon the gates of hell will be written in flaming characters, to be opened no more throughout eternity." Another preacher, Thomas Walker says: "The death-bed of the impenitent is surrounded by the powers of darkness, and the curse of an incensed God, and when he dies he is driven away in his wickedness to become the laughing-stock of hell;" and yet another preacher, James Bromley, says: "Infamy and guilt and wretchedness will be the portion of your cup, a dark cloud charged with the thunders of the Almighty's wrath will hang over you, fiends of rage and despair will haunt the chamber of your fate, and hell will move from beneath to meet you at your coming." Another, Joseph Beaumont, says: "He will meet you as a bear bereaved of her whelps and will rend the caul of your heart. As you would not lie down in sorrow, nor make your abode in the flames of hell, nor dwell where the howlings and cries of damnation break forth unceasingly, nor be fastened upon by a worm that can never be shaken off, nor consumed by a fire that can never be quenched."

One of the most pious and learned Presbyterian ministers, Samuel Rutherford, indulges in this rhetorical flight: "Suppose we saw with our eyes for twenty or thirty years together a great furnace of fire, of the quantity of the whole earth, and saw there Cain, Judas, Ahithophel, Saul, and all the damned, as lumps of red fire, and they boiling, and leaping for pain, in a dungeon of everlasting brimstone, and the black and terrible devils, with long and sharp-toothed whips of scorpions, lashing out scourges on them—and if we saw our neighbors, brethren, sisters, yea, our dear children, wives, fathers and mothers, swimming and sinking in that black lake, and heard the yelling, shouting, crying of our young ones, and fathers blaspheming the spotless justice of God; if we saw this while we are living here on earth, we should not dare to offend the majesty of God." Bede, a clergyman of the Church of England, usually called the Venerable Bede, while preaching on the Christian Sabbath supposes that St. Paul and St. Michael had petitioned that the lost souls might have rest on Sundays from their punishment. He says: "It was the Lord's will that Paul should see the punishment of that place. He beheld trees all on fire, and sinners tormented on those trees; and some were hung by the feet, some by the hands, some by the hair, some by the neck, some by the tongue, and some by the arm. And again, he saw a furnace of fire burning with seven flames, and many were punished in it; and there were seven plagues round about this furnace—the first, snow; the second, ice; the third, fire; the fourth, blood; the fifth, serpents; the sixth, lightning; the seventh, stench; and in that furnace itself were the souls of the sinners who repented not in this life. There they are tormented, and every one receiveth according to his works; some weep, some howl, some groan, some burn and desire to have rest but find it not, because souls can never die."

Some of the poets have given terrible descriptions of the lost. Dante's "Three Visions" refers to it. Young, on "The Last Day," says:

"Enclosed with horrors, and transfixed with pain,
Rolling in vengeance, struggling with his chain,
To talk to fiery tempests, to implore
The raging flame to give its burning o'er;
To toss, to writhe, to pant beneath his load,
And bear the weight of an offended God.
When I have wept a thousand lives away,
When torment is grown weary of its prey,
When I have raved ten thousand years in fire,
Ten thousand thousands, let me then expire."

These descriptions of the lost are mere flights of the imagination. We often read of the terrors of the wicked, and of the misery that awaits them beyond this life, but what instruments are to be employed in the infliction of retributive justice is not directly and positively stated. That memory will act a leading part in the infliction of punishment on the wicked cannot be doubted. Young says:—"Sense, reason, memory, increase my woe." It may be fairly inferred from our Saviour's description of the final judgment, where an appeal is made to the sinner's memory ; the judge is represented as saying :—" I was an hungered and ye gave me no meat." Remorse contains in it the very essence of the anguish of hell. The lost will carry in their bosoms their own tormentors. Milton puts into the mouth of Satan "Which way I fly is hell, myself am hell." All our actions are said to be recorded in the book of God's remembrance.

> "Then on the fatal book his hands he lays,
> Which high to view supporting seraphs raise ;
> In solemn form the rituals are prepared,
> The seal is broken, and a groan is heard."

Some suppose a man may write his history upon the material universe in an enduring and indelible record. Take the idea of Babbage, indulations of the atmosphere caused by our words go on for ever, sounding now in the ear of God, and hereafter to sound in our own ear. Again, take the idea of Flammarion, that the light flying off from our deeds into the infinite space, flies without ceasing, so that hereafter we may travel along these lines of light from the beginning to the end, and with our own eyes see all the events of our life from first to last. Who shall say that the universe may not be a great photographic book, so to speak, in which we shall yet be brought face to face with ourselves in all the evil we have thought. The great Lord Bacon, in the midst of his troubles under impeachment for misuse of office, among other items of self-defence, said :—" When the book of hearts be opened, I hope I shall not be found to have the troubled fountain of a corrupt heart." That God has a book of human lives is a common conception among us ; but that he has a book of human hearts is a form of the same idea. A heart book then lies before God, and when that great book is opened how wonderful will be the revelations ? Our Lord went during the intermediate state into the lower regions of Hades, the world of departed spirits, and preached in the prison-house of the universe that the year of jubilee was come at last. At the resurrection "death and Hell," or Hades, will be cast into "the lake of fire, which is the second death." Death as it now exists will be no more, and Hades, the intermediate state, will exist no longer.

"The Uncrowned King."

IN reply to Mr. Ash's inquiries : " Was Charles S. Parnell a Protestant, and if so, to what denomination did he belong. What is your opinion about Home Rule ?" etc. If you had looked at the papers, you would have read that the funeral services of Mr. Parnell, at the church and at the grave, were performed by clergymen of the Church of England and the Church of Ireland. On his first visit to America, I met Mr. Parnell twice in company with Timothy Healy. Mr. Parnell informed me that he was a member of the Church of England, or rather, I should say, a member of the Church of Ireland, because, after the disestablishment of the Church in Ireland, it was called the Church of Ireland. He was elected a lay delegate to the synod of the Irish Church, which met in Dublin, and he had more to do with the pastor of the parish where he resided than anybody else. In personal appearance Mr. Parnell was comparatively youthful, slender, but decidedly a handsome man, gentle and unassuming in his manner. I had long talks with him, and was very pleased with my intercourse with him. It was with sincere sorrow I heard of his unfortunate downfall. For many years I was accustomed to receive rents from Parsonstown, Ireland, for a lady in Ontario. I conducted all the correspondence between her and her tenants. During the last six or seven years, there has been a great falling off in the payment of her rents, the back rents now due her amounts to over five hundred dollars. I wrote Mr. Parnell to use his influence to induce the tenants to pay their rents, but he did not interfere in the matter. I then invoked the aid of Archdeacon Chester, who was rector of Parsonstown—Birr—now the Bishop of Killaloe, who took great interest in the matter, saw some of the tenants, and got them to pay fourteen pounds. The Archdeacon advised that legal proceedings should be taken. I accordingly employed two solicitors of Parsonstown to collect the rents, but they appeared to be in collusion with the tenants, and sent me only five pounds. The land belongs to Lord Ross, to whom head-money is annually paid. He is a son of Lord Ross, of big telescope celebrity. The family name is Parsons, hence the name Parsonstown. I mention about the rents to show how difficult it has been to get rents in Ireland, even when willing to take half the rent for full payment. I am not a politician, and my opinion about Home Rule is not worth much. The mass of Roman Catholics, and some Protestants, are in favor of Home Rule. On the other hand, the mass of Protestants, with some Roman Catholics, are against Home Rule. I think that by continuous, persistent perseverance, Home Rule will eventually be given to Ireland, perhaps not exactly in the same way that the Home Rulers would like. It will also probably be given to Scotland, and perhaps Wales, and then possibly will come Imperial Federation, when all the colonies will be represented in the Imperial Parliament. There is no possibility of denying the long misgovernment of Newfoundland. In many respects she has been more oppressed in the past than Ireland. I therefore hope the Government of Newfoundland will not rest satisfied until it gets complete Home Rule—that, with unfaltering tenacity of purpose, it will knock at the door of Imperial Government until the French evacuate St. Pierre and Miquelon, and are cleared out of Newfoundland, bag and baggage;

not until then will there be complete Home Rule in Newfoundland. I should be sorry to see the French expatriated, as were the Acadians from Nova Scotia, to suffer privations, hardships, and even death. I only spoke of their removal, so as there would be no obstruction or interference from them to the Newfoundland fishermen in prosecuting their fisheries. They, of course, could still reside at St. Pierre and Miquelon by becoming British subjects, as in Quebec, at the time of the conquest. I have the greatest respect for the French, and have always received the greatest attention and kindness from them in Canada and elsewhere. I have frequently stayed with some of the principal French families on the St. Lawrence river, and was always treated with the greatest hospitality and kindness. My last stopping-place in the Bay of Chaleurs, last summer, was with the French priest of the parish of Port Daniel, by whom I was treated in the most courteous and sumptuous manner. He was full of *savoir favre, en calier.* I am of French origin on my father's side. My forefathers were natives of the Island of Jersey. Jersey, Guernsey, Alderney and Sark are the only possession belonging to Great Britain which belonged to the Dukedom of Normandy from the time William the Conqueror became King of England. The late Count De Tocqueville, French statesman and author, is said to have been a relative of mine. And my wife, according to the genealogical journal published in Boston, U.S., has descended from one of the Norman Plantaganet Kings of England, and her grandfather, on her mother's side, was a native of Guernsey, a relative of the late Marshal Canrobert, who was one of the French commanders in the Crimean war. So there is no reason why I should dislike the French. Yesterday I got an autograph letter from Rome, dated the 4th January. It was from the Right Hon. the Most Noble, the Marquis of Dufferin and Ava, who is the British Ambassador to the Italian Government at Rome. I became personally acquainted with him when he was Governor-General of Canada. He is a man of imperial ability—popular throughout Europe and America. When I saw that the Marquis was appointed Ambassador to France, I thought it a good time to write him about the French claims on the Newfoundland coast. I gave him all particulars, and sent him the report of the Newfoundland Commissioners on their mission to England as the people's delegates, so that he might have a thorough understanding of the whole affair. I pressed on him that when the negotiations came up, if any, between the British and French Governments, to endeavour to induce the French to give up their claims, in lieu of the British giving them a certain sum of money, or some place of equal value to their claims on Newfoundland. The Marquis, in his letter to me, says:—"I beg to thank you for the pamphlet you have been good enough to send me, which I shall read with great interest. At the same time, I would take the opportunity of congratulating you on the useful efforts you have been making to acquaint the Canadian public with the resources of your native colony; and thanking you for the kind terms of your letter."

Degrees and Titles.

I NOTICE that several persons had degrees conferred upon them. D.D.'s are not so much sought after as B.D.'s, which just now appear to be all the rage. Forty-one years ago, the honorary degree of A.M. was sent me by the faculty of Lawrence University, Appleton, Wis. This Institution was largely under the influence of the Methodist Episcopal Church. Two of the professors were among the most learned and popular preachers in the city of Boston when I resided there and with whom I was personally and intimately acquainted. The diploma was not sent me on account of my acquaintance with the learned languages, or of my knowledge of the ancient literature of Greece and Rome, but simply, I presume, because of their great friendship for me. In their letter to me the Faculty says :—" We have sent you the degree of A.M. because we think we confer greater honor than if we sent you the degree of D.D., which has become so cheap that self-respecting men would not receive it." Dr. Schaff, one of the patrician scholars of the United States, says :—" You will make no mistake in Dutch reformed classics by addressing every man as 'Doctor.'" There are many ministers who are as well, and some of them better, entitled to the honor of D.D. than some who have received it. There are some men whose scholarship is undoubted, and by this I mean general classics, theology, scientific culture,—lovers and readers of first class books —students of the past and present. To avoid invidious distinctions, I do not see why all clergymen should not be called "Doctor," as they have the cure of souls as well as the medical men have the cure of bodies. The New York *Observer* says:—" All regular physicians are called Doctors of Medicine, and all regular ministers ought to be called Doctors of Divinity." Old Mr. Harper, of the great publishing house of New York, used to address me as " Doctor," over forty years ago, as being the proper title for ministers.

I well remember how proud and glad the Rev. Charles Blackman felt when he received the honorary degree of A.M., conferred on him by Dr. Howley, the then Archbishop of Canterbury. Mr. Blackman was at that time Principal of the Church of England Theological Institution, St. John's, Newfoundland. He felt so elated that he said to me, " When I am appointed Bishop of Hong Kong, if you like to come, I will place you in a good position," etc. This weakness of poor human nature we are all more or less tinctured with. Sometimes honorary degrees have been given for some great achievements as a *substitute* for learning, to a notoriously unlearned man. "Some years ago the Rev. Mr. Darling, late Rector of Holy Trinity Church, Toronto, and one of the most indefatigable and hard-working parish priests, was offered a degree, but he refused to accept or wear a distinction which, he said, 'proclaimed a lie.' The community applauded, and his personal popularity greatly increased. The Rev. Dr. McLeod, who was the first editor of the *Wesleyan* newspaper published at Halifax, N.S., removed to the United States. After a year or two he again visited Halifax, and returned to the United States with a list of names, upon whom he got one of the Universities to confer the degree of D.D. George Cubitt, who was one of the ablest, if not the very ablest Wesleyan minister ever stationed in Newfoundland, had no parchment conferring on him a degree, but he was an intellectual giant. He remained in St. John's three or four years, then returned to England, when he became editor of the *Methodist Magazine*, published in London, and also of the *Youth's Instructor* and other publications.

University degrees of late years, even when they are not given " *pro honoris causa,*" but supposed to be won in due course, the "due course" often proves, upon examination, to be simply a course of money transactions without any test of scholarship. "Thus the only 'distinction' that a degree indicates as existing between wearer or winner and his confreres in age, work and academic standing, is the possession of spare cash. Time was when to be an English Dean or Canon *meant something* in the way of antecedent achievement in letters, if not of church work of some kind. Can we say the same now ? It looks sometimes as if the question of *political service* were acknowledged to be the chief factor in estimating the claims of rival candidates for the plums of ecclesiastical patronage." D.D. is sometimes given to a man merely because he is a respectable and socially influential gentleman, occupying a conspicuous position to whom the title would be an additional ornament only—done to please his congregation or his rich father-in-law, or his wealthy aunt, or his influential brothers or sisters—thus buying favors perhaps, with this cheap distinction, when the recipient might, perhaps, be " plucked or stuck," as the college boys say in analyzing the first word in the Hebrew Genesis, or flounder in an examination in church history of the first century, or, perhaps, call in somebody to translate his Latin diploma. " We read in modern English literature about families who owe their titles to having been Mayor in some provincial town when royalty passed through on a certain occasion, or to some improvement in making shoe blacking, the manufacture of malt, or some other invention." All this has an effect in discounting the value of even imperial knighthood or baronetage. The Hon. A. McKenzie, ex-Premier of Canada, and the Hon. Edward Blake, both refused imperial knighthood.

The Bocothics or Red Indians of Newfoundland.

THE miniature of Mary March (Demasbuit), was drawn and painted in water colors, by Lady Hamilton, wife of Admiral Sir Charles Hamilton, the Governor of Newfoundland in 1819. When Lady Hamilton left the Island, she made a present of the portrait of Mary March to Mrs. Dunscombe, wife of the Hon. John Dunscombe, and mother of Mr. Dunscombe, late collector of Customs for the Port of Quebec. Mrs. Dunscombe lent it to me to take a copy of it, which is, I believe, the only one extant. Mary March—so called from the month in which she was taken. She appeared to be about 23 years of

Mary March, Red Indian or Bocothick of Newfoundland.

age, and of a gentle disposition. She acquired a number of English words. Her hair was much like that of a European, her complexion was of a copper color, with black eyes. She was active, and her whole demeanor agreeable—in these respects different from all other tribes of Indians with which we are acquainted.

In 1819, Mr. Peyton, who was engaged in the salmon fishery at the mouth of the River Exploits, and constantly suffered from the depredations of the Indians, resolved, if possible, to hold friendly intercourse with them. Accordingly, early in the spring, accompanied by his father and eight of his own men, he proceeded into the interior, and on the 5th of March on Red Indian Lake, which was then frozen, a number of the Indians came in sight, who, on seeing the party, ran away; but on Mr. Peyton making signs of pacific intentions, one of them stopped, who proved to be a woman. The rest of the Indians then approached with hostile intentions. One of them seized the elder Mr. Peyton, intending to take his life, to prevent which the Indian was shot, when all his companions, save the woman, fled. The woman was taken by Mr. Peyton and his party to Twillingate, and placed under the care of the Church of England clergyman residing at that place. It was ascertained that she had a child three or four years old. It therefore became an object of solicitude to restore her to her tribe. The man shot was her husband, said to be a man six feet high, of noble and commanding figure. The woman was called Mary March. She was taken to St. John's, where she remained a year, and experienced the kindest treatment from the inhabitants. She was sent back to the river Exploits under the care of Captain Buchan, R.N., who had before, when lieutenant, been engaged in expeditions to the Indians, with presents to her tribe; but unfortunately she had contracted sickness and died on board the vessel. Captain Buchan proceeded on his journey, taking with him the dead body, which was wrapped in linen, placed in a coffin, and left on the margin of a pond, where it was likely to be found by her tribe, and where it was discovered by some of her own people, who conveyed it to their place of sepulture, and where, very much to the surprise of Mr. McCormack, he found it some years after, lying beside the remains of her husband.

The Boothicks or aborigines of Newfoundland painted themselves with red ochre, hence they were called red Indians. They called themselves Bethucks or Bocothicks. We have no authentic history of their origin. They are supposed to have descended from one of the tribes inhabiting the American continent. When Cabot discoved Newfoundland in 1497, he held intercourse with the red men, who were dressed in skins and painted with red ochre. He carried away three of the Indians on his voyage to the American coast.

Jacques Cartier, who visited Newfoundland in 1534, describes the natives as "of good size, wearing their hair in a bunch on the top of their head, and adorned with feathers." In 1574, Martin Frobisher, the celebrated mariner, visited Labrador, when, probably forced by the ice, he touched at Newfoundland. On that occasion some of the Red Indians went on board his ship, and on their return to land he sent five sailors ashore with them. The men did not return, he took one Indian to England where he lived but a short time. For centuries the red men where hunted like beasts, alike by Europeans, Micmacs, and Esquimaux, until not one of the race has been seen these seventy years past. All are supposed to have been exterminated. Of the whole race of the Red Indians only two are known to have been brought to adopt the mode of civilized life. Their names were William June and Thomas August, so named from the months in which they were taken. They were both taken young. One of them went master of a fishing boat for many years out of Catalind. The Red Indians of Newfoundland never knew the use of the gun, nor were they ever blessed with the services and companionship of the dog. The art of pottery was not known to them, as no earthenware remains have been found. They used the bark of the birch for buckets, dishes, and other culinary purposes. The only relics of this once powerful tribe are a few stone implements, consisting of axes, gouges, chisels and arrow and spear heads, with a skull in the museum at St. John's.

The Red Indians were considered as the fair game of the Micmacs, the English and French furriers, and the northern settlers. They inhabited the north-eastern and north-western parts of the island, and in the vicinity of the Bay of Exploits, and on the shores of the Grand Lake and Red Indian Pond, lakes of the interior. In 1760, Scott, a master of a ship, went from St. John's to the Bay of Exploits to open a communication with them; but being unarmed, he was killed with five of his men, and the rest fled to their vessel, carrying off one of their companions whose body was full of arrows, from the effects of which he died.

During the administration of Admiral, afterwards Lord, Gambier, of the Government of Newfoundland in 1803 a reward was offered for the capture of a Red Indian, or Bocothick, as they called themselves, and in 1804 a fisherman of the name of William Cull brought an Indian woman from Gander Bay to St. John's, and was paid for his trouble the sum of $250. She was treated kindly, and sent back in charge of Cull to the place whence she was brought. From some cause this was not immediately done, and the woman remained with her captor all the winter. The man in charge of her was entrusted with a quantity of clothing and a variety of articles as a conciliatory present, to be left with her and her tribe. What became of this poor woman, who was at the mercy of such a man as Cull, who is said to have shot a number of Indians, has never been stated. Dr. Chapell and others think that this woman never reached her tribe, and that she was made away with on account of the value of the presents. In 1809, under the auspices of the Governor, Admiral Holloway, another attempt was made to open up a friendly intercourse with the aborigines. Lieut. Spratt proceeded in an armed schooner to the Bay of Exploits, with a painting representing friendly intercourse between the Indians and Europeans; but none of the tribe was found. After this the notorious Cull, already spoken of, and several others, were engaged to make a journey into the interior during the winter in search of Indians. Cull and his companions saw two of the natives on their way to the place where their winter provisions were stored, but the Indians saw their party and fled, and the party gave up any further exploration. In 1810, Sir John Thomas Duckworth, the Governor, issued a new proclamation for the protection of the Indians, and soon after sent to the Bay of Exploits an armed schooner, under the command of Lieut. Buchan, R. N., to winter there and open a communication with the Indians. He succeeded in discovering an encampment, and prevailed on two of the Indians to go on board his vessel, leaving the marines with the Indians as hostages, while he proceeded in search of another party. Lieut. Buchan did not return at the time appointed by him, and the Indians, suspecting that cruelty was about being practised upon them, murdered the marines and fled. When Lieut. Buchan returned to the spot and did not find his men, the two Indians he had taken immediately decamped, and never were heard of afterwards. In 1811 a reward of $500 was offered to any person who would bring about a friendly understanding with the Red Indian tribe.

In the spring of 1823 Cull, whose name has appeared before, while hunting, fell in with an Indian man and an old woman. The man fled, but the woman approached Cull and led him to where her two daughters were—two young women. All three were conducted by Cull to Twillingate, and placed in charge of Mr. Peyton, the

Magistrate. Shortly after Mr. Peyton accompanied them to St. John's. It soon appeared that one of them was in consumption, and the health of the other two failing. Two of them were sent back in charge of Mr. Peyton, with presents for their tribe, but what became of them does not clearly appear. Shanandithit, the one left in St. John's, was very kindly treated. She lived six years, dying of a pulmonary disease in the hospital in 1829. She lived in Mr. McCormack's house until he left the island, and then with the late Judge Simms, at that time Attorney-General, by whom she was kindly cared for.

In 1827 a Bocothick Society was formed in St. John's, having for its object the civilization of the native savages, and an expedition was undertaken by W. E. Cormack, president of the society. Mr. Cormack commenced his expedition with an Indian of the Abenakie tribe, from Canada, a mountaineer from Labrador, and a Micmac, a native of Newfoundland. In the journey of 30 days they traversed the whole island from east to west, and made a complete circuit of 200 miles in the Red Indian territory, but not a single Indian was fallen in with. Much curious and valuable information, however, was obtained. A chain of lakes was discovered, extending westerly and southerly, which emptied their waters into the River Exploits, about thirty miles from its mouth, thus favoring a route for the Red Indians by water to the interior and to the sea. Here was seen the remains of one of their villages, consisting of eight or ten wigwams of large size, and intended to contain from eighteen to twenty persons. The winter wigwams had pits dug in the ground, lined with bark, to preserve their stores, etc. In this village was also discovered the remains of a vapour-bath. At the margin of Red Indian lake the ruins of summer and winter wigwams were seen. One of the singularities of these wigwams is that, although conical and the frame made of poles, covered with skins or birch bark, like those of the Canadians, each had small cavities like nests dug in the earth near the fire-place, one for each person to sit in, by which it is conjectured that these people slept in a sitting posture. A smoke-house for venison was still perfect, and the wreck of a large bark canoe lay thrown among the bushes.

But what were most interesting were their wooden repositories for the dead. These were differently constructed, according to the rank, as was supposed, of the persons entombed. One of them resembled a hut, ten feet by eight or nine and four or five feet high in the centre. It was floored with square poles, the roof covered with bark, and every part well secured against the weather and the intrusion of wild beasts. In it were found the bodies of two full grown people laid out at full length on the floor and wrapped in deer skins, with a white deal coffin containing a skeleton neatly shrouded in white muslin. This was the remains of Mary March, who was captured in 1819, and whose body after her death was left by Capt. Buchan some years before on the shore of a lake. In it also they thought they observed the corpses of children, and one body had not been placed there more than five or six years. In this cemetery were deposited a variety of articles, and in some instances the property and utensils and trophies of the achievements of the deceased. There were two small wooden images of a male and female, meant to represent husband and wife, a small doll or image of a child, several small models of canoes, etc., a bow and quiver of arrows, which were placed by the side of the body supposed to be Mary March's husband, and two fire stones (radiated iron pyrites, from which the Indians used to produce fire by striking them together as flint and steel) lay at her head. There were also several other things.

Another mode of sepulture was the wrapping of the body in birch bark, and with the property placed on a scaffold about four feet from the ground, formed of posts about seven feet high to sustain a kind of crib five feet

P

and a half in length by four in breadth, with a floor made of small, squared beams laid close together, and on which the body and property rested.

A third mode of disposing of the dead was when the body was bent or doubled up, wrapped in birch bark, and enclosed in a kind of box on the ground. This was four feet by three, and two or three feet deep, well lined with birch bark to exclude the weather, and the corpse laid on the right side.

A fourth and most common mode of burying among these people has been to wrap the body in birch bark and cover it well with a heap of stones; but sometimes the body was put a foot or two under the surface and covered with stones; in one place, where the ground was soft and sandy, the bodies appeared to have been buried deeper and no stones placed over them.

This singular race appears to have shown great respect for the dead, as seen in their sepulchral stations on the sea coast at particular chosen spots to which, it seems, they were in the habit of bringing their dead from long distances. With their women, it appears, they only buried their clothes, but no property. From Red Indian Lake to the sea is about seventy miles. Mr. Cormack says:—" What arrests the attention most while gliding down the stream, is the extent of the Indian fences to entrap the deer. They extend from the lake downwards continuous on the banks of the river for at least thirty miles."

During the time of the French dominion in the southwest part of Newfoundland, nearly two hundred years ago, and when Plaisance (Placentia) was their capital, it appears the Red Indians incurred the displeasure of the French authorities, and a reward was offered for the heads or persons of some of their chiefs; and for this purpose a number of the Micmacs were brought from Cape Breton and Nova Scotia. As the Micmacs had learned the use of fire arms, they had a decided advantage in the wars of extermination that followed, and the poor Red Indians were hunted like wolves ever afterwards, both by Micmacs and Europeans. Mr. Cormack says :—" A short vocabulary of their language consisting of 200 or 300 words, which I have been enabled to collect, prove the Bocothicks to be a distinct tribe from any hitherto discovered in North America. One remarkable characteristic of their language, and in which it resembles those of Europe more than any other languages do with which we have had an opportunity of comparing it, is its abounding in dipthongs."

The Bocothicks had some idea of religion, though dark and mixed up with errors and superstitions. They believed that they were created by the Great Spirit out of arrows, and that after death they went to a distant country to renew the society of their friends. Thus they believed in those great doctrines of the Christian revelation, the existence of a God, and the immortality of the soul. Reason never could have discovered the doctrine of the soul's immortality to them, because there is nothing in nature, unaided by revelation, from which the doctrine could be deduced. The ancient Greeks and Romans, with all their learning, eloquence and refinement, could not discover, without doubt, the soul's immortality. What they asserted in regard to it at one time, they doubted at another. Sunk in ignorance as they were, we cannot suppose that the red men were sufficiently acquainted with the operations of nature in the vegetable kingdom, or the principles of philosophy by which the laws of rest and motion are governed, as to draw any analogy between them and the resurrection of the human body. Therefore the knowledge of a future state must have been communicated to them by a divine intuition. The dealings of Jehovah are frequently dark and mysterious. " Clouds and darkness are round about His throne."

Once the Red men sported along the shores of Newfoundland in perfect security ; their hunting grounds unintruded upon and their peace unbroken by their cruel persecutor—the furrier. But as soon as the Europeans began to settle in the country, the French and English furriers, perceiving the skin dresses of the Indians, and the rich furs which served them as bedding at night, conceived the diabolical purpose of shooting them for the valuable furs which they possessed, and thus commenced a cold-blooded war against these unhappy people, who were thought as little of by these so-called civilized men, as a seal or a bird. The poor Indians were hunted like wild beasts by these merciless and unfeeling barbarians, the white men, till at last, of all this noble race, at one time a powerful tribe, scarce a trace is left behind. No canoe is now seen gliding noiselessly over the lakes. If we go to the River Exploits, no sound of the Indian is heard breaking the silence of these gloomy solitudes. If we visit Red Indian Lake (their last retreat) no smoke is seen curling from their wigwams, their fires are extinguished, no footstep is traced, all is desolation. Where, then, are the Red men? They are gone, passed away forever, and are now in the far-off land of the Great Spirit. The philanthropist cannot contemplate the destruction of the aborigines of Newfoundland, without dropping a tear over the melancholy and sad destiny. It is astonishing that such a length of time should have rolled on, and so little effort made for the accomplishment of one of the sublimest objects in which man can be engaged, the civilization of his fellow-man. Had the Government in the beginning sent a devoted Christian missionary to this degraded race, to charm them with the music of a Saviour's dying love, he would have been the true pioneer in the march of civilization; the hearts of these savages would have been tamed, their ferocity restrained, their passions subdued, and the bow and arrow exchanged for the "olive branch of peace."

The Cod Fisheries of Newfoundland.

Mr. McGregor, in his "British America," says: "Newfoundland, although occupying no distinguished place in the history of the New World, has, notwithstanding, at least for two centuries and a half after its discovery by Cabot, in 1497, been of more mighty importance to Great Britain than any other colony; and it is doubtful if the British Empire could have risen to its great and superior rank among the nations of the earth if any other power had held the possession of Newfoundland; its fishery having, ever since its commencement, furnished our navy with a great proportion of its hardy and brave sailors."

And the London *Times* says: "It is about one hundred years ago that the first Mr. Pitt, in declaring upon the national interests of Britain, affirmed that one point was of such moment as not to be surrendered though the enemy were masters of the Tower of London. We shall be thought, perhaps, to be robbing the idea of its grandeur when we proceed to explain that the point so characterised was simply the Newfoundland Fishery; but the inhabitants of that colony would not themselves be willing to make much abatement from the estimate the great minister has put on record. In their own eyes the Newfoundland Fishery is everything, and everything it certainly is to Newfoundland."

The Europeans first began the fishery on the Newfoundland coast in 1502. The Portuguese were the first, and subsequently the Biscayans and the French. In 1578 the Portuguese had 50 vessels engaged in the fishery; the English 50, and the French and Spanish 150. So important had this fishery become that in the year 1634 France consented to pay a tribute of five per cent. to the British Government rather than relinquish the privilege of fishing on the coast This rebate continued until the reign of Charles II., or during a period of forty-one years. In

1763 France abandoned all her pretension to Nova Scotia for the privilege of fishing on the northern parts of Newfoundland. From this time the French fishery rapidly increased. In 1721 France employed 400 ships in the Newfoundland fishery. The Grand Bank or deep-sea fishery at one time gave employment to 400 British ships, manned by 7,000 men, and during the wars of 1815, 700 ships were employed on the Banks.

Fishing by the British commences in some places in May, at other places not until June. The great staple of the island is fish. Dried codfish is the main support of the population and is obtained from the seas either on the coast of the island and its dependency, Labrador, or on the Banks of Newfoundland. The Banks extend southward of the island 500 miles in length and 200 miles in breadth. They are distant from the nearest part of Newfoundland forty or fifty miles. The bank fishing is prosecuted by the French, Americans, Canadians and Newfoundlanders. The banking grounds being on the high seas do not belong to any nation, but are the common property of all. These banks have been fished for over 380 years without showing any tendency towards exhaustion. The Bank fishing fleet, in 1892, numbered 279 vessels of 15,212 tons; the number of men employed was 3,719; the quantity of fish taken was 147,948 quintals. The average catch per schooner was 530 quintals, and the average catch per man was 40 quintals. The largest catch for the season by any one schooner was 2,350 quintals. A quintal is 112 pounds weight, so that the the total catch last season was 16,520,176 pounds. The French have adopted a mode of fishing on the Banks called the Bultow system. The vessel is provided with two or three large boats, of a size fit to carry out for considerable distances large supplies of rope and line, with moorings and anchors sufficient to ride at anchor on the open Bank in rough weather. These boats carry out from five to six fathoms of rope to which are fastened

Conception Bay, showing the Stages and Fish Houses of the Fishermen.

leads, with baited hooks at certain distances from each other. These are carried out from the vessels in different directions and let down and secured with suitable moorings to prevent their being carried away by the strong currents that usually prevail on the Bank. They are then laid out at certain distances from each other, with several thousand hooks well baited, and frequently occupy several miles of ground. On the next day they are taken up and overhauled, the fish taken off, the hooks fresh baited and let down again. This proceeding is repeated over and over again during the voyage. In this way they capture the largest fish. It is estimated that the French, Americans, Canadians, and Newfoundlanders take annually in the North American waters 3,700,000 quintals of codfish, valued at $14,800,000. The value of the Newfoundland fisheries alone annually amounts to $7,482,715. The exports of dried codfish by the French from St. Pierre in 1889, were 594,529 quintals, while Newfoundland exported 1,175,720 quintals in the same year. Besides the codfish there was exported 2,946 tierces of salmon, and 257,362 barrels of herrings.

The industry of preserving lobsters by canning is of only a few years' growth. In 1890 the value of the export amounted to $430,000. Halibut, turbot, brett, tunny-fish or horse mackerel and other fisheries as yet undeveloped. These fisheries are inexhaustible and of great value, surpassing all the fisheries of the world. The fish is caught in seines, nets, traps, jiggers, and hook and line. The harvests of the sea like the harvests on the land are subject to great variations. There is great elasticity in the Newfoundland trade, there have been great ups and downs during the last three hundred years. The number of persons employed is over 60,000. These fishermen earn their daily bread under circumstances of greater labor, hardship, toil and privation than any other class of men. The ocean is, in a great measure, the home of the Newfoundland fisherman. His life is daily exposed above the ordinary and common exposure to danger and death. Not a season passes without shipwreck and loss of life. The coast is sometimes swept by heavy storms carrying away wharves, stages and fishing-boats; but some of the merchants engaged in the Newfoundland trade have made large fortunes and retired to Europe to spend them.

After the Treaty of Paris, in 1763, Labrador was annexed to the Government of Newfoundland. This extensive coast, commencing at the estuary of the St. Lawrence, and stretching far north to the regions of perpetual snow, is one of the most barren and desolate in the world. It seems that nature has removed the means of supporting human life from the land to the waters which surround it, the abundant production of which offer inducements, and reward the industry and perseverance of thousands of adventurers who resort to it from Europe and America. Capt. Loch, R. N., in his Report to the Earl of Dundonald, says :—

"The fisheries round the island of Belle Isle north are very valuable. The fisheries are capable of yielding 40,-000 quintals in a season, and I am told the French take upon an average 30,000. I could not visit the establishments at Chatauw, owing to the bay being blocked up by icebergs—83 were counted between Belle Isle and the coast of Labrador." It is estimated that 25,000 Newfoundlanders fish from June to about the middle of October. Many of them take with them their wives and children, who reside in temporary shanties or tents built of boards and covered with the rind of trees and sods. Here they reside three or four months. The catch of Labrador used to be for a crew of three men 200 quintals for the season, but of later years the average has not been more than 100 quintals. The Labrador fishing, in 1891, the best for many years, amounted to 643,824 quintals, and this was independent of what was caught along the shores of Newfoundland proper. There are about 1,700 vessels from 20 tons upwards, employed in the fisheries,

Some of the schooners make two voyages loaded with dry cod-fish, back to Newfoundland during the summer and fall; while several merchant vessels proceed from Labrador with their cargoes direct to Europe. A considerable part of the cargo of the second voyage is in a green, salted state, and is dried afterwards at Newfoundland. The fish is shipped to various ports of Spain, Portugal, Italy, Brazil and the West Indies. The price is regulated by the demand for it in the foreign markets. The different qualities are, large merchantable, small merchantable, Maderia, West Indies, Tolqual, and inferior.

Where the vast swarm of fish around Newfoundland go for food is a natural question often asked. The late Senator, Hon. John McDonald, who visited Newfoundland, says :—" The Arctic current which washes the coast of Labrador, Newfoundland, Canada, and part of the United States, chilling the atmosphere, bearing on its bosom huge ice argosies, is the source of the vast fish wealth which has been drawn on for ages, and which promises to continue for ages to come; wanting this 'cold river in the ocean,' the cod, seals, herrings, mackerel, halibut, pike, etc., which ever crowd the northern seas would be entirely absent. The great fishing interests are as dependent upon the Arctic currents as the farming interests on the rain and sunshine which ripens the crops. The Arctic seas swarm with every form of life. Prof. Hind says:—'In many places a living mass, a vast ocean of living slime, and the all-pervading life which exists there affords the total solution of the problem which has so often presented itself to those engaged in the fisheries, where the food comes from which gives sustenance to countless millions of fish which swarm on the coast of Labrador, in the Dominion and United States waters, or wherever the Arctic currents exert an active influence.' In the Arctic seas the waters are characterised by a variety of colors, and it is found that if a fine insect net be towed after a ship it becomes covered with a film of green in green water and with a film of brown in brown water. These films are of organic origin. 'It is,' says Hind, 'a living slime, and where it abounds there are also to be found swarms of minute crustaceans, which feed on slime, and in their turn become the food of larger animals.' Dr. Brown has shown that the presence of this slime extends over a hundred thousand square miles, provides food for myriads of birds that frequent the Arctic seas in summer, and also furnishes sustenance to the larger marine animals up to the gigantic whale. Thus the great battalions of icebergs carry with them the same food on which minute crustaceans live. These in their turn furnish food for the herring which swarm on the Great Banks where this food is so abundant, and the herring, with multitudes of other forms, is devoured by the cod."

A large fish hatchery it established at Dildo Cove, in Trinity Bay, and there are hatcheries at other places, while an association has even been organized for stocking the fresh water ponds in the vicinity of St. John's. The first importation of ova was in 1886. At Long Pond, and other ponds, Lochleven trout, and the magnificent Rainbow Trout of California have been introduced; also white fish and salmon trout, which are doing well. The French possess the right by treaty of catching and drying fish from Cape Ray, on the west, as far as Cape St. John, northward along a stretch of land usually called the French Shore, but they are not allowed to make any fortifications, or any permanent erections, nor or they permitted to remain longer than for the time necessary to cure their fish. This line of coast extends 398 miles. The whole line of shore in exclusive use of Great Britain is 535 geographical miles. Public meetings were held in different parts of the country, at which resolutions were unanimously passed "That the treaties with the French should be terminated, and that the territorial and maritime rights of the whole coast of Newfoundland should belong solely to Newfoundland." In the report of the Royal Colonial Institute it is said, "The time has arrived when national policy imperatively demands that the question be finally settled, so that British subjects may no longer be deprived of the rights of fishing in their own waters, and colonizing and developing the resources of their own territory; the interests of the Empire require that its right of sovereignity within its own dominions should be maintained inviolate." Resolutions to the same effect were passed by the Legislative Assembly of Newfoundland. Sir Robert Pinsent, one of the judges of the Supreme Court of Newfoundland, when in London, says: —" I can claim to be as high an authority as anybody upon the Fisheries Question, which so gravely concerns the interests and destinies of Newfoundland, and which is a very much more important subject than the Behring Sea question, having regard to the extent and value of British rights and property effected by it. The *modus vivendi* between France and Great Britain in reference to the rights of lobster fishing and canning will shortly expire with the statute which gives it legal force; and an intimation has been given that since the Local Legislature of Newfoundland declines to pass the permanent act, which contemplates arbitration, the Imperial Parliament will shortly be asked to adopt it. The lobster industry is rapidly dying out and ceasing to be remunerative by the reason of the depletion of the breeding grounds. On that part of the coast where the French possess treaty rights this branch of the Newfoundland fisheries is subject to no control by the Fisheries Commission or by the Legislatures of Newfoundland or France, and consequently, as in the case of the fur-bearing seals of the Behring Sea, it would seem much more desirable that an agreement for the preservation of the lobster, and the resuscitation of the industry should be arrived at in the interests of all parties, than a prolonged diplomatic fight should take place over it. What legislation and diplomacy should be directed to is the final solution of a situation which mars the well being of an important British colony. The time must be rapidly approachiag when the **French Treaty** question will again come on the *tapis*."

Fires of St. John's, Newfoundland.

THE great fires of St. John's, Newfoundland, date back to 1816. On the 12th February, 1816, a most destructive fire desolated a great part of the town of St. John's. The property destroyed amounted to more than $500,000. In the following year, 1817, on the night of the 7th of November, another great fire broke out at St. John's, and in nine hours thirteen large mercantile establishments well stocked with provisions, and one hundred and forty dwelling houses were destroyed. The estimated value of the property thus destroyed was $2,000,000. This distressing calamity was succeeded by another on the 21st of the same month, when fifty-six more houses besides stores and wharves were consumed. During the winter great distress prevailed, and, owing to the failure of the crops in Europe, the usual quantity of supplies were not imported in the fall and the merchants circumscribed the usual credit system. Numbers, rendered desperate by want, broke open the stores. Volunteer companies were embodied and armed to prevent further depredations, and committees of relief were organized to issue small quantities of food at stated periods. St. John's was visited by smaller fires in 1839 and in 1840. The next great fire was on the 9th June, 1846, which took place when all the mercantile establishments were well stocked with every article of merchandise, and the seal vats full of oil. By this conflagration 2,000 houses were consumed, and property to the amount of $4,000,000 destroyed. On that occasion, contributions in money, provisions, clothing and building materials were sent from Nova Scotia, New Brunswick, Quebec and the United States. The British Government gave a munificent donation of $150,000, to which was added, under the sanction of the Queen's letter, addressed to the Archbishops of Canterbury and York, to make collections in the churches, the further sum of

$157,580; making a total of $307,580; in addition to which the sum of $106,236 was received from various parts of Great Britain and Ireland, the British Colonies and the United States, making a grand total in money of $413,816.

The great fire of July 8th, 1892, originated in a barn on Long's Hill, by a man lighting his pipe and throwing the match among the straw. The high wind which prevailed caused the flames to spread with great rapidity among the wooden buildings in the vicinity. The gale carried the live embers in all directions, and soon the fire was raging in a score of places at once. The fire department was utterly helpless. There were about fifty firemen, but a supply of water could not be obtained, owing to the water being turned off for repairs of the main pipe. For twenty-four hours the flames raged with irresistible power when the fire had spent itself, the area from the parade ground on the north-west, down to Beck's Cove on the water front, then sweeping easterly, destroyed everything in the entire area, between the water front on the south and military road on the north, up to Signal Hill near the entrance to the harbor. The exception being the Roman Catholic cathedral, the Union Bank building and the block of brick houses known as Devon row, east of the burned district. The buildings which escaped were the Parliament house, Government House, and all the residences north of the military road. Not only was there an appalling destruction of property, but loss of life. Two women and two children were burned to death. A woman who fled for refuge to the open fields, gave birth to a child. Five men were either burned or drowned by the burning of a steamer, and other vessels lying at the wharves. Those vessels which could not get out into the stream, were burnt at their docks. A man dropped dead from fright during the fire. The public buildings destroyed were the English Cathedral, the Masonic Temple, St. Patrick's Hall, Orange Hall,

Church of England Cathedral, as it appeared before the fire of July, 1892, St. John's, Newfoundland.

Star of the Sea hall, Total Abstinence Hall, Mechanics' Hall, Athenæum Hall and Library, Custom House, Methodist Church, Presbyterian Church, Congregational Church, the Atlantic Hotel, all the newspaper offices, the Court House, the Government and Civic Offices, all the great shops and stores, and fish and oil warehouses on that street, and over 2,000 houses. The burned district extended over a mile in length, by nearly a half mile in width.

It is estimated that 1,950 families, of about 10,219 persons were burned out. On July 16th, about two thousand persons were camped. There were 66 streets burned containing over 1,572 buildings, of which 781 were lessees and 452 freehold. Loss about $15,000,000 ; insurance effected, $4,850,000.

During the fire in the city, forest fires broke out in different places near the city A forest fire at Kilbridge burned the Roman Catholic Church at that place and farm houses, and threatened the west end, and only remaining portion of the unburnt portion of the city. The city contains a population of over 33,000. Half of these, comprising mostly the work people, lived at the unburnt west end of the town ; the other half was distributed over the rest of the city, comprising two-thirds of its area. The bulk of the food supplies were stored in the burnt district. Newfoundland is dependent on other countries for its supplies of food. All the flour, meal, and nearly all its meats, butter and vegetables are imported. St. John's is the only city of any importance in the island, the seat of the Government, and the commercial emporium. It is the one great market for the products of the fisheries, and here was stored the provisions for feeding the people along a line of coast of two thousand miles. The burning of St. John's, therefore, meant loss to the whole colony.

The magnificent cathedral of St. John the Baptist, destroyed by the fire, was a gem of gothic architecture designed by the late Sir Gilbert Scott; superintendent of the work, Mr. Wm. J. Fay Mills; 188 feet long and 9 feet broad, with tower and spire, its vaulted roof 80 feet high from floor to ridge of the roof. It was partly built of stone obtained on the island, and partly of cut stone imported from England, Ireland and France, with flagged floors It was, perhaps, more like the old English Cathedrals, than any this side the Atlantic. Its estimated cost was $400,000, which, together with the burning of the bishop's residence, clergy house, synod hall, schools, orphanage and academy, amounted altogether to nearly $1,000,0 0. The Cathedral was insured for $40,000. The orphanage was valued at $5,000, and insured for $2,000. Synod hall and academy, worth $10,000, insured for $5,-000. Sunday-school building and furniture, valued at $4,000, insured for $2,000. Central schools of the Continental and Colonial Church Society, worth $10,000, insured for $4.000. The bishop's residence, chapel, library, and furniture, worth $25,000, but what amount of insurance, if any, on this property, we have not heard. Another great loss was the church ship *Havelock*—the " Floating Cathedral," by which the bishop visited the remote parts of his diocese, and in which he held services. The cathedral was insured for $40,000, but virtually uninsured, for the policy was not available for rebuilding, as it was security for debt, still outstanding, on the original cost of the building. It was deemed fire-proof, and not likely to be burned. It is remarkable that the surplices in the vestry were not scorched and all the papers were safe, which is only accounted for by supposing that some masonry fell in and blocked the staircase and door. Bishop Field used to say it took three bishops to build a cathedral, but this cathedral took four bishops to build it—Bishops Spencer, Field, Kelly, Jones. During the episcopate of Bishop Spencer, the sum of $20,000 was raised in St. John's, and $10,000 in England, towards the erection of the building. The foundation stone was laid by the first bishop of Newfoundland, Right Rev. Dr. Aubrey George Spencer, August 21st., 1843, who was translated to the Diocese of Jamaica the same year, so that the cathedral took nearly fifty years building, and a few finishing touches still wanting to certain parts of the interior when it was destroyed. The choir and transepts were erected by the recent Bishop Jones.

The following is a transcript of the inscription on the plate inserted in the foundation stone:—

D. O. M.

HUJUS ÆDIS,

SANCTO JOHANNI APOSTOLO

DEDICATÆ,

Impensis Anglicis, Simul Colonicis Exstructæ,

Auspicante Johanne Harvey Equte
Provinciæ Rebus Bene Præposito,
Cleri Autem, Civiam

NON SINE PRECIBUS AUBREIUS,

PRIMUS DIŒCESEOS TERRÆ NOVÆ
EPISCOPUS,

Primum Lapidem Posuit

XXI. AUG.

ANNO SALUTIS MDCCCXLIII.

Beneath the plate were deposited the seal of the Lord Bishop, a glass bottle containing coins of the then reign, a parchment with copy of inscription, and numbers of the *Royal Gazette* and *Times* newspapers, in which were published a programme of the proceedings.' His Excellency Lieut.-General Sir John Harvey, the Governor, attended by his aide-de-camp private secretary, and staff, delivered an appropriate address on that occasion. The bishop delivered an address in the parish church to a crowded congregation. The eloquence and beauty of his Lordship's language, excited universal admiration, and his touching reference to his first coming to Newfoundland as a missionary, his subsequent return as the first bishop of the island, and his approaching separation from his beloved flock, went home to every heart. At the conclusion of the ceremonies, the band of the Royal Newfoundland Companies played the national anthem. During the episcopate of Bishop Spencer, the sum of $20,000 was raised in St. John's, and $10,000 in England, towards the building of the cathedral. The plan and style of the building was altered from what Bishop Spencer intended it to be.

Immediately after the great fire of 1846, Bishop Field visited England, and obtained the consent of the Secretary of State for the Colonies to the appropriation of $75,000 out of $157,580, which had been collected in the churches of England under the sanction of the Queen's letter to the Archbishops of Canterbury and York, towards the building of the cathedral in the room of the parish church, which had been destroyed by the fire. The cathedral was opened for worship by Bishop Field in 1850, the nave of the church being all at that time erected and finished. The finish, externally and internally, was elaborate and beautiful. Experts have examined the walls still standing, and pronounced most of them firm and good, and can be built on. The choir, aisles and transepts are to be permanently roofed, and other necessary work for the holding of Divine service. The nave is also to be protected from the weather, by a temporary roof of board and cement. The cathedral will probably be ready for service in the spring. The amount taken up in the various churches of the diocese of Toronto for the restoration of the cathedral amounted to $1,561. It would have been much larger but that most of the church people had previously liberally subscribed to the general fire fund. The Bishop of Newfoundland has asked the Anglican Church throughout Great Britain and Ireland and the Colonies to assist in rebuilding the cathedral, and has received encouraging replies from the presiding Bishop of the American Church, the Primates of New Zealand and Australia, the Metropolitan of Canada, and the Primus of Scotland, and here I will make a digression to introduce a little bit of ecclesiastical history.

It is said that the cathedral was erected on the historic spot where the service of the Church of England was first celebrated in the New World, but this, I think, is a mistake. It is recorded in the historical records of the State of Maine that the Rev. Mr. Sermour preached at St. George's Island, a locality within the State of Maine. The colony that settled there had a clergyman of the Church of England in their number, who was their chaplain, was a sworn assistant, and regularly officiated in the church built within their fort. The common notion that Plymouth, in Massachusetts bay, was the first place in which any kind of Protestant religious worship was steadily kept up, is evidently unfounded. The "Pilgrims" landed on Plymouth rock in 1620. In the summer of 1578 a landing was made by a colony of Episcopalians in the forest of Maine, divine worship was performed, and the administration of the Lord's Supper, 42 years before the landing of the "Pilgrims"; so that the site of the cathredral was not the spot where the service of the Church of England was first performed in the New World. The Cabots visited Newfoundland in 1497; Frobisher visited the coast in 1576; Gasper de Cortercal in 1500; Jacques Cartier in 1534; Hackluit and Whitebourne in 1588; Rut in 1527; Hore in 1536; Sir Humphrey Gilbert in 1583. Sir Humphrey (half brother of Sir Walter Raleigh), took formal possession of the island for Queen Elizabeth, in the presence of the assembled merchants and fishermen. "There were delivered to him in token of submission, the feudal symbols of turf and twig, and there he raised the English flag and erected a wooden pillar, to which were attached the arms of England engraved on lead. In declaring the chief points of the law, he spoke of religion and of loyalty to the Queen, pronouncing that " in public exercise it should be according to the Church of England." But we do not find any record of a religious service being held by any of them. It would seem that a clergyman of the Church of England accompanied Frobisher's expedition and celebrated the Holy Communion on the mainland of America, five years before 1583. In the charter given to Sir Humphrey Gilbert, it is declared to be " for the honour of God, compassion for poor infidels captured by the devil."

It was on St. John the Baptist's day, 1497, that Newfoundland was discovered, by Cabot The day is perpetuated in the name of the city and of the cathedral. The first missionary of the Church of England stationed at St. John's, previously, was the Rev. Mr. Jackson, in the year 1703. " In the American *Antiquarian* for 1889, is a sketch of the tradition found by Cortes in Mexico, of a visit to that country by a white man who had crossed the sea in a winged boat, had won the esteem of the people, and by his teaching had inaugurated for them a golden era. Research into the history of missionary enterprise in Ireland, between A D. 500 and A.D. 800, has disclosed an obscure and almost forgotten record of a transatlantic voyage of an Irishman, named St. Brendan. MSS. of the original Latin narrative, and versions in Irish, Dutch, German, Italian, Spanish, and Portuguese are extant in Continental libraries, and it is also among the Cotton MSS. It is submitted that in St. Brendan we have the first preacher to the people of Mexico, more than 800 years before the voyage of Columbus."

" It is a well-known fact that the Basques, both Spanish and French, were a great seafaring people. They were the first to capture whales and seals in the Gulf of

St. Lawrence. Sydney, Cape Breton, is still called in the maps 'Spanish Bay.' El Coe de Premio Real, the late learned Spanish Consul for Quebec, wrote a very interesting pamphlet on the Basques in North America. His view is that the Basques fished in Newfoundland and the the Gulf before Cabot's discovery." Possibly some religious service might have been held among them at that early period.

The following bit of church history may not be uninteresting. Dr. Pilot says:—" In the year 1634, an Order-in-Council was made by Charles I., at the instance of Archbishop Laud, by which the members of the Church of England in the Colonies and in foreign parts were placed under the jurisdiction of the Bishop of London. This system prevails to this very day where jurisdiction has not been given to some regularly commissioned bishop. The Church of England congregation of the French Island of St. Pierre, distant about ten miles from Newfoundland, is subject to the Episcopal Order of the Bishop of London, and the clergyman officiating there has his license direct from that dignitary. The Bishop of Newfoundland exercises episcopal acts there only as a Bishop *in partibus*. The anomaly is apparent. A Bishop being in one hemisphere and one of his churches in another." The consolidation of the church in Canada will perhaps remedy this anomalous state of things. As will also the annexation of Newfoundland to the Dominion of Canada. The largest revenue ever collected at the custom house at St. John's was immediately after the fire, for the fiscal quarter ending the 30th October, which amounted to $530,717.

The loss to the Methodist Church at St. John's was:— The spacious new College valued at $45,000; Orphan Home $5,000; Model School $2,000 brick Church $25,000; Parsonage $4,000. Insurance on all $55,000.

Presbyterian loss:—The Presbyterian Church valued at $30,000; the Manse valued at $4,000.

The Congregational stone Church valued at $20,000.
The Roman Catholic Church at Kilbridge valued at $20,000, with schools, halls, orphanage, etc.

Collections were taken by the different denominations to rebuild these churches in St. John's.

Generous donations of money, food, clothing and building materials were sent from Great Britain and Ireland, from the various Colonies, the Dominion of Canada, and from the United States. And from British residents in France, Spain, Portugal, Italy and Germany. I am sure the sufferers of St. John's feel very grateful for the Christian sympathy, munificent subscriptions, and timely aid given to them by the Canadian people. Toronto has done nobly, the ready response of the Ontario Government, the City Council, and the liberal gifts of the Board of Trade, the merchants, the millers, butchers and citizens generally, have relieved much distress and suffering.

The Imperial Government gave a donation, $75,000, the Lord Mayor of London received at the Mansion House, $100,000 The whole of the contributions amount to probably $500,000.

Newfoundland would be a great acquisition to the Dominion, with its great fishing, mineral and lumbering resources. Newfoundland holds the key of the St. Lawrence. Separated from Cape Breton, Prince Edward Island, Nova Scotia and New Brunswick by the Gulf of St. Lawrence, and from Labrador by the Straits of Belle Isle, it affords two ocean highways, a northern and southern entrance to the Gulf of St. Lawrence. Her population of 203,000 gives a large market for the agricultural products and industries of Canada. Her harbors and her fish-bait supplies are necessary to the successful prosecution of their business by Canadian fishermen. A railway is now building from Hall's Bay to St. George's Bay in Newfoundland, through the undeveloped heart of the country, whence a steamer conveying goods and passengers will be despatched to

Shippigan, in New Brunswick, to meet the Intercolonial Railroad. It has been proposed to run a railway from Quebec to the Straits of Belle Isle, with a ferry across the Straits, thence a railway to meet the road which is now being built at Hall's Bay, north of St. John's. This would reduce the ocean voyage to England and America three days. It would involve the construction of about 700 miles, including 300 miles across Newfoundland, from Chicoutimi, this being the lowest point of which the Saguenay river could be bridged.

Mineral Resources of Newfoundland.

In the sandstone at Shoal Bay, near St. John's, a vein containing crystals of sul huret and green carbonate of copper was worked, in 1775, by some English miners, but was afterwards abandoned in consequence of not paying the expense attending the working of it. Captain Sir James Pearl, of the Royal Navy, re-commenced the working of this mine in 1839, but his death occurring in 1840 the work was suspended. Minerals of various kinds are found scattered all over Newfoundland. The principal mine is at Tilt Cove, on the northern coast. It was discovered by Mr. Smith McKay in 1864. This mine yielded in 1868, 8,000 tons of copper ore. In 1869 a fine vein of nickel was discovered intersecting the copper, from which in two years ore was taken which realized $38,600. Another copper mine is worked at Burton's Pond, south of Tilt Cove. In his annual report to the Colonial Office in London, in 1868, Governor Hill says:—

"In the first year the exportation of copper ore of a very superior quality was commenced, and at this time more than 2,000 tons have been shipped. On my recent visit to Labrador I stopped at Tilt Cove, in Notre Dame Bay, for the purpose of seeing a mine which is now in most successful operation, and which I trust is only the first of many which will soon be worked with profit to the proprietors, and great advantage to the population in affording new employment which is so often sorely needed in the winter season. I was much interested in what I witnessed. The quality of the ore is said to be equal to the best known from any other place. The fine kinds are worth as much as $100 per ton, and the average value of the sales of shipments to England is equal to about $50 per ton. Before the end of the year it is expected that a quantity worth from $400,000 to $500,000 will be shipped, and the ore now being extracted is even better than that first obtained. One hundred and seventy men and boys are now on the new pay list, and about 500 people altogether now reside at the settlement, which was not in existence three years ago. Some of the men make as much as $80 per month, the average being from $40 to $84. Seventeen of the men employed, including the captain of the mine, are Cornish miners, but the remainder are Newfoundlanders. I spoke with several and found them well pleased with their position and circumstances, which are indeed greatly preferable to those in which they had frequently been placed in seasons when the fishery had been unsuccessful and their subsistence depended wholly on its result If, as I believe will be the case in a very short time, many other mines equally productive should be worked, it will scarcely be possible to over-value the beneficial effect of this new industry upon the circumstances of the laboring population."

It is said that Tilt Cove mine was purchased by an English company for $750,000. In 1879 Tilt Cove mine yielded nearly 50,000 tons of copper ore, valued at $5 2,-154. The mine at Betts' Cove and other places amounted to 23,556 tons, the whole valued at $2,982,836 Little Bay is said to have one of the most valuable copper mines in the world. Up to 1879 the total value of copper ore exported amounted to $5,000,000. Regarding Little Bay mine, Judge Little says, in 1892 :—

"As gathered from the magisterial and other reports, we find that at Little Bay some 400 persons are employed. The output for the year about 15,000 tons. There were shipped 1,125 tons of ingot copper last year, and 20,000 tons of ore as flux were purchased from the Cape Copper Company, now working Tilt Cove mine. At the last mentioned place we find there are 500 men at work, with a pay-roll of $14,500 per month. The result of their labors is most satisfactory. The output has already exceeded the anticipations of those in charge of Pilley's Island. There are 250 men engaged. The output is 4,000 tons per month, and the monthly pay-roll averages $6,700." Mr. Howley, the geological surveyor, says :—
"The discovery of the deposit at Tilt Cove, in Notre Dame Bay, in 1857, since named the Union Mine, gave a new impetus to copper mining in the country, though mining operations were not actually prosecuted there till 1864. The deposit consisted chiefly of yellow sulphuret of copper and iron, averaging about 12 per cent. of copper, though it has reached as high as 30 per cent. Betts' Cove mine was worked with extraordinary activity for ten years, during which period 130,682 tons of ore and regulus were exported therefrom, besides 2,450 tons of iron pyrites. In the course of excavating some enormous pockets of ore were come across. Several other copper mines were opened up during this period, and more or less ore derived from each.

"The principal localities which gave most promise were Burton's Pond, the Colchester Mine, South-West Arm, Shoal Arm, Little Bay, Lady's Pond, Whale's back, Hall's Bay, Sunday Cove Island, Rabbit's Arm, and Thimble Tickle, Seal Bay—all within the great Bay of Notre Dame. But the most celebrated of all the copper mines yet developed in this region is the Little Bay mine, which has been in constant and active operation since 1888. Operation were only commenced here in August of the above year, yet before the end of the season some 10,000 tons of ore were raised and shipped to Swansea. Between 1880 and 1885, 61,796 tons were shipped from this mine, and since that date to the end of last year, 1893, over 40,000 tons of ore, regulus and ingots of copper are given by the Customs' returns. Between 1880 and 1882 the South-West Arm mines yielded 490 tons; Hall's Bay 240 tons; White Rabbit's Arm mine—which was only worked for one year—yielded 1,260 tons of ore, averaging 28 per cent. copper. At Lady Pond mine the ore is a rich yellow sulphuret, with a large proportion of beautiful purple and bluish erabescite, generally occurring in pockets. Some of the copper deposits in this bay, notably those of Sunday Cove Island, consist of wide bands of fine, soft, shelly chloritic slate, impregnated with iron and copper pyrites, and containing bands of yellow copper ore, varying from mere strings to layers of several inches thick. Here also very beautiful arborescent filaments of native copper are found on the cleavage plains of the lode rock. Metallic copper occurs at the Union mine, Tilt Cove, in thin sheets or plates, lining the walls or crack or slips in the lode rock. It has been found on the west side of the island, in Port-au-Port and Bay of Islands. The other localities where ores of copper have been found are too numerous to mention. It will be sufficient to state that the indications of these ores occur on all sides of the island, and in every one of the great bays at hundreds of localities. During the past six months a new discovery of copper has been made at South-West Arm, Green Bay, near the old Colchester mine. This lode is said to average six or seven feet wide, with two feet of solid ore." In 1891 were shipped 7,060 tons of copper ore; 3,226 tons regulus; 1,139 tons ingots; total value of these ores $965,850. Value of all the ores exported in 1891, $624,-750. Newfoundland ranks as one of the chief copper-producing countries in the world. Iron pyrites is found all over Newfoundland, and occurs in all the copper mines, some masses of which is said to be over 200 feet thick. An immense deposit is now being mined at Pilley's Island, in Green Bay, which is the great Bay of Notre Dame. It is said that 70,000 tons were shipped from there in 1891, principally to the United States. The lode containing the ore is sixty feet wide, and contains fifty-five per cent. of sulphur. This mine is lit up by electricity with incandescent lamps. Iron ores, such as clay ironstone, pyrites, bog iron ore, magnetic iron sand, and several other varieties are found in many parts of Newfoundland. Near the Grand Pond is a deposit of iron ore three feet thick. Lead, chiefly galena, is disseminated through all rock formations of the island. In 1857 a lead mine was opened at La Manche, at the head of Placentia Bay, at that time 150 tons were shipped off. From 1857 to 1868, 2,375 tons of galena were taken from this mine. Another mine is the Silver Cliff mine, of Little Placentia. The ore of this mine gave 70 per cent. of metal. A deposit of galena is found at Port-au-Port Bay, on the west coast, and many other localities. Nearly all the galena ores contain more or less silver. Many years ago the working of a silver mine commenced at Lawn, Placentia Bay. Several lumps and strings of dark colored metal appeared, which proved to be native silver mixed with other ores. Specimens were brought to the notice of chemists, who pronounced it to be chloride of silver (horn silver), native silver and ruby silver, or light red silver ore. When the miners became acquainted with the value of the ore, it is said they appropriated most of it, and sold it to jewellers at St. John's and the French island of St. Pierre. Specimens analysed contained 65 per cent. of metal. From some cause or other the working of this mine was discontinued. Nearly all the galena ores contain silver. One deposit in Little Placentia gave specimens showing as high as 356 ozs. to the ton of ore. In 1880 some good specimens of gold were discovered in quartz veins at Brigus, Conception Bay. Gold has been discovered in two other places. Some free gold was obtained in quartz veins at the Bay of Islands, but the most promising specimens yet discovered was at Ming's Bight, on the north-east side of the island, where was found a lode charged with gold. One nugget of several ounces in weight was obtained. A specimen now in the museum at St. John's is about two inches square. The presence of gold in most of the copper ores of Notre Dame Bay had been detected by the color of the flame in the smelting of the ores. More recently a quantity of gold was found in the low grade ore from the Union mine, Tilt Cove. Gold to the value of $50,000 was extracted from this ore in the process of refining during the last year. Bituminous shales are found on the Humber River in the Carboniferous group of rocks. Crude petroleum is often found floating on the surface of the water at Port-au-Port Bay and at Sandy Bay, and collected in little cavities in the rocks. Recently a fine flow of oil has been struck at a depth of 1,000 feet. It is thought there is oil-bearing strata at Cow Head, west coast. Rock salt is supposed to be found in St. George's Bay, as several brine springs exist there. Plumbago and mineral pigments abound in many places.

Competent miners assert that the serpentine rock between Port-au-Port and George's Pond contains an immense belt of asbestos of the best quality. Mr. Hayes has started working one mine, situated one and a-half miles inland from Port-au-Port, and the Hon. Captain Cleary another. The opening up of these mines will be a source of wealth to the people of the locality, and yet asbestos is only one of the leading deposits which are to be found in this metalliferous portion of Newfoundland. Experts who have carefully gone over the ground say the supply is inexhaustible, and that the place must eventually become one of the most celebrated in the world for this mineral. Asbestos is said to be worth the enormous sum of $265 per ton, with a probable further increase. It is believed the coming spring, 1894, will witness great activity in prospecting for this mineral substance. Its great price and comparative scarcity render it an object much sought after. The antimony mine at Moreton's Harbor gives employment to 50 men. Many tons of fine ore have been extracted. It has only recently been worked.

The first geological survey of Newfoundland was made in 1838. Professor Sedgwick, of the University of Cambridge, recommended J. B. Jukes, a graduate of that University, a member of the Geological Society of England, and afterwards a professor of geology in Trinity College, Dublin, and author of several works, as a competent person to make a geological survey of Newfoundland. Sir William Logan, the head of the Geological Survey in Canada, told me that Mr. Jukes was one of the highest authorities they had on geology. Mr. Jukes was employed by the local government for two years, 1838 and 1839, to make a geological survey. He was but poorly provided for making the survey; he had no geological probe or instrument for boring. Owing to the want of roads he merely coasted along the coast in a small sloop, made only a partial survey of the sea coast and went nowhere into the interior, except twelve miles from St. George's Harbor on the west coast. His geological report, however, laid before the legislature, was exceedingly interesting and gave the only information ever known of the geological structure of the island. He found on the west coast of St. George's Bay and Bay of Islands a coal field occupying an extent of 30 by 10 miles and $3\frac{1}{2}$ feet in thickness. The coal is bituminous and caking and is identical with the coal of Cape Breton. He also found gypsum, or plaster of Paris, in large fibrous veins, and also in thick beds, soft, powdery, and finely laminated in large quantities in the cliffs of Codroy Harbor. Limestones, building stones and marble of every quality and color. After an interval of many years, the late Alexander Murray, formerly of Sir William Logan's staff in Canada, was engaged by the Government to make a geological survey of the island in 1866, to continue for several years. He found a vast exposure of gypsum between Codroy Island and Codroy River, and that the carboniferous formation of St. George's Bay is an extension of the same rocks which constitute the coal fields of Cape Breton. Mr. Murray concludes, that within the area supposed to be underlaid by the seam coal, spoken of by Mr. Jukes, there were 54,720,000 chaldrons. Respecting the coal formation, Mr. Murray says:—" One of the most important of these detached troughs or basins of coal measures is in the Bay of St. George, where the formation occupies nearly all the lower and more level tract of country between the mountains and the shores of the bay; and another lies in a somewhat elongated basin from between the more northern ends of the Grand and Deer Ponds and White Bay; the eastern outcrop running through Sandy Pond, while the western side probably comes out in the valley of the Humber River, near the eastern flank of the long range of mountains. There is reason also to suspect the presence of a smaller trough of the same rocks, between Port au-l'ort and Bear Head, towards the Bay of Islands, the greater part of which, however, is in the sea; and from local information I received from the Indians, as well as some residents at the Bay St. George, I think it not improbable that another trough of the formation may occur in the region of the Bay of Islands." Mr. Murray says:—" Of three other seams having an aggregate thickness of eight feet, a seam of coal one foot thick would give per square acre 1,500 tons, per square mile 960,000 tons; multiplied by eight and the result would be 7,680,000 tons." It is said this estimate equals the whole annual output from all the Cape Breton mines. James Howley, F.G.S., the present head of the geological staff of Newfoundland, says:—

"There are two distinct carboniferous basins in this island—on its western side. The first known as the St. George's Bay trough. It occupies a fringe of the south side of that bay, about sixty-eight miles long by twelve wide, comprising an area of about 816 square miles. Other small outlying patches on the north side of the same bay, and again in Port-au-Port Bay, would probably bring the total area up to 900 square miles. The second, called the central carboniferous trough, is situated in the valley of the Humber River, which flows into the Bay of Islands, at the head of the Humber Arm. Although lying in a direct line from each other, and corresponding with the general trend of the physical features of the country, the two areas are separated by between sixty and seventy miles of distance, though they were at one time probably connected. The central basin comprises a superficial area of about 500 square miles. By far the greater portion of both basins is occupied by the lower and unproductive portions of the series, especially the carboniferous limestones and millstone-grit formations. The entire southern side of St. George's Bay exhibits the above strata, frequently broken by faults, and repeated again and again. One great inticlinal fold running parallel with the shore, extends up and down the coast, with a westerly dip on the outside, towards the waters of the Gulf of St. Lawrence, and an opposite dip inland, where the strata which holds the coast are repeated, and at a distance of some six or seven miles from the shore, the middle or true coal measures are exposed on the surface. A long, narrow trough, of some three or four miles wide, is here brought in, which holds some fairly good seams of coal. The lower measures come again to the surface on the inner side of the trough, where they finally rest against the Laurentian mountain range in the rear. What the longitudinal extent of this coal trough may be has not been definitely ascertained, and it can only be determined with certainty by the use of the boring-rod.

In 1889 a more thorough investigation resulted in the finding of several seams of good coal, which were uncovered at their outcrops and traced for some distance, so as to obtain accurate and reliable measurements and good average specimens of the quality of the mineral. Altogether 14 seams of coal, of varying thickness, from a few inches up to six feet, were uncovered on one small brook; three seams on another two miles distant, and four small seams on a third brook, still further eastward some two and a-half miles. These, with some smaller ones, aggregate a thickness of twenty-seven feet of coal in the section, which is repeated by being brought again to the surface on the other side of the synclinal trough. There is reason to believe that these do not represent the seams in this section. In the central carboniferous trough, which was the object of special investigation, several seams of coal were found in the region of the Grand Lake, occupying another long, narrow synclinal trough. Two sections cross this trough, and at two miles distant from each other on the strike, were measured, with the result that in the first one sixteen outcrops of coal were observed, and in the second twenty-eight outcrops. These are not separate and distinct seams, but the same seams repeated by the doubling up of the strata. So sharp is this trough in one case that twenty-four of those outcrops are crowded into a horizontal distance of 600 feet. None of the seams are large; only a few averaging three feet of coal each. Many of the smaller seams of good coal are so close together, being divided only by five or six feet of loose, shaly strata, and all in vertical position, that I believe several of these could be worked as one seam by a single drift along the strike. All the coal as yet discovered in this island is of the soft, bituminous variety; some of it approaches cannel coal. One seam in St. George's Bay, 'the Shear's seam,' has a very clear, shining black lustre, and hardness approaching the softer kind of anthracite. Neither of these coal areas have

R

been thoroughly explored as yet; the difficulty of carrying a close investigation where so much of the surface is covered with loose debris renders the use of the boring-rod absolutely necessary to further prove the character and extent of these coal deposits."

Mining generally in Newfoundland is an industry of great promise. There is no doubt but that thorough and extensive prospecting would bring to light hidden treasures of immense value for the investment of capital. A railway is now being constructed from Bay of Exploits, in the north-west part of the island, to St. George's Bay, in the west through the undeveloped part of the country, a distance of over 200 miles, to the coal region. This in the near future will lead to the opening of the coal and iron mines and the erection of smelting works. Newfoundland, the oldest colony of Great Britain, and nearer than any possession in British North America, yet for 396 years, up to the present time, not a single ton of coal or iron ore has been extracted and sent to market, though possessing coal and iron mines of great value. The opening up of these mines would be a safe investment for capitalists. Here we have the chaotic elements of future greatness, and the elements to set in motion iron works and manufactures. The strong arm of England is said to be her coal and iron. Recently, 1894, a very valuable iron mine has been discovered at the Island of Bell Isle, Conception Bay, and is now being worked. This summer, 1895, a seam of coal four feet thick has been discovered in the vicinity of the Grand Pond close to the railroad.

Agricultural Developments of Newfoundland.

WHITBOURNE and other early adventurers who visited Newfoundland, speak in high terms of the productiveness of the soil. As early as 1610, John Guy, who had established a colony in Mosquito Cove, in Conception Bay, speaks of the climate not being so severe as in England; he also raised garden vegetables. In 1623, Governor Wynn, in his communications to Sir George Calvert, from Ferryland, speaks of wheat, barley, and oats being eared on the 17th of August, and that the garden vegetables had arrived at perfection. Sir Richard Bonnycastle says:—" Whitbourne was ridiculed when he talked of the productiveness of the soil of Newfoundland, and Lord Baltimore was almost ruined by choosing to build his castle on a bleak and desolate part of the coast, instead of upon the western shores, or in the interior. Had he chosen the fine healthy climate of St. George's Bay, or the Bay of Islands, for the seat of the Calverts, Newfoundland would now have professed a capital, rivalling that he afterwards founded in the pestiverous swamps of Maryland, and which by dint of perseverance and labor, has since risen to rank as the fourth city of the union, notwithstanding its ancient insalubrity. Alas! its capabilities have never been truly appreciated; they interfered with the certain gains derivable from the Bank fishery, a false policy prevented the settlement of the fairest half of the island, superior to parts of the opposite continent; and has continued until nearly the present moment, because Great Britain was unnecessarily generous to the conquered French, and because it was originally the open and undisguised policy of a few rich merchants to keep the trade limited to the Bank fishery, thereby ensuring wealth to them at home, and to those they employed in the island as their chief factors. The climate is less severe on the western side of Newfoundland, the land more rich. It is therefore to that portion that we must hereafter look as the seat of a population dependent upon an inexhaustible field of agricultural resources. But with all its natural advantages in the scale, we must not allow it the whole weight; for already the eastern half of Newfoundland is cultivable to the extent of supporting a population which can be gradually thrown into it, either for the fishery or for settlement."

The first settlers in nearly all the British colonies were aided by the Imperial Government to cultivate the land, whereas not a single shilling had ever been expended on Newfoundland down to the present time, either for cultivation or any other improvement. It cost the British Government upwards of $5,000,000 for the colonization of Nova Scotia. The cost for the colonization, protection, and settlement of Canada, goes beyond counting. It may be stated by tens of millions. The following is an extract from the Petition of the House of Assembly in 1837, to Her Majesty, the Queen, on the subject of Crown Lands:—

"It is only within the last twenty years that general permission has been given to the inhabitants to cultivate the soil of Newfoundland. It will scarcely be believed at this happy era of your Majesty's accession to the throne of your ancestors, when the people in the most distant parts of your extensive empire look forward with unbounded confidence and hope to the just, mild, and merciful government of your Majesty, that for upward of two centuries the cultivation of the soil in Newfoundland was considered a criminal offence, and prohibited under the severest restrictions and prohibitions; this withering and desolating policy was the cause why your Majesty's colony of Newfoundland did not improve in the same progress with the colonies in its neighborhood.

"Representations have been made from the earliest period to the present Government, that the extreme severity of the climate and the sterility of the soil of Newfoundland formed insurmountable obstacles to cultivation. If these representations are correct, the House of Assembly would humbly submit to your Majesty, that there can be no necessity for creating further obstacles beyond those raised by nature herself.

"But may it please your Majesty, these were false representations made by persons, who, from corrupt or interested motives of their own, attempted to arrest the order of Providence, and prevent the people of Newfoundland from receiving that support and sustenance from the soil which God and nature intended it to afford.

"The House of Assembly, therefore, have most humbly to bring the subject under your Majesty's benign consideration, and with certain hope that your Majesty will be graciously pleased to give every encouragement, and remove every restriction to the cultivation of the soil of your Majesty's ancient and loyal colony of Newfoundland."

The late Colonial Treasurer of Newfoundland, the Hon. Patrick Morris, says:—

"About the year 1806, the late Dr. William Carson, arrived in Newfoundland; he at once saw the great injustice that was done, both to the country and the resident inhabitants, by the semi-barbarous policy that prevailed which prohibited the cultivation of the soil. He raised his voice against it, wrote some excellent tracts on the subject denounced it in the strongest terms, incurring no small risk of being transported for his temerity for arraigning the venerable system that had prevailed for centuries. He became the most strenuous advocate for the cultivation of the soil, which he represented as fully equal in quality to that of his native country, Scotland; he was opposed by the local authorities, by the merchants, and a great portion of the inhabitants; he was ridiculed as a visionary. Notwithstanding, in good report and in evil report, he persevered until he saw, for some time before his death, his views and doctrines almost unanimously approved of by all parties.

"Dr. Carson may be called the parent of agriculture of Newfoundland, he not only encouraged it by precept but likewise by example. In the year 1818, he obtained a large grant of waste land from the then Governor, Sir Charles Hamilton, which he cleared and cultivated at considerable expense. The land cleared and cultivated by Dr. Carson forms one of the most valuable farms in the vicinity of St. John's."

In the year 1828, one of the principal merchants of St. John's, Henry P. Thomas, obtained a grant of 250 acres of waste land, four miles from the town, which he cleared and cultivated and occupied for some years, until he was repaid for the whole expense of the outlay, he then let the ground on lease to an intelligent Scotch farmer, the same person who had the superintendence of it from the beginning, at a rent of $1,000 per annum, who, in a few years, some twelve or fourteen, after paying his rent, realized a sum of not less than $16,000. Twenty years before, this land was a wilderness, not producing a cent, unapproachable even by a footpath. Since that time, numerous farms have been cleared, many miles beyond it. Within a circuit of two or three miles from this farm, there are now thousands of acres in profitable cultivation, in the occupancy of some hundreds of industrious families.

On the arrival of Sir Thomas Cochrane as Governor of Newfoundland in 1825, he became the advocate of agriculture. He cultivated lands surrounding his private residence, "Virginia Waters," situated three miles from town. He opened a road from St. John's to Portugal Cove, and Cochrane street, in front of Government House. During the administration of Admiral Prescott, in 1839, about $175,000 was voted by the Legislature for the opening up of roads. The sea was the great highway, and no roads leading back from the shore not even for a mile. On the arrival of Lieut.-Gen. Sir John Harvey, the Governor in 1841, he endeavored to dispel the prejudice which had existed for centuries against the cultivation of the soil. In 1842, an agricultural society was organized under his patronage. The following is an extract from his address to the society:—

"Newfoundland is in reality something more than a mere 'fishing station,' and possesses resources beyond the mere 'rocks on which to dry the nets of the fishermen,' in a word, I saw in it the undoubted evidence of a capability for agricultural pursuits far beyond what I had imagined to exist, and I likewise saw that by no other means can the great staple of this country, its fisheries, and the great national objects, the nursery of seamen and the consumption of the manufactures of the parent state, be so effectually promoted as by bringing the homes of the fishermen nearer to the scene of their pursuits and operations; in a word, by encouraging settlement and the cultivation of the soil—an encouragement which contemplates the rapid increase of its population, consequently of its fishermen and mariners, as well as of brave, hardy, loyal, and permanent settlers, who would constitute the 'constitutional defence' of the colony, and whose labors as auxiliary to the fisheries, might, at no remote period, go far to render the island independent of all foreign countries for the means of feeding those engaged in them. Of which no more convincing proof can be required than the specimens of produce now before you, consisting of wheat, barley, oats, turnips, potatoes, etc., equal in size, in weight and in quality to the productions of any other country, England not excepted. It may be asked, 'how is this to be explained with reference to the reputed sterility of the soil of Newfoundland, and to the length and severity of its winters, and the consequent shortness of its open season?' The answer is, 'by the productive qualities of the soi., to which the imputation of sterility so unjustly attaches; by the fineness of its autumnal season which affords ample opportunity for the preparation of the ground for the spring crops; and by the almost unexampled rapidity of vegetation during the summer, by which the shortness of that season is amply compensated.'"

At a ploughing match in 1844, Sir John said:—"Almost from the first moment of my arrival in this island, my eyes were opened to the fact of which the inhabitants themselves evidently appeared not to be sufficiently aware viz., that it possessed agricultural treasures, capabilities, and advantages, as well of soil as of climate, which, if not unequalled, are yet certainly not surpassed by any of the surrounding colonies."

The Hon. Mr. Morris says:—"It may be said that landed property quadrupled in value during the eminently successful government of Sir John Harvey. The most important measure of Sir John Harvey's Government, in reference to the agricultural improvement of Newfoundland, is the law for the sale and regulation of the Crown Lands. Her Majesty consented, and with a truly royal bounty, to grant the whole of the land to her loyal subjects in the Colony. Newfoundland is no longer to be hoarded as a 'royal wilderness.' The people will ever entertain a grateful sense of Her Majesty's royal beneficence. It is only those acquainted with the partial mode of disposing of land which prevailed in Prince Edward Island, and in most others of the modern North American Colonies, that can form a correct estimate of the vast boon that has been conferred."

The Right Rev. Dr. Mullock, Roman Catholic Bishop, says:—"Wheat will ripen very well, especially if the proper variety of seed adapted for a northern country be procured. I have never seen finer barley than the growth of Newfoundland, and all persons who have bought, as I have done, Newfoundland oats, at nearly double the price of the husky grain imported here, will find that he has gained by his purchase. Hops are most luxuriant, and so are strawberries, currants, gooseberries, cherries, and many other species of fruit. The hawthorn flourishes here when planted, and I have seen as fine hedges of it laden with haws here as in the home country. And I mention this as a proof of the comparative mildness of our climate, for I find in Russia, as far south as Moscow, it is a hot-house plant. My estimate, then, of the agricultural capabilities of Newfoundland, comparing it with what I have seen in the North of Europe, is that if we had a large agricultural population we could support them in comfort, and that as population increases we must attend more to the land, then more general wealth and comfort will be diffused a hundred-fold than now, when our population is, I may say, wholly maritime, and we depend almost altogether on other countries for our food. Introduce settlers, encourage domestic manufactures, home-made linen and home-spun cloth, and Newfoundland will become the paradise of the industrious man. The soil in general is thin, but kind, easily worked, and besides the legitimate manure of the farm-yard, can always be enriched near the sea by sea rack and fish offal. The climate is comparatively mild, and all we want are hands and industry."

The Report of the St. John's Agricultural Society for 1849, says:—" Our wheat is found to weigh with few exceptions, not less than 60 lbs. to the bushel, and our oats and barley maintain a proportionate character. Butter and cheese have been attended with the happiest results. Measures have been taken to import and secure the services of a man and his wife to instruct those who may be desirous to learn the operation of spinning and weaving flax and wool. It is well known that one pound of wool will produce one yard of good warm cloth, and of much better texture than is usually purchased in the shops; and as the expense in producing it is scarcely anything beyond the time, which in too many instances is unprofitably spent, it is hoped that the homespun of Newfoundland will soon become as generally known and valued as the other productions of the country. It is highly gratifying to see enrolled among the members of the Agricultural Society, the names of so many of the respectable merchants who have been spending their lives in pursuing the trade and fisheries; it affords the strongest evidence of the fallacy of the opinions formerly prevalent, but of late years rapidly disappearing, that to encourage agriculture and promote the cultivation of the soil, would necessarily create separate and conflicting interests. The facts already prove the contrary, for not only are the ordinary pursuits of the fisheries not impeded or in anywise interfered with, but it has now become evident that the best interests of the trade, and the moral and social condition of the people, are equally promoted by bringing to our aid all those valuable auxiliary resources."

Five hundred dollars per annum was given by the local government to the above society, but last year, 1892, the sum of $10,000 was given by the Government to the various Agricultural Societies, besides the annual subscriptions of the members. A great change is silently but surely taking place in the agricultural horizon of Newfoundland. The clouds of ignorance and prejudice against agriculture are being dispersed by the organization of Agricultural Societies throughout the country. The Agricultural mind has burst from its slumber, the surface has been broken, the rock has been perforated, and the water has begun to flow to swell the stream of inquiry which is now meandering through the mind of the country. Will Newfoundland ever become an agricultural country? Inquiries are now aroused where till lately the deepest quiescense prevailed. This is a favorable symptom of the increasing intelligence of the people. In these Agricultural Societies we see nebulous beginnings of a new order of things, when Newfoundland garnished by the plough, will be clothed with grain and fruits for the sustenance of its inhabitants, and become the scene and happy abode of the toil-worn, heroic, and brave fisherman. Newfoundland, throughout the whole extent of its bays, harbors and inlets, is skirted by a belt of cultivated land, well cultivated to reward the labor of the agriculturist. Captain Loch of H.M.S. Alarm, says of St. George's Bay in 1849 :—"The cultivation of grain has been commenced with success, wheat, barley, and oats ripen well; and turnips, potatoes, and garden stuffs grow particularly fine. In 1839, Mr. Jakes says in the report of his geological survey :—" On the South side of St. George's Bay, along the sea cliffs, on the banks of the rivers, or wherever the surface is drained and cleared of trees; it is covered with beautiful grass; and the few struggling settlers scattered along the shore exist almost entirely on the produce of their live stock. The aspect of their houses put one in mind of the cottages of small farmers in some parts of England. There is every reason to believe that the same fertility would be characteristic of the country round the N. E. of the Grand Pond. The whole of the district, even the primary hills, is covered with wood of a far finer description than the generality of that on the east side of the island."

A Prince Edward Island farmer who visited Codroy says of it :—" At the homestead where I passed the winter, a farm of not more than fifteen acres of roughly cultivated land supported a stock of twenty head of cattle and thirty-five sheep, wholly upon hay. I passed over rich fields where clover had been grown luxuriantly for more than thirty years without manure, with no signs of decay or loss to the soil." Another who visited Codroy a short time ago, says:—" We travelled for about fifteen miles on either side of the river. The extent and appearance of this rich interval struck me so forcibly that I stopped to examine carefully the nature of the soil. I could see along the banks that the soil was exceedingly good and four feet in depth, while the grass, balsam and balm of gilead trees and tall alders gave proof of its surpassing fertility." It is estimated that the valley of the Codroy river alone contains 56,862 acres of very fertile land.

The late Very Rev. Monsignor Sears, who resided many years in this part of the country, says of it:—As the soil here is surpassingly productive, especially in the growth of various grasses, I believe there is no country in our latitude to surpass it for grazing sheep and cattle. Wherever the trees are removed by fire, wind or other causes, a spontaneous growth of grass springs up. Meadows have given hay for the last nineteen years, the last crop being better than the first." George Nichols, from Nova Scotia, who has been living on the banks of the Humber river, says of it :—" I consider the soil in the Humber valley superior to any I have ever seen in Nova Scotia. The climate is warmer and freer from frosts which would injure plants. Since I have lived here I have had no crops of any kind injured by frosts, I consider the soil admirably adapted to raise cereals such as wheat, barley, oats and even buck-wheat."

The joint committee of the Legislature of Newfoundland in their report says :—" For grazing purposes we have large tracts that we believe cannot be surpassed in British North America, and when we regard our proximity to England and the all important consideration of a short voyage for live stock, the advantages we possess in this are too manifest to be the subject of question or argument." Mr. James Howley, F.R.G.S., of the Geological Survey, says in 1892:—"I sent a small parcel of the Lady (Russian) wheat, introduced here by His Excellency Sir Terence O'Brien, a few years since, to Mr. George Nichols, a farmer, residing on the Humber River, near the head of Deer Lake, in order to test the character of the soil in that locality. Nichols sent me about two gallons of the grain raised from this seed during the past summer. It is of a very superior quality, hard, firm, and large grained; far exceeding the original seed. It was examined by several persons competent to give an opinion thereon, some of whom are well acquainted with the various grades of Canadian wheat. All these pronounced it first-class grain, fully up to the average Canadian. One gallon was weighed carefully, and found to slightly exceed nine pounds, thus giving seventy-two pounds per bushel, while the average weight per bushel of the best Manitoba wheat is given is 62 pounds. Now, this wheat was raised on land situated about 26 miles from the mouth of the Humber River, or some 60 miles inland from the outer coast line, on the western side of the island. I think that may be safely reckoned as the interior of Newfoundland. Of course this is not the first, or only time, wheat has been successfully raised, both at Deer Lake and Codroy. Scarcely a season elapses that some person or other on the west coast does not grow a small quantity." Thus have I brought forward a host of witnesses to testify to the agricultural capabilities of Newfound and.

Mr. J. L. Ross, of the Grove Farm, a suburb of St. John's, testifies to the mildness of the climate, by stating that he did some ploughing every month of the winter of 1892. He also testifies to the successful manufacture of home-spun by his weaving a suit of home-spun, made from the fleece of sheep bred and raised in Newfoundland. Siberia, a few years ago, was considered uninhabitable, on account of the severity of the climate, and the sterility of the soil. Now agriculture is pursued there to a considerable extent, and it is fast becoming a habitable country, producing the necessaries of life. The fall and winter of 1891 in Newfoundland were very mild. In the month of January cauliflowers and lettuce were raised in the open garden of the Police Magistrate, Mr. Stabb, at Bona Vista, and in the month of February, in the garden of Sir Robert Pinsent, at Salmoniet, a bed of flowers burst into bloom, and the autumnal peas were over the ground. According to the returns of 1889, the last census, the quantity of land under cultivation was 47,460 acres; number of oxen, cows, and calves, 19,886; sheep, 40,326; goats, 8,126; swine, 2,964; horses, 5,536;

wheat and barley raised, 1,000 bushels; oats, 6,121 bushels; potatoes, 762,622 bushels; hay, 28,518 tons; turnips, 58,116 bushels; other root crops, 56,380 bushels; cheese manufactured, 1,260 pounds; butter, 396,220 pounds. There were raised a large quantity of other roots, cabbages, carrots, fruits, and berries. The whole estimated at the annual value of $1,500,000 Meadow lands all over the country have been cropped year after year for forty and fifty years without manure; most of these meadows, however, have never been ploughed, most of the hay, wild hay. In some places the "bog meadows" are very productive, producing large quantities of natural grass.

On the granting of a Constitution to Newfoundland by William IV., in 1832, every one thought the country would rapidly advance and become equal to Nova Scotia and New Brunswick. It caused great excitement throughout the island. Some of the merchants and others at Carbonear went three miles from the town, and each spotted trees, with their names painted in full, for farms of a half-mile. The writer's name was also painted with black paint for a half-mile farm. We built a fire and had a jolly time. Next year one of the principal merchants sent a lot of men, who spent some weeks cutting down trees on the farm which he had selected, and that was all that was ever done with it. Within the last few years quite a settlement has sprung up on those embryo farms, called Victoria village. Newfoundland is destined to become a rich grazing country for cattle and sheep, and stock raising. Cattle ranches will, no doubt, soon be established in localities with such inexhaustible natural resources. Natural grasses are abundant throughout the country, which will some day be the feeding ground for innumerable herds of cattle and flocks of sheep. For nearly four hundred years the agricultural development of Newfoundland has been a very slow process. Out of 2,800,000 acres, which is the area of the island, not 50,000 have yet been cultivated. It is popularly supposed that the extent of land capable of cultivation is quite insignificant. The amount of land under cultivation is, no doubt, small when compared with the whole area of the island; yet it is very considerable, considering the short time that some of the fishermen have turned their attention to agriculture. Fishing unfits them for working on the land. How shall the agriculture of Newfoudland be developed? By opening colonization roads, railways, and emigration. There has been no regular emigration for the past sixty years. Seventy and eighty years ago, Irish merchants residing at St. John's, used to get, every spring, from one hundred to over three hundred emigrants, come in their own vessels from Waterford and Cork. The English merchants used to get from ten to forty, come in their vessels from England. They were all called " youngsters." They were brought not for tilling the land, but to be employed in the fisheries. The Scotch merchants imported their clerks and tradesmen from Glasgow, and Greenock, where they had branch establishments. In this way Newfoundland became gradually populated. The Newfoundland Government ought to have emigration agents, like all the other colonies in Great Britain and Ireland. To atone for her opposition and neglect in the past, the British Government ought to give Newfoundland five hundred thousand dollars, for settlement and cultivation of the lands, as well as to provide the means of living for her own redundant and impoverished population. At a meeting of the Church of England Emigration Society, held in London, emigration and colonization were proposed, to relieve the distress arising from the superabundant masses of the people. Another society has been started, called the " Church Colonization Land Society," whose object is to take up land and plant colonies of church people upon it. The emigrants are assisted to the place of destination, money is advanced to them for two or three years, to be returned when able to repay it. They assist the kind of men who are fit for colonization; not those from workhouses and prisons, but men physically and morally strong to fight their way in the world. Perhaps the Government of Newfoundland may be able to make some arrangement with these societies by which the cultivatable lands may be settled. A farming population could be settled along the lines of railways, and the various fertile bays of the island. Shanties, called in Newfoundland "tilts," should be built for the settlers, and they should be supplied with a cow and two or three sheep, etc., the Government to be repaid at the end of from three to five years. This has been done in various parts of Canada.

Until recently, the interior of the country was a *terra incognito*. The railway now building from Bay of Exploits to St. George's Bay, will open up the country for settlement. A chain of lakes extend from the Bay of Exploits on the north-east to St. George's Bay on the west, about two hundred miles. There is the Grand Pond which commences at about fifteen miles from St. George's Bay. It is 54 miles long and from six to twenty miles wide. It is of great depth, no bottom having been found with three fishing lines, or about ninety fathoms. Its depth is further proved that its S.W. half is never frozen over in the hardest winters. Red Indian Lake, forty miles long; Deer Pond, fifteen miles long. The Red Indian Lake discharged itself about four miles from its north-east end, and its waters form the River Exploits. From the lake to the sea is estimated seventy miles. From Badget Bay, Great Lake, a chain of lakes extend westerly and southerly, and discharge themselves by a brook into the River Exploits, about thirty miles from its mouth. This tract of country, comprehends the interior from New Bay, Badget Bay, Seal Bay and Hall's Bay, these being minor bays included in Green or Notre Dame Bay, at the north-east part of the island. There are two easy methods of crossing from north to south with a canoe. The first bay proceeding from St. George's Bay, through the Grand Pond to Hall's Bay, the second from White Bear Bay, through the third pond to the Bay of Exploits. Here we have an extensive inland water-way, and a grand field for emigration and colonization. There are no navigable rivers in Newfoundland. The Humber, the largest, only six or seven feet deep, extends twelve miles, encumbered with several rapids, to the Grand Lake. These lakes are destined to play an important part in the future development of the country Tourists will yet be wending their way to them as one of the most delightful watering places and summer resorts. In the vicinity of the Grand Pond in the valley of the Humber, last year, was discovered a coal basin said to extend four miles by twelve, covering about fifty square miles, and a deposit of iron three feet thick. This district is level, containing five hundred square miles of timber. The forests of Newfoundland consists of pine, spruce, birch, fir or balsam, juniper, alder, mountain ash, balm of Gilead and a variety of smaller shrubs. While all the islands and continent of America are adorned with the beautiful foliage of the maple, cedar, elm, beech, oak, butternut, chestnut and other beautiful trees which add such beauty to the American forest, not one of these trees is indigenous to Newfoundland. It is said, the scenery everywhere in the interior is a wealth of beauty, a magnificent panorama of woods, hills and ponds, with prairie-like plains, enameled with a great variety of wild flowers meet the eye. These prairie-like plains may turn out to be like the Canadian beaver meadows, which supply hay for the lumber shanties to feed their horses and oxen. The forests around those lakes are yet uncut, some of them are still the abode of wild beasts, but the knell of their empire has sounded. It is heard in the ring of every woodman's axe as he fells the trees; it is heard in the crack of every hunter's rifle, in the jingle of the sleigh bells, and the railroad whistle. There is something

s

exhilirating in contemplating the future settlers levelling the forests and converting the wilderness and solitary places before them into farms and gardens, and making hamlets and villages to spring up, where the wild beasts now prowl. Around these lakes are plenty of limestone, freestone and hills of marble of every quality and color. These lakes may yet be the seat of a magnificent city, with streets of marble houses. Steam, with its revolving wings, will yet be fretting the bosom of these beautiful lakes, conveying argricultural produce and passengers. A silent, slow, but sure change is going on in Newfoundland, and the time will surely come when she will raise enough agricultural produce so as to be independent of other countries for the necessaries of life.

Aggressive Work of the Church.

THERE is no more comprehensive description of the Church than that it is a great missionary organization. The commission originally given by the Saviour was, " Go ye into all the world and preach the Gospel to every creature." What effect upon missions will result from the limitation of a diocese to a single city and its appropriate portion of surrounding country ? It is the chief argument against the division of dioceses that the weaker is cut off from the stronger part. But where new dioceses have been formed in England, in New Zealand, in Australia, in the United States and in Canada, so far from the Church suffering, her missionary work is in a much more vigorous and aggressive condition than before, and a fresh impulse given to all kinds of Church work. Multiplied dioceses have always resulted in multiplied co-workers. It is not development, but reconstruction on the primitive model, we want, when from metropolitan to deacon every one was the centre of influence. We have bishops, but the Church burdens them with vast fields of labor, which they must constantly travel over, and it is difficult for them to undertake what the apostles and primitive bishops regarded as one of the first duties of a Christian Bishop, the fellowship of the ministering to the saints, the care of the poor of Christ, of His widows and orphans, the sick, etc. The present cumbersome episcopal jurisdiction should be divided. The question of the proper limits of a Bishop's jurisdiction is regarded by many too exclusively from a single point of view. It is considered a matter in which the Bishop chiefly is concerned, to be decided by the powers of physical endurance, the convenience, comfort and comparative dignity of the diocesan. These things are worthy of consideration, and were the Episcopate merely an ornamental appendage to the ministry, might perhaps exercise a controlling influence. Each parish clergyman, however, realizing that Episcopacy is an integral part of the Church, the source of all vital energy, whose power and guidance should be everywhere felt and acknowledged, just as the head of the human body controls the action of each member, will be conscious to himself how absolutely essential to the permanent success of his own labours is the right termination of that question now engaging the attention of the Church. " One Bishop for a city, and one city for a Bishop." At the time of the meeting of the Council of Nice, a city and a diocese were evidently considered synonymous. In the Epistle and Canons set forth by the Council, it is evident that a city, a church, a parish (otherwise a diocese in the modern sense), are used indiscriminately one for the other. What inference are we to draw from this, except that it was an acknowledged right for every city to possess its own Bishop. The Apostolic Canons show conclusively that a city means a diocese.

The lay element now largely employed will be felt in

the aggressive work of the Church. The course of popular opinion tends strongly towards a sort of democratic equality in the Church, which recognizes the people as the source of all power. Compare the popular standing of the ministry of all denominations as a body at this day with their status of fifty years ago. There was at that time a degree of reverence, respect, and profound regard which is largely wanting in the present day. "Presbyter" says: "I believe all our dioceses would be glad to see a largely increased episcopate, but they want the dignity of the office kept up by a large stipend. The American Church has shown us that her Bishops lose none of their dignity because their salaries are small. Archbishop Lewis used to say that respectability and dignity were killing the Church. "Is there no way in which the present endowment funds of the various sees could be divided, so that as each Bishop dies, the four or five thousand dollars he gets may be used for two successors instead of one. I believe the late Metropolitan Bishop of Fredericton during the last eleven years gave half of his stipend to the coadjutor, and both these Bishops seemed none the worse for their comparatively small pay."

The Roman Catholics, with a population of 66,000 in Newfoundland, have three Bishops, while the Church of England, with a population of 60,000, at the present time has but one Bishop.

In 1851, a fund was raised in England, Ireland and Scotland, the interest of which, together with annual subscriptions, went to the salaries of the seven Scottish Bisops, each of whom received from $550 to $900. The bishopric of Argyle is endowed by a separate fund. Each of the seven bishops in Scotland now receive a salary of $2,000 per annum. The Scottish Church has not been idle in these days of revival—great progress has been made and a number of churches have been built within the last twenty years. The stipends of the Roman Catholic Bishops are not large.

www.ingramcontent.com/pod-product-compliance
Lightning Source LLC
Chambersburg PA
CBHW030819230426
43667CB00008B/1288